Enjoy the Same Liberty

The African American History Series

Series Editors:
Jacqueline M. Moore, Austin College
Nina Mjagkij, Ball State University

Traditionally, history books tend to fall into two categories: books academics write for each other, and books written for popular audiences. Historians often claim that many of the popular authors do not have the proper training to interpret and evaluate the historical evidence. Yet, popular audiences complain that most historical monographs are inaccessible because they are too narrow in scope or lack an engaging style. This series, which will take both chronological and thematic approaches to topics and individuals crucial to an understanding of the African American experience, is an attempt to address that problem. The books in this series, written in lively prose by established scholars, are aimed primarily at nonspecialists. They focus on topics in African American history that have broad significance and place them in their historical context. While presenting sophisticated interpretations based on primary sources and the latest scholarship, the authors tell their stories in a succinct manner, avoiding jargon and obscure language. They include selected documents that allow readers to judge the evidence for themselves and to evaluate the authors' conclusions. Bridging the gap between popular and academic history, these books bring the African American story to life.

Volumes Published

Booker T. Washington, W.E.B. Du Bois, and the Struggle for Racial Uplift
    Jacqueline M. Moore
Slavery in Colonial America, 1619–1776
    Betty Wood
African Americans in the Jazz Age: A Decade of Struggle and Promise
    Mark Robert Schneider
A. Philip Randolph: A Life in the Vanguard
    Andrew E. Kersten
The African American Experience in Vietnam: Brothers in Arms
    James Westheider
Bayard Rustin: American Dreamer
    Jerald Podair
African Americans Confront Lynching: Strategies of Resistance
    Christopher Waldrep
Lift Every Voice: The History of African-American Music
    Burton W. Peretti
To Ask for an Equal Chance: African Americans in the Great Depression
    Cheryl Lynn Greenberg
Loyalty in Time of Trial: The African American Experience During World War I
    Nina Mjagkij
The African American Experience During World War II
    Neil A. Wynn
Through the Storm, Through the Night: A History of African American Christianity
    Paul Harvey
Enjoy the Same Liberty: Black Americans and the Revolutionary Era
    Edward Countryman

Enjoy the Same Liberty

Black Americans and the Revolutionary Era

Edward Countryman

ROWMAN & LITTLEFIELD PUBLISHERS, INC.
Lanham • Boulder • New York • Toronto • Plymouth, UK

Published by Rowman & Littlefield Publishers, Inc.
A wholly owned subsidiary of The Rowman & Littlefield Publishing Group, Inc.
4501 Forbes Boulevard, Suite 200, Lanham, Maryland 20706
http://www.rowmanlittlefield.com

Estover Road, Plymouth PL6 7PY, United Kingdom

British Library Cataloguing in Publication Information Available

Library of Congress Cataloging-in-Publication Data

Countryman, Edward.
  Enjoy the same liberty : Black Americans and the revolutionary era / Edward Countryman.
    p. cm. — (The African American history series)
  Includes bibliographical references and index.
  ISBN 978-1-4422-0028-9 (cloth : alk. paper) — ISBN 978-1-4422-0029-6 (electronic)
    1. United States—History—Revolution, 1775-1783—African Americans. 2. United States—History—Revolution, 1775-1783—Social aspects. 3. Slavery—United States—History—18th century. 4. Antislavery movements—United States—History—18th century. 5. African Americans—History—To 1863. I. Title.
  E269.N3C68 2012
  973.30896—dc23

2011033236

Printed in the United States of America

For My Mother-in-Law Lyn Mitchell,
One of the Finest People I've Had the Privilege to Know

"Has the GOD, who made the white man and the black left any record declaring us a different species? Are we not sustained by the same power, supported by the same food, hurt by the same wounds, wounded by the same wrongs, pleased with the same delights, and propagated by the same means? And should we not then enjoy the same liberty and be protected by the same laws?"

—"A Man of Colour" [James Forten], 1813

Contents

~

Preface

To most Americans, the revolutionary era of the late eighteenth century is a heroic time of great white men. George Washington, Thomas Jefferson, Benjamin Franklin, John Adams, James Madison, and their like dominate understanding of how the British colonies broke with Britain and turned themselves into the United States. Such men's achievements were enormous and they deserve the honor they receive. But they did not act alone. Every single human being, female and male, black, native, and white, urban and rural, rich and poor, patriot and loyalist, within the huge zone that became the young United States, took part one way or another in the transforming era that they all lived through. Living through it changed them, and, one way or another, they changed their lives and their world. Taken together, they transformed what might have been a mere break over the problem of belonging to Britain while living in America into something much larger. Those people included free white men of all sorts, the women with whom those men shared their lives, Native Americans, and the hundreds of thousands of black people who were held almost entirely in slavery at the point of independence. This short book explores what those black men and women did with the chances that their time gave to them.

During their time the institution of human slavery underwent enormous changes. As of the middle of the eighteenth century, slavery was age-old and almost world-wide. It existed throughout the colonized western hemisphere. By the end of the revolutionary era, its world-historical destruction was underway. It was gone or dying, not just in some parts of the United States, but in much of the rest of the Americas. It had turned from an ugly but unavoidable fact of life into a problem that would not go away. Communities of free black people were taking form in the United States and elsewhere around the Atlantic basin.

Those people achieved something remarkable. Seeking their own freedom, they also sought something much larger, the destruction of human slavery itself. In part, they achieved that goal. Without what those people did during the revolutionary era, human slavery might have continued unchallenged, not just in the United States, but throughout the Americas and probably around the world. They could not destroy slavery alone. They had allies, and even with their allies they could not have destroyed slavery outright. It was too ancient, too important, too profitable, for that. In the American South, slavery flourished rather than withered, leading to the attempt by the would-be Confederate States of America to create a separate republic based unapologetically on slavery. But the American revolutionary era marked the beginning of slavery's end. *Enjoy the Same Liberty* tries to tell the story of the important, necessary part that black people took during that enormous change in the course of human events.

~

Acknowledgments

Jacqueline Moore, who coedits the Rowman & Littlefield series in African-American history, invited me to write this book during the year she spent as a research fellow in the William P. Clements Center for Southwest Studies at Southern Methodist University. I demurred for months. I don't count myself a specialist in African-American history, but she persisted and I gradually realized that I might learn something important about the American Revolution if I took the project on. I owe Jackie a lot, because I did learn, a lot. I want to thank her coeditor Nina Mjagkij almost as fulsomely. Between them, they cajoled, pushed, chided, and edited me as I turned some ideas that were a lot rougher than I had thought at the beginning into a finished manuscript.

During the drafting process, Nina asked one of her graduate students at Ball State University to read the manuscript with a student's eye. What that student found helped me greatly as I struggled to get my prose and argument right. I tried out some of the ideas in the book in a junior research seminar at SMU in the fall semester of 2010. Seminars are about exploring, and my thanks are deep to the students who joined me over that semester in the exploration that was leading to this book. I want to thank Ms. Sharon Speight, docent at Mother Bethel African Methodist Episcopal Church in Philadelphia, for giving me a detailed tour of the church museum and sanctuary and introducing me to what Mother Bethel's people have achieved during the congregation's proud history.

I owe thanks to my former students David Waldstreicher of Temple University and Corey Capers of the University of Illinois, Chicago, and to my colleagues Kenneth Hamilton and Elizabeth Russ of SMU for readings of the manuscript. Like Jackie and Nina, they pushed me hard to do better when I thought in my innocence that I had it right. I tried out my ideas with several audiences. One was professional, the ever-stimulating Dallas Area Social History Group. I thank all of its members for a spirited discussion in August 2010, and in particular its organizers Stephanie Cole and Gregg Cantrell. Another was a Teaching American History group that Corey Capers organized at the Newberry Library in Chicago in October 2010. Like every TAH session I've done, it was a great experience. The project's unveiling, in the summer of 2010, was not to academics, students, or teachers. It was to the Dallas Chapter of the Sons of the American Revolution, a group of patriotic men who care deeply about the founding era of the United States, and who gave an enthusiastic hearing to what I had to say about black people, slavery, and freedom during that era.

Almost at the last moment, SMU undergraduate student Scott Howe posed a question to me that forced me to reconsider the import both of Lord Mansfield's decision in *Somerset v. Steuart* in 1772 and Thomas Jefferson's language in the Declaration of Independence in 1776. The result appears in chapter 3. SMU undergraduate Taylor Harkness forced a similar change to chapter 1 with a point he raised in his term paper. I owe deep thanks to Mustafa Ibrahim for a really remarkable correspondence over what now is a very long period. He's a brave, honest man in terrible circumstances, and his letters remind me without his having to say so of the importance of trying to tell black history.

In an old-fashioned but necessary gesture, I asked a truly remarkable woman who has spent her life far from the world of academic American history, and far from the United States as well, if I might dedicate this book to her. She thought about it for a moment, and then said yes. I'm humbled and deeply grateful. She knows why. Evonne knows why too.

~

Chronology

1751   End of ban on slavery in Georgia; in Maryland Benjamin Ban-
            neker creates first clock made entirely in America
1754   Philadelphia Quaker yearly meeting begins campaign against
            Quakers buying slaves; other meetings follow
1764   James Otis of Boston links American resistance to British
            imperial policy changes with problem of slavery in the
            colonies in early revolutionary pamphlet
1765   Slaves rally in Charles Town, South Carolina, crying "Liberty!"
1767   Massachusetts Assembly votes prohibitive tax on import-
            ing slaves, but bill is vetoed by Royal Governor Thomas
            Hutchinson
1772   *Somerset v. Steuart* decided by Lord Chief Justice Mansfield in
            Court of King's Bench, London
1773   Pennsylvania adopts prohibitive tax on importing slaves
1773   Black protest writing begins in Massachusetts; Phillis Wheat-
            ley publishes her book *Poems on Various Subjects, Religious
            and Moral*; she journeys to London where she meets promi-
            nent British figures
1774   First Continental Congress adopts "Continental Association,"
            including absolute ban on slave trade; first separate black
            church is founded at Silver Bluff, South Carolina
1775   "Society for the Relief of Free Negroes Unlawfully Held in
            Bondage" established in Philadelphia; slaves in Williams-
            burg, Virginia, approach Royal Governor Lord Dunmore
            with offer of help after news of war arrives in April; in
            November Dunmore offers freedom to slaves "pertaining
            to rebels" in Virginia who will assist in putting down colo-
            nial rebellion; George Washington dismisses black soldiers
            when he takes command of the Continental Army at Bos-
            ton in July, but welcomes their services within months. In
            December, Thomas Paine publishes anti-slavery pamphlet
            in Philadelphia
1776   Thomas Jefferson tries to make slavery a grievance against the
            king in his draft of the Declaration of Independence; par-
            tially black Rhode Island regiment rescues American Army
            from entrapment on Long Island
1777   Vermont becomes a separate state and abolishes slavery
1779   British commander-in-chief Sir Henry Clinton issues proclama-
            tion offering freedom to all slaves of rebellious Americans

1780   Pennsylvania begins gradual emancipation

1781   At Battle of Yorktown, which ends mainland war, British commander Lord Cornwallis dismisses slaves who had sought his protection; George Washington allows Rhode Island black regiment a prominent place in final assault on British emplacement

1782   Virginia adopts law permitting masters to grant freedom to slaves; about one hundred thousand eventually are freed

1783   Definitive peace treaty requires departing British to return "Negroes" who had escaped from American slavery; Sir Guy Carleton, final British commander-in-chief, opens "Book of Negroes" to enroll as many refugees as possible; thousands are enrolled and leave America with departing British troops. In Massachusetts, Chief Justice William Cushing abolishes slavery by decree in *Quok Walker* case; gradual abolition begins in New Hampshire

1784   Methodist Church in America adopts requirement to members to free their slaves; gradual abolition begins in Rhode Island and Connecticut

1784–1787   Series of "Northwest Ordinances" organize territory north of the Ohio River for American occupation, leading to ban on further expansion of slavery into that region

1785   Virginia Methodists reject policy of granting freedom to slaves; New York Manumission Society is established; New York State Legislature passes act for gradual manumission, but act is vetoed by the state's "Council of Revision" on ground of creating unequal free population

1787   United States Constitution is written by Philadelphia Convention; several clauses grant special privileges to slavery; in Philadelphia Richard Allen buys land that will become site of his African Church; Thomas Jefferson publishes English edition of *Notes on the State of Virginia*; British anti-slavery activists found Sierra Leone in West Africa as refuge for former slaves

1788   Constitution is ratified, after national debate, in which some opponents raise slavery question

1790   Congress adopts first Immigration and Naturalization Act, opening easy access to citizenship for Europeans only

1791   Richard Allen establishes the African Church in Philadel-
            phia, first congregation of what became the African Meth-
            odist Episcopal Church; Benjamin Banneker sends strong
            response to Jefferson about his disparaging remarks about
            black people in Notes on Virginia
1792   Black self-emancipators who had fled the United States to
            Nova Scotia begin migration to Sierra Leone
1793   Eli Whitney of Connecticut invents cotton gin
1792   Migration of 1,196 former American slaves from Nova Scotia
            to Sierra Leone
1791–1794   Violent revolution ends slavery in Ste. Domingue
1793   Black Philadelphians come to city's rescue during yellow fever
            epidemic and are later accused of profiteering
1794   French National Assembly decrees end of slavery in all French
            possessions
1797   Congress rejects petition from free black Philadelphians on
            behalf of escaped North Carolina slaves
1799   New York begins gradual abolition
1800   Gabriel Prosser's attempted insurrection in Virginia
1802   Under Napoleon Bonaparte's rule, France tries to reestablish
            slavery in Caribbean colonies; massive resistance in Haiti
            defeats the project there
1803   United States acquires Louisiana, where slavery already exists
1804   New Jersey begins gradual abolition, although persons already
            enslaved will remain so for life; Haiti declares indepen-
            dence, forming second republic in the western hemisphere
1807   Britain ends African slave trade
1808   Congress ends African slave trade to United States
1810   Abolition of slavery begins in Mexico, followed by other Latin
            American republics
1811   Slave revolt in Louisiana, put down by French sugar planters
            with aid of United States officials and troops
1816   American Colonization Society established with goal of send-
            ing free black people from the United States to West Africa
1822   Denmark Vesey's "conspiracy" in South Carolina
1824   Liberia established as colony under sponsorship of American
            Colonization Society
1827   Publication begins of Freedom's Journal, first black newspaper
            in the United States; slavery ends in New York State on

PROLOGUE

~

"Proud of My Country"

Early in the 2008 presidential campaign, Michelle Obama provoked a media storm by saying that "for the first time" she was "proud of my country."[1] In political terms, it was just a misstep, from which the campaign recovered. Not long afterwards, however, images appeared on the Internet of the Obamas' pastor, Reverend Jeremiah Wright, who was not proud of America at all. Instead, he damned it in an angry sermon to his Chicago congregation. Candidate Barack Obama used the occasion to talk seriously to a vast audience about race in American history and life, and the Obamas resigned from Wright's church. Both flaps passed, and Barack Obama won the election, inspiring much of the world. Even months afterwards, Asians and West Indians in Britain showed obvious delight at meeting an Obama voter.

No America-hater, Ms. Obama revealed a deep problem about how to understand American history. Dominant American culture celebrates a past full of great events and great heroes, utterly different, it seems, from the unhappy history of most countries, utterly different as well from the complex, messy United States of the present day. In that picture, the tangled, vibrantly human American past in which people lived, faced their problems, resolved some, and failed at others collapses into the Good Old Days, a kinder, gentler, better, triumphant American time that never actually was.

Take just two examples, both of them remote from the actual subject of this book. It is obvious that for native people the arrival of Columbus in 1492 was a disaster, beginning the destruction of their world. It is just as obvious that, for *Nuevo Mejicanos* and *Californios*, the armies that wrested the

Southwest from Mexico brought conquest and often displacement, rather than liberation. What, then, of the main American story for people whose ancestors (including Michelle Obama's and Jeremiah Wright's) came from Africa in shackles, endured centuries of slavery, struggled for another hundred years against white supremacy that was written into the very laws, dealt with the terrorism of lynching and the Ku Klux Klan, and faced always what W. E. B. Du Bois called the "double consciousness" that went with being both black and American within an unquestionably racist United States?

Many black Americans prior to the Obamas and Reverend Wright have pondered that question. Consider Martin Luther King. During the great campaign that overthrew racial segregation, and in the short remnant of his life before his murder in 1968, he had harsh things to say about the United States. Yet always his great call to his country was that it live up to its proud rhetoric of liberty, equality, and justice. Never was he more eloquent in that call—"Let Freedom Ring!"—than in his moving speech to the hundreds of thousands of African-Americans and their supporters who gathered in Washington, D.C. in August 1963. Like American reformers and protestors of all races and all sorts, Dr. King looked back to the founding era of the Republic, the time we call the American Revolution, which is the subject of this book. He found in it not only promises still unfulfilled but also a model for determined action and good reason for hope.

But consider King's contemporary, West Indies–born Black Power leader Stokely Carmichael/Kwame Ture, who (like Du Bois) finally rejected the United States and finished his life in Africa. He called up the Republic's founding in much the same way. "Constitu, Constitu, Constitu," he would say to 1960s college-student audiences. "Funny, I can only say three-fifths of that word."[2]

His reference, of course, was to the clause in the United States Constitution that drastically increased the political power of white southerners by counting "persons held to service" as three-fifths of human beings for representation in the House of Representatives and in the absurd Electoral College that actually chooses American presidents. Not until the Thirteenth Amendment in 1865 and the Fourteenth Amendment in 1868 did such constitutional privilege and protection for just one special interest, slave owners, come to an end. The privilege and the protection were products of the American Revolution's final great political act, the making of the Constitution. Colonial slave owners had not needed either special privilege or special protection, because during the colonial era slavery was everywhere. By the time of the Constitution, slavery's slow, difficult destruction had begun. In a backhanded way, the Constitution's recognition that slavery indeed was a special interest suggests, correctly, that the Revolution put slavery in danger. But as Carmichael/Ture and King both knew, the same revolution also set the basis for slavery in the United States gaining new, enormous strength that required a long, destructive, and deadly civil war for it to die.

Twentieth- and twenty-first-century African-American leaders are only the latest participants in a long, turbulent stream of historical argument, all referring again and again to the large-scale presence of black people and the problem of their massive enslavement during the American founding. The United States Supreme Court's very worst moment came in 1857, when Chief Justice Roger B. Taney, a non-slaveholding Marylander, announced in *Dred Scott v. Sandford* that no black person, whether free or slave, enjoyed citizenship under the Constitution, access to the federal courts, or "rights that any white person need respect." Taney based his opinion on his reading of the Revolution's history. White abolitionist William Lloyd Garrison, who campaigned against slavery for three full decades, concurred with Taney's historical analysis (though not at all with his moral attitude toward slavery), publicly burning a copy of the Constitution and calling it a "covenant with death and an agreement with hell" because of how it protected slavery, including the fugitive slave and three-fifths clauses.

Yet in a widely circulated speech given on July 5, 1852, black abolitionist Frederick Douglass, who had escaped from slavery in Taney's Maryland, described the same Constitution as a "glorious liberty document." He heaped praise on the people who wrested independence from Great Britain and created the American Republic, including slaveholders Washington and Jefferson. For Taney the heritage of the Revolution was complete, and it belonged to white people exclusively. Reluctantly, Garrison agreed. But for Douglass, as for still-obscure Abraham Lincoln in Illinois, the founding era had been only a beginning, particularly on the question of slavery.

This book will explore some of the historical problems that Michelle Obama raised in 2008, and that Martin Luther King, Frederick Douglass, William Lloyd Garrison, and Roger B. Taney all called up as well. What is the relationship between the institution of human slavery and the founding era of the American Republic, what we call the American Revolution? Approaching that problem requires understanding how slavery became a hugely important and powerful part of the colonial American world. It means exploring what black people did with the opportunities that the revolutionary era presented. It means understanding how what they did changed the nature and the direction of the Revolution itself, by challenging slavery in every way they could. But it also means realizing that the American Revolution set the conditions in which the Cotton Kingdom flourished and, eventually, the Confederate States of America appeared. In one sense the Revolution marked the beginning of slavery's world-wide end. In another, it led straight to the most powerful, self-confident slave society that the world ever has seen.

Others have dealt with the same issues, of course. I could not write here without drawing on their deep research, their serious thought, and their own attempts at big-picture accounts. I have borrowed widely, ideas and information alike, and I acknowledge my debts at the end of the book. But the story is worth telling and telling again. The intertwined questions of the American Revolution and slavery and of what black people did with the opportunities that the Revolution presented are just as central to understanding the Revolution as are the familiar stories of the Declaration of Independence, Valley Forge, Yorktown, and the Federal Convention. Showing greater nerve than wisdom, perhaps, I plan to tell the story somewhat differently from previous accounts.

There are many ways to approach and frame such a project. One might be to center on the intellectual and legal problem that slavery posed among a revolutionary people who claimed to value liberty above all and who announced as they stepped into world history that all men are created equal. Another is to discuss the efforts of some white people to do something about slavery. Neither of those subjects can be ignored, but the central interest here will be with the black people who lived through the revolutionary era: what they had to confront, how they seized their chances, what they said, what they wrote, and what they made of themselves and their time.

What they did was more than remarkable; it had no precedent in all of history. Whenever a chance to break out of slavery has appeared, enslaved people have seized the time and sought their freedom. Almost everywhere prior to the late eighteenth century they simply joined the existing society and accepted its rules, including the enslavement of others. Instances abound, from the ancient world to the pre-revolutionary western hemisphere. What the black people of revolutionary America did was profoundly different, because they set out to bring down slavery itself. Taken this way, the book is not about the Revolution's failure to abolish slavery within the new United States. It is about the beginning of slavery's end, not just in the United States but in the whole Atlantic world, and about how black Americans had a major part in bringing that about.

Taking that perspective helps to resolve a problem that has haunted understanding of the revolutionary era ever since London literary figure Samuel Johnson asked, in 1775, "how is it that we hear the loudest *yelps* for liberty among the drivers of negroes."[3] It is not enough to excuse well-meaning but ineffectual white people because "the time was not yet ripe." Nor is it enough to ask why the Revolution did not abolish slavery, or even whether it could have done so. It is not enough to ask whether the Founding Fathers (George Washington, Thomas Jefferson, Benjamin Franklin, and their like) could have ended it if they had lived up to their stated ideals, invoked their own prestige, and given a firm example.

We need instead to place the whole matter in a larger context, spanning the whole age of eighteenth- and early nineteenth-century democratic revolutions in the Atlantic world. The era of revolutions began small in the mid-1760s, with British colonial tax protests. By the time the era ended, about 1830, Britain's North American empire was broken, the American Republic had taken form, the great revolution in France had brought permanent consequences all across Europe, two separate world wars had been fought, and new western hemisphere republics stretched from Haiti and Mexico to Argentina and Chile.

What of slavery during this time? In 1760 slavery was a pan-American fact of life, from Quebec (where most enslaved people were Native Americans) and Boston to Rio de Janeiro and Buenos Aires. Continuing enslavement of Native American people was nearly (though not entirely) over. But whether the enslavers spoke French, English, Dutch, Danish, Spanish, or Portuguese, being of African descent had become their prime criterion for regarding other human beings as their prey. Full-blown slave societies, whose whole basis was labor wrested from unwilling bodies by fear and violence, flourished in the Chesapeake Bay, the Carolina and Georgia low country, the Caribbean, and Brazil. Colonial-era slavery's tentacles entangled the Americas and Africa together in a huge slave-plantation complex, all of it organized for the benefit of Europeans and of the white colonizers who tried to rebuild Europe in the New World. Understanding colonial-era slavery, not just in the Southern colonies or even just in British America, but in the world of its time, is the first great theme here.

By 1830 much was changed. Within the United States slavery was gone or well on its way to death in the northeast. Law forbade it to expand into the "Great West," north of the Ohio River. It had become a pressing subject in American public life that would not go away, however many times people turned their heads and pretended that they just didn't see. How slavery became a problem, rather than simply a fact of life, during the revolutionary era and what black people of the day did with the opportunities that their time presented to them forms the second great theme.

Like the political revolutions that transformed colonies into independent nations, monarchies into republics, and subjects into citizens, what began in

North America spread across huge distances. The greatest example is how the hugely oppressive slave system in French Ste. Domingue exploded into a violent revolution that drove out the French, completely destroyed slavery there during the 1790s, and led to the creation of independent Haiti. Britain banned the African slave trade in 1807, and the United States followed a year later, as soon as the Constitution allowed, in both cases with consequences for Africa. Two new African countries started to emerge as refuges for former slaves, Sierra Leone and Liberia. Slaveholding President Thomas Jefferson signed into law the act of Congress that ended the United States trade, his last major action against slavery. By 1830, Britain was nearing the point of freeing the 800,000 slaves who still labored in its West Indies colonies. The new republics of Latin America were ending slavery as well.

Yet in the United States slavery was spreading and prospering westward from the original southern colonies to beyond the Mississippi. It was spreading as well from Louisiana, which brought slavery with it when it entered the United States. Outside the United States slavery still flourished as of 1830 in the Empire of Brazil and in still-Spanish Cuba and Puerto Rico. Its destruction in the independent republics of South America was almost as drawn out as in New Jersey, where there still were a few slaves as late as 1860. Though Mexico had abolished slavery, it was resurgent in Mexican Texas, as Anglo settlers and their black so-called "servants" moved in from Arkansas, Louisiana, Mississippi, Alabama, and Tennessee. Despite the Haitian Revolution, France did not end slavery in its remaining sugar colonies, Guadeloupe and Martinique, until 1848, the same year that the Danes ended it in their Virgin Islands. The Dutch took even longer in Surinam and Curaçao, ending slavery there in 1863, the same year as the American Emancipation Proclamation. The United States was not at all alone in continuing slavery well into the nineteenth century.

Against this background it becomes clear both that the American Revolution did help to start the demolition of world slavery and how difficult and drawn-out that task proved to be. Without what black people did as the British colonies turned themselves into the United States, it seems doubtful that white colonists' American Revolution would have taken an anti-slavery turn at all. It seems probable that slavery's destruction elsewhere would have been long delayed.

But the Revolution also fostered the creation of the strongest slave regime that the world has ever seen, strong enough to wage a titanic struggle between 1861 and 1865 for its own survival. The South's main post-independence product, cotton, underpinned nineteenth-century industrial development in both Britain and the northeastern United States. The legal African slave trade closed in 1808. But as the Republic celebrated its first half-century in 1826, the South's enslaved population was increasing almost as fast as its free white people. A domestic slave trade was still ripping black families and communities to shreds in order to serve enslavers' needs. Nowhere else in the Americas did a slave population grow by natural increase rather than African imports. By 1860, when white Southerners were making up their minds to destroy the United States rather than accept Abraham Lincoln's election to the presidency, they ruled four million slaves, a vastly larger population than the West Indies or even Brazil ever possessed at any single time.

The book's final theme returns to the problem of historical memory posed by Michelle Obama, Jeremiah Wright, Martin Luther King, Frederick Douglass, and many others. It explores how black people, rather than the dominant culture, understood and tried to use the revolutionary past, including events outside the United States, how they drew upon that past for their own purposes, and how others sought to turn that past against them. It will do so against the background of the world struggle against slavery that the American Revolution helped ignite, but also against the background of slavery's strength within their United States.

The fundamental premise of slavery is to deny a slave any choice at all, on any matter whatsoever. The Greek philosopher Aristotle thought of slaves as being perfectly bound to the will of their masters and mistresses. The reality of American slavery was to deny most choice, on most matters, even the choice of people's names for themselves and their children. But the Revolution ruptured American society, bringing many separate moments when meaningful, serious choices became possible for slaves. No choice is without its costs. Every yes also is a no. But enslaved people did get their chances to join the British, or to stay with the Americans, to fight, to write, to petition, to demand, to seek assistance, and to go to court. As free men and women they would have the choice of staying in America or of leaving it. They made all sorts of choices. The only possible generalization is that, given the moment, almost all of them made those choices in the hope of bettering themselves and of doing something about slavery.

Tens of thousands of black people abandoned America, finding their freedom with the British. They were not betraying the Revolution in the manner of Benedict Arnold. They were making the most of its possibility of freedom, for themselves. Some people who stayed at first thought of abandoning the country later, as Du Bois and Carmichael/Ture were to do in their own times. Among them was New Englander Paul Cuffee, sea captain and seafarer. But most black people in the young United States understood in their bones that Africa lay far away and far behind, however important were the memories of it that that they cherished and handed down. They had been born in America and had had a large hand in building it. Among *them,* after some thought of leaving for Africa or Haiti, were James Forten, Philadelphia businessman and community leader, and African Methodist Episcopal Church founder Bishop Richard Allen.

Whether "returning sail" to Africa or remaining in America, these people placed themselves among the founders of a major American tradition. From the time of the Revolution onward, they insisted that the fine words of the Declaration of Independence about the "self-evident" rights of all men to "life, liberty and the pursuit of happiness" and of the Constitution about securing "the blessings of liberty" were meaningless, if they did not reach far beyond the gentlemen in powdered hair and silk stockings who wrote them.

The credit for the fine words is to the gentlemen Americans still rightly honor as "the Founding Fathers," a point that Frederick Douglass fully understood. But the credit for taking that language seriously goes to the women and men who reached out during the American Republic's founding time and who have continued reaching ever since then to claim that language and its consequences for themselves. Nobody had to reach across greater obstacles, nobody had greater difficulty grasping the American Revolution's promise. But reach and grasp they did, no matter how slippery the prize seemed to be, no matter how much it continued to elude them.

In one sense, then, what Michelle Obama said in 2008 about being proud of America for the first time was just a tactical political mistake, made by a relative newcomer on the national stage during the intense heat of a presidential campaign. But like most mistakes it was revealing, not in regard to her but because she posed a central question in regard to American history itself. This book explores some of that question's dimensions, from the point of view of people who started with no reason to be proud of America at all, but who claimed what is best about it for themselves, and who changed American history for the better because they did so.

Notes

1. blogs.abcnews.com/politicalpunch/2008/02/michelle-obam-1.html (accessed February 27, 2011).

2. Personal Recollection, Cornell University, 1967.

3. Quoted in David Brion Davis, *The Problem of Slavery in the Age of Revolution, 1770–1823* (New York: Oxford University Press, 1999), 275.

~

CHAPTER ONE

"Fire, Fire, Scorch, Scorch"

Enslaved Africans in the Colonial World

"Fire, Fire, Scorch, Scorch, A Little, Damn It, Bye-and-Bye."

—Quack, A New York City slave, 1741

Between Christopher Columbus's first westward voyage in 1492 and the American revolutionary era, Europeans invaded and transformed the western hemisphere. Great opportunities lured them. They could bring their Christian faith to native people. They could practice the kind of Christianity they wanted. They could spread the glory and dominion of their kings and queens. They could remake what they found in Europe's image. Some, who were lucky, ruthless, or both, might become very rich. Most thought they could create better lives for themselves. Westward, the land seemed bright. For many of the European migrants, that proved to be so.

But everywhere they went, the explorers, invaders, colonizers, and settlers brought human slavery. During the colonial period a vastly greater number of Africans than Europeans crossed the Atlantic to the Americas. For them, there was no reason for the land or what they found there to seem bright at all. They went as captives, and they joined captured Native American people in slavery. More than any other institution, slavery became the great unifying colonial institution, throughout the whole hemisphere.

We cannot appreciate what black people did during the American Revolution, which is the subject of this book, unless we understand what they faced as colonial America developed, from the time of Columbus onward. Nor can we cannot appreciate slavery in the places that became the United

1

States without the background of slavery throughout the hemisphere, at least in outline. Three powerful images, the first in words that a settler wrote down in earliest Virginia, the second a painting from late eighteenth-century South Carolina, and the third a map of New York City as of 1741, plunge us into colonial-era slavery. Each image is North American; each is very specific. But none of them displays its full meaning except against a world and hemispheric background.

The first image comes from the pen of Virginia colonist John Rolfe, after Rolfe returned from a visit that he and his famous Native American wife Pocahontas made to England. She died there, and he left behind their newborn son, whom he never saw again. Rolfe discovered that Caribbean tobacco would grow well in Virginia soil. He and other growers began using indentured English servants to plant, tend, harvest, and cure the crop. But at the end of August, 1619, Rolfe wrote, "came a dutch man of warre that sold us twenty Negars" whom the Dutch had seized from a Portuguese trader that was bound from west Africa to the Caribbean.[1] The outline story of those twenty people is familiar, the stuff of textbook accounts. They had been captured into slavery in Africa, they had been slaves at sea, and it is easy to assume they remained slaves in Virginia. It is just as easy to fast-forward from them to the four million enslaved black people laboring all across the South on the eve of the Civil War, with nothing to separate them except the enormous growth in their numbers. But doing so would be wrong.

Rolfe's word-sketch has three separate dimensions. It presents a bare historical fact, which is that twenty Africans did arrive. It raises a historical probability, which is that these were the first black Virginians. That is not absolutely certain, but Rolfe most likely would not have noticed them otherwise. It also poses a historical problem, which is whether these were the first Virginia slaves. To appreciate the problem, consider another early arrival, identified as "a Negro" and bearing the Christian Portuguese name Antonio. He landed at Jamestown on an English vessel, the *James*, a year after those first twenty. Apparently he had been born in the Kingdom of Kongo, which had been Catholic since the mid-fifteenth century. Whatever his route from there to Virginia, Antonio was the sort who learned and adapted fast. After a few years of service he gained his freedom and gave himself a new name, Anthony Johnson. He prospered, acquiring property (including legally-bound servants on the same terms he had experienced), marrying a black woman who also had survived servitude, and earning his neighbors' respect. He seemed set to pass both his African heritage and his Virginia freedom on to his children. One of the Johnsons' sons chose the name Angola for the farm he acquired in Maryland. The New World proved about as good to him and his family as to European colonists. More than that, if his story holds for other early arrivals, how did Virginia become a place of slavery?

To answer that question we need to look much wider than Virginia and much deeper in time than 1619 or 1620. Looking at it that way, we can see that there was slavery all around the earliest Virginians' world, but not in Virginia itself. When Christopher Columbus crossed the Atlantic in 1492, slavery already existed across much of the world, including the Italian city of Genoa where he was born, and Spain, whose monarchs Ferdinand and Isabella sponsored his voyages. Columbus and his fellow voyagers enslaved Taino Indians almost as soon as they met them, and brought some back to Spain. The Spanish conquistadors who followed began enslaving Native Americans on a large scale, some to take to Europe, others to grow crops and dig for gold. Native Americans enslaved Spaniards as well. Columbus saw African slavery directly. He profited from it himself at least once, in the year 1479, on a voyage to the Atlantic island of Madeira for a cargo of slave-grown sugar. By then, Portuguese and Spanish seafarers had been carrying captive African people to sugar slavery in the Atlantic Islands for years.

Black Africans also practiced slavery. For them, in broad terms, slaves were signs of prestige and valuable objects in trade. Status, not race, separated masters from slaves in their world. They might adopt their slaves into freedom and full community membership. Light-skinned North Africans raided across the Sahara and down Africa's east coast, bringing people darker than themselves to slavery in Egypt, Turkey, Arabia, and as far as South Asia. During Europe's Middle Ages slaves came from Africa to cultivate sugar on the islands of the Mediterranean Sea. But they also came from Eastern Europe and Central Asia. Some medieval slaves in both the Muslim and Christian worlds were black, some olive-skinned, and some blond and blue-eyed. Muslims captured at sea might be enslaved by Christians, and Christians by Muslims. Medieval Norse raiders enslaved Anglo-Saxons and Celts from the British Isles, as well as French, Spaniards, Portuguese, Lithuanians, Poles, and Russians. The English word "slave," the French *esclave*, the Spanish *esclavo*, and the German *Sklave* all are cognate to Slav, because many Slavic people became enslaved. The Arabic term *abd* simply means servant, without any ethnic reference.

Europeans went to colonial America willingly, by the hundreds of thousands. Africans went, in far greater numbers, by the millions, because other Africans captured and sold them. One group of enslavers, called the Imbangala, ranged widely south and east of the Kingdom of Kongo during the seventeenth and early eighteenth centuries. They were mostly male and they were strong enough to force alliances upon the monarchs of settled African kingdoms. They laid waste wherever they went, and they made it their business to capture other Africans, transport them over long distances, and trade them as slaves. The Imbangala and people like them created one of several moving slave frontiers that swept across Africa, gathering human beings as they went. The Imbangala's captives and others from Mozambique on Africa's east coast most likely ended up in Brazil, after their captors force-marched them to Luanda. Still others, from western and central Africa, and from as far away as the island of Madagascar, were bound for the Caribbean sugar islands and the British mainland colonies.

The concept of an advancing frontier is familiar in the mythology of the American West, and it does not usually include the idea of slavery. To Americans, at least, it usually brings up images of freedom and opportunity spreading across the continent. The frontier that spread across Africa brought not freedom but rather enslavement on a huge scale. Many other groups besides the Imbangala took direct part in African enslavement. All along the African coastline and deep into the African interior there were kings and rulers who cooperated in the slave trade and profited from it, and who, in return, received relative immunity.

All of the enslavers were brutal, including the Africans who captured their fellow Africans, the European seafarers who received the captives, the merchants who dispatched the ships, and the colonists who awaited the captives at their journey's end. So, for that matter, were the Native American enslavers who added their own captives to the ones brought by the African trade. The Africans and Native Americans probably would have practiced slavery of some sort without the Europeans. But the Europeans provided the market to which the enslavers brought millions of people for sale.

Law, history, and sacred scripture, including both the Christian and Jewish versions of the Bible and the Muslim Qur'an, all seemed to justify the enslavement of some people by others, given the right circumstances. Such circumstances could include being "infidel," meaning in Muslim eyes Christians or a believers in many gods, or, for Christians, Muslims or, again, believers in many gods. Medieval Eastern European Orthodox Christians who did not acknowledge the pope were fair game for Western European Catholics. A person whose life was forfeit in war might be killed or enslaved at the victor's choice, although Western Europeans were ceasing enslavement of one another's soldiers. A slave in the Ottoman Turkish Empire could rise to a high position, including the sultan's office of grand vizier in Istanbul. Enslaved European Christians became *Mamluk* soldiers in Egypt. But the slave-vizier had no real legal rights, and could be sent to the galleys at the sultan's whim.

Slavery has been a nearly universal fact in world history, but enslavers always have sought some justification for what they are doing to other people. As Europeans started to move to the newly found western hemisphere "race" did not figure among such justifications. The concept of race did not exist, not in the biological sense that some physical trait (such as the color of skin or the texture of hair) supposedly betokens all of a person's qualities, and not in the cultural sense of belonging to a group with a genetic heritage and a history in common. Africans had no sense of themselves as "black" and the western hemisphere's people had no sense of themselves as "natives" or "red," let alone "Indians." Europeans did not look at them in such terms either, or at themselves as "white."

King Charles V of Spain decreed an end to his subjects' enslavement of Native Americans in 1550, after listening to a ferocious debate on the subject. During the debate, the Catholic priest Fray Bartholomé de las Casas argued passionately against Indian enslavement. Las Casas had taken part in it as a conquistador, until he changed his ways and joined the Dominican Friars. But as the black American writer David Walker was to note with great anger centuries later, even as Las Casas was condemning Indian slavery, he also declared that there was an endless supply of readily available Africans. In the Spanish priest's view it was not race that determined the difference, but rather that Africans supposedly had refused their chance to embrace Christianity and Native Americans had not the chance at all.

Despite the Spanish monarch's decree, native enslavement continued for centuries under all the colonizers, Spaniards, Portuguese, French, Dutch, and English alike. Massachusetts enslaved hundreds of native people in 1676, after it defeated a coalition led by the Wampanoags in King Philip's War. It shipped them to Carolina, the West Indies, and even to Africa. South Carolina employed Westo Indians to capture other Native Americans from nearby and from deep into the continent, and then enslaved the Westo themselves when it defeated them in a war in 1680. In 1673 the French Jesuit priest Jacques Marquette spotted Indians with firearms near modern Memphis, Tennessee. In all probability they were on a slaving mission for Spaniards in Florida or for the English who had begun settling South Carolina. In 1722 the five *Haudenosaunee* (Iroquois) Nations negotiated an agreement with the governor of Virginia. They would be safe if they stayed west of the Blue Ridge when they journeyed southward to make war against their Catawba enemies. But if they crossed the mountains, enslavement awaited them, as they recognized and accepted. They side-stepped the governor's request that they return escaped Virginia slaves who, as he and they both knew, had found refuge among them.

Their Catawba enemies enjoyed no such option. They faced nearby South Carolina's wrath, which meant facing their own enslavement and extinction, unless they tracked down escaped black slaves and returned them. As late as 1776, South Carolina leader William Henry Drayton promised Cherokee land and Cherokee slaves to frontier settlers who joined the revolution. Far to the west, the Comanche established a powerful, long-lasting horse-borne empire on the Great Plains, basing its economy partly on enslaving other native people. Some of their captives went to Spanish Texas and New Mexico. They traded others to French Louisiana and Canada. Still others found their way to the British settlements. Spanish, Portuguese, French, Dutch, and British alike, the conquistadors, colonizers, and settlers took slavery with them, or developed it wherever they went.

But they did so in different ways. Full-blown, legal slavery existed in Spain and Portugal at the time of Columbus. Spanish slave law reached back through the Middle Ages to Ancient Rome. The conquistadors who took over Hispaniola, Cuba, Mexico, and Peru simply imported it. But when the English founded Virginia, slavery had not existed among them in their country for centuries. On the Caribbean Islands and in the mainland places that the English claimed, the settlers created it themselves.

The law of British-American slavery took shape piecemeal, colony-by-colony, starting in Barbados in 1636. The Barbados code denied to slaves all the rights that Englishmen and women enjoyed under English law. Killing or maiming a slave would be no crime. The only requirement that the law imposed on the masters was to clothe the slaves. On the mainland, Massachusetts, rather than Virginia or Carolina, established the first slave law, in its "Body of Liberties" of 1641. Supposedly these Puritan settlers declared there would be no "bond slaverie, villinage or Captivitie amongst us." But they allowed themselves two big exceptions, "lawfull Captives taken in just warres, and such strangers as willingly selle themselves or are sold to us."[2] "Taken in just warres" was among the rationales that slave merchants on the African coast were using, and the passive-voice "are sold to us" completely begged the question of how the victim had been enslaved. These Puritans said that they abhorred slavery, but they were willing enough to have it among themselves and, eventually, to join enthusiastically in the African slave trade and take advantage of it. Others like them who tried to settle at the same time on Providence Island in the Caribbean just got on with the business of buying slaves.

Seventeenth-century Virginia shaped its slave law over several decades. Step-by-step, white Virginians stripped black servants of their property, denied them firearms, forbade the men among them to have sexual contact with white women, banned all black-white marriages, treated their servitude as for life, and decreed that enslaved women's children would follow the condition of their mothers, whoever was the father. Imitating Barbados, Virginia's assembly enacted a law in 1660 that protected a master who "casually" killed a slave during the course of punishment. A year later, in 1670, it provided that all non-Christian "servants" brought in "by shipping . . . were to be slaves for life."[3] Slavery was not long in coming to colonial Virginia, but another possibility did exist when those first twenty "Negars" arrived. British colonists made it for themselves.

Because British colonials made their own law of slavery, what they made varied from province to province. Under Dutch rule, the slaves of seventeenth-century New Netherlands enjoyed the possibility of half-freedom, which meant that the Dutch West Indies Company owned them but left them free to run their own lives. When the English conquered New Netherlands in 1664, renaming it New York, that privilege ended. Pennsylvania's Quaker founders practiced slavery, but they lived from the start with a tension between it and their fundamental principle that all human beings contain God's inner light. Carolina, whose first settlers came from overcrowded Barbados, simply imported the island's slave law. Georgia tried to do without slavery after its founding in 1733. But it turned to slavery in 1751, borrowing its law intact from South Carolina, just as South Carolina had borrowed intact from Barbados.

Unlike Spanish practice, colonial British slave law gave no recognition to slave marriages or slave parenthood, so masters could separate husbands and wives or parents and children as they chose. Only in a few places did it permit slaves to purchase their freedom. In Virginia a master who wanted to free his slaves could not do so without a special act of the House of Burgesses. Most colonies banned teaching slaves how to read. Insubordination to any white person, not just to a slave's master or mistress, justified physical punishment. Except for allegations of illegal enslavement (primarily based on having a free female ancestor), no slave could go to court, other than as a defendant in a criminal case. If that happened, the slave would be judged under different rules and procedures from a white person facing the same charge. Slaves who witnessed a master torture or murder one of their fellows could not testify against the perpetrator. British colonials wanted the slavery that surrounded them. They made the laws, and they bought the slaves.

Turn to the second image, a painting that hangs in the Gibbs Museum of Art in Charleston, South Carolina. It shows a plantation called Mulberry, as artist Thomas Coram viewed it about the year 1800. In Coram's painting

Image 1.1. Many plantation landscapes emphasized the planter's "great house." Thomas Coram's "Mulberry Plantation" puts the slave quarters and the people who lived there at the front of the frame instead. ©Image Gibbes Museum of Art / Carolina Art Association

Mulberry looks much as it had since 1714, when colonial politician Thomas Broughton had it built, and as it still does, but with one difference. Seen as Broughton intended, from the West Branch of the Cooper River, the building is handsome, a testimony in brick to its owners' wealth, good taste, power, and commitment. Such a house was not the property of an absentee owner or of somebody who wanted to leave when he had made enough money. Broughton was making a statement. He was in South Carolina to stay.

Coram, however, showed the house from the rear. Eight slave huts, closer to the point of view than the house and invisible from the river view, dominate and structure his painting. They stand in two straight lines, presumably by the planter's order, and they seem as Coram painted them to be solidly built of brick. Main house and slave huts alike, the plantation's architecture derived from models and memories far away. Like George Washington's Mount Vernon or Thomas Jefferson's Monticello, the design of the main house is rich-man's imitation-European. The huts, however, seem to be African, particularly their steeply pitched roofs of thatched straw. Coram also showed some of the people who dwelt in them. They are deep in the frame and they have their backs to the viewer, so we cannot see their faces. The most clearly defined are a man and a woman, each bearing a heavy iron hoe.

Unlike Anthony Johnson, these people indubitably were slaves. Again unlike Johnson, their names are lost. But in all probability, they did not bear names that they chose for themselves. A story from early eighteenth-century Virginia, after slavery there had congealed, probably applies to Mulberry's Africans too. Virginia's greatest planter of the day, Robert "King" Carter, was receiving arrivals from Africa. Carter took upon himself the biblical Adam's privilege of bestowing names upon them. As he told one of his overseers, "I named them . . . [and] I am sure we repeated them so often to them that every one knew their names." Some slave names, such as Cuffee (Kofi), were African-derived. Most were degrading, fit for gods and goddesses (Venus, Juno, Jupiter), or children (Jack, Billy), or animals (Jumper), but not for adult human beings. None of Carter's captives would have a family name, linking that person to ancestors or descendants. The overseers on Carter's far-flung properties were to take "care that the negroes . . . always go by ye names we gave them."[4]

Both the clash of building styles at Mulberry plantation and Carter's little ceremony of renaming his newly arrived slaves suggest the violent, bitter conflict that underpinned all American slavery. Colonizers and settlers were in America because they wanted to be there, pursuing their happiness. The inhabitants of the huts at Mulberry, and of slave quarters from Canada to Argentina, were there because they had no choice. In the words of an old-school white Southern historian, "the slave was, by the very nature of slavery, engaged in continual warfare."[5] Nobel-laureate novelist Toni Morrison makes the same point in *Beloved*, her great account of slavery in nineteenth-century Kentucky: "Not a house in the country ain't packed to its rafters with some dead Negro's grief."[6]

The women and men in Coram's painting seem to be returning from the rice fields, as enslaved people had been doing at Mulberry for three-quarters of a century by the time he painted them, and as they would do for six long decades to come. They were survivors, both of rice-growing's lethal conditions and of the African slave trade. In the early years of Carolina rice slavery, when Mulberry was built, growing the crop had been so difficult that South Carolina's black population increased only because new imports from Africa were larger than the death rate among people already there. Add the most careful estimate for the number of Carolina slaves alive in 1736 (26,000) to the number of Africans brought in by 1740 (15,000) and the total is about 41,000. But in 1740 only about 39,000 black South Carolinians were alive, despite the massive imports, and despite the birth of African-American children. Without the slave trade, Carolina's black population could not sustain itself. This place was a killer.

It still was a killer when Coram touched brush to canvas sixty years later. Unlike Virginia, whose slave population was starting to grow naturally by the mid-eighteenth century, South Carolina and its neighbor Georgia kept on importing all the Africans they could, until the United States ended its African slave trade in 1808. Coram's people may have had direct memories of a free life far away. People like them came to Carolina primarily from the West African "Rice Coast." English planters valued them for what these Africans knew about growing this warm-climate, wet-country crop, as well as for the work power of their muscles, sinews, and bones.

Without understanding human biology or medicine, the planters also knew that the Africans had some sort of resistance to the otherwise deadly "fever and ague" (*falciparum* malaria), which haunted the region from springtime, when the mosquitoes appeared, to first frost, when the insects finally died away. They seemed to have resistance to yellow fever as well. Nobody, black or white, linked resisting malaria to the ghastly pain and short life of a baby born with the sickle-cell condition that parents could pass to their children. Genetically, a man or woman who carries the hereditary trait for the condition has a better chance of resisting malaria, which is why the trait evolved. But if a man and a woman both carry the trait, they have a one-in-four probability that they will have a child with full-blown sickle-cell disease. The red blood cells of a sufferer can deform and clump together in the blood vessels, leading to severe suffering and early death. The disease would not even have a name until the twentieth century. But it was part of life at Mulberry.

The slaves at Mulberry were just a few of the Africans who crossed to the western hemisphere over three and a half centuries following Christopher Columbus's first trans-Atlantic voyage. In numbers, these Wolof, Serber, Fula, Wangara, Jalunga, Susu, Temne, Yoruba, Ibo, and many more vastly dwarfed the French, Britons, Dutch, Swedes, Danes, Spaniards, and Portuguese who established and named new-world colonies. Historians dispute the exact figures, but the most recent and thorough estimate is that about 9,599,000 slaves survived the journey and arrived in the New World. The greatest numbers went to Brazil and the Caribbean, about 3.9 million and 4.65 million respectively. By the same count, about 361,000 reached the British mainland colonies and, after the Revolution, the independent United States. Another careful study of the post-Revolution United States slave trade raises that figure to about 600,000. The only really safe generalizations are that a huge number of people were torn from Africa, that deaths on the journey to slavery were high, and that the British colonies/United States accounted for a small proportion of the whole trade.

In the sugar regions, as in early rice-growing Carolina, conditions and hard exploitation killed enslaved people faster than they could reproduce. The worst instances came in the West Indies, and knowing about conditions there gives a frame of reference for North America. Jamaica imported about a million Africans altogether, but its population at the end of the eighteenth century was barely more than three hundred thousand. But in North America, people started to survive, despite the psychological shock and the physical horror of capture, despite their journey, despite their justified fear of what awaited them (including the prospect that they had been captured in order to be slaughtered and eaten), and despite the despair and endless hard labor that actually awaited them at the voyage's end. As the survivors began having children, the imbalanced sex and age ratio of the slave trade (roughly two men for every woman) righted themselves naturally. There began to be more births than deaths, and more children had a chance of living past infancy. Black life expectancy in North America began to climb and the population began to grow. In the eighteenth-century West Indies, however, life expectancy remained a bare seven years after arrival from Africa.

By 1825 the United States had about a quarter of the western hemisphere's black population, despite having received at most 6 percent of the forced travelers. When Britain ended West Indies slavery in 1834 about eight hundred thousand people became free. They were what remained from the millions whom the slavers had captured and taken there. When the United States took its fifth census, in 1830, there already were far more enslaved African-Americans, just over two million of them. That number doubled again, to four million, over the next thirty years. By hemispheric standards, North American slavery began small. But the plantation slave system in the Southern colonies and states grew for as long as United States slavery lasted, ultimately dwarfing all the others. On three separate counts, eighteenth-century Mulberry was an outpost. Economically, it stood at the very edge of a plantation world that was far more developed in the Caribbean and Brazil. Culturally, it represented Broughton's desire to create a British place for himself in America. For the people who actually built the great house, lived in the quarters with their African-style roofs, and labored in the rice fields, it was an outpost of faraway Africa, just one of many in the African-Atlantic world.

Silently but firmly, the roofs that Coram showed on Mulberry's slave quarter present one possible way for the captured people to survive. This was holding on to memory. The people who lived in those dwellings knew who they, or their ancestors, had been before the enslavers caught them. Open rebellion was another way, dangerous and not to be done lightly. In 1739 South Carolina slaves rose near the Stono River, arming themselves, killing whites who opposed them, and starting toward Florida, where they knew they had a chance of receiving Spanish freedom from the colony's governor. The Stono Rebellion was more than just a rising of rage against an unbearable situation. The rebels were not ignorant, and they had a rational goal in mind. Some of them seem to have been Catholic Christians, from Kongo. Had the rebels reached their Spanish fellow Catholics, they might have joined the armed black community that Florida's governor had established north of St. Augustine, known now as Fort Mose or Musa. The fort's people were former slaves of the English. Catholic Spaniards could have asked for no more willing protectors against their Protestant English enemies than these. But those Spaniards also practiced slavery. Escape to them did not challenge slavery itself, nor did reaching a Maroon community of people who had freed themselves and taken refuge in some place that the masters found difficult to reach. There was one in Jamaica's Blue Mountains, with which the lowland British sugar growers actually negotiated a treaty. By mutual agreement, the planters would not destroy the Maroon community, as long as the community turned new escapees away.

Enslavement separated wives and husbands, parents and children, and sisters and brothers from one another, almost always never to meet again. But people caught up in slavery's web sometimes crossed paths again, far from where they first met. One such encounter took place after American independence in Natchez, Mississippi, when a white man on horseback and a slave on foot recognized one another. The white man addressed the slave as "boy," as Southern custom required by then. The black man knew that, whatever white people called him, he remained Abdul Rahman Ibrahima Ibn Sori, and that he had been a prince. He and the white man, Dr. John Cox, had met in Africa once, at the court of his royal father. Leading his father's army in war, Prince Ibrahima had met defeat, which took him to his Mississippi enslavement. He did find release after his case became known, but he died on his way back home.

Like many Muslims, the enslaved Prince Ibrahima was literate in Arabic, and he struggled to retain both his reading knowledge and his Islamic faith. The Africa from which he came was no land of untutored savages. Africans had mastered iron smelting and they could forge their own metal tools, pots, and weapons. They grew cotton, wove it into fine, brightly dyed fabrics, and turned the fabrics into elegant clothes. Like Ibrahima, many could read and write Arabic. Timbuktu, now to most people a byword for remote backwardness, had housed a great Islamic university since Europe's so-called "Dark Ages," attended by both light-skinned North African and black sub-Saharan people. People along Africa's east coast were thoroughly familiar with long-distance coastal seafaring, as far north as the Red Sea and the Persian Gulf and even on to India. Savannah-dwelling Africans had mastered open-range cattle herding on horseback, a skill that some enslaved cowboys practiced in South Carolina before the province's turn to rice culture early in the eighteenth century. After the rice revolution, white Carolinians long debated the origins of their staple crop, speculating on the Orient and Italy as possible sources. The rice-growing zone along the African coast seems far more likely, with Carolinians melding African knowledge of the plant and English understanding of how to drain wetlands and how to flood them with fresh water when the crop required.

Turn once again, to the third image. It is David Grim's map of New York City in 1742, drawn as he remembered the city seventy-two years later, in 1813. Grim's map shows two places where slaves and people linked to them died that year by public execution. One was a gibbet where thirteen slaves and four white people were hanged. The other was a pyre where four black New Yorkers burned to death. Their crime, supposedly, was trying to burn New York down. Decades later, as an old man, Grim still was haunted by the memory. Like John Rolfe's word sketch of the first Africans at Jamestown or Thomas Coram's image of Mulberry, Grim's map of colonial New York City opens up a whole world of slave experience.

As of 1742, slaves made up about one-fifth of New York's population, and the city could not have done without them. They toiled on its docks, loading and unloading ships. They swept its streets. They labored side by side with white men building houses and ships, carting goods and driving rich people's coaches, baking bread, hauling water and firewood, handling grain and flour, making sails, forging iron, and spinning rope. Black women cooked much of New York's food. They nursed babies, spun yarn, wove cloth, and sewed garments. Black people did virtually all of the city's really dirty work, including, in the absence of sewers, taking away the reeking tubs of "night soil" that New Yorkers' bodies voided.

New York City was hundreds of miles from the northernmost plantations, but it thrived because of plantation slavery. New York ships carried slave-grown West Indian sugar and molasses up the coast from the Caribbean and across the Atlantic to Britain. They transported slave-grown Chesapeake tobacco and slave-grown Carolina rice, in barrels made of wood hewn (sometimes by slaves) from New York trees, bound with hoops that New York blacksmiths (who often had slaves to assist them) had forged from New York iron, which slaves might have dug and helped to smelt. New York distilleries transformed West Indian molasses into rum. Some of the rum, along with

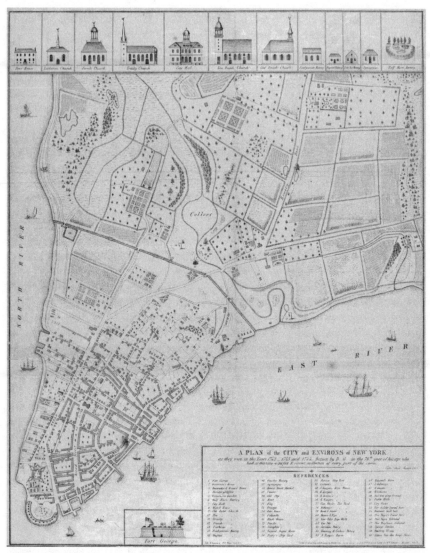

Image 1.2. David Grim, Map of New York City, 1813. Courtesy of the New York Public Library

other colonial and European goods, went to Africa in New York ships, to pay for more slaves. Then the vessels carried new captives from Africa to slavery at any Atlantic port where a vessel flying Great Britain's proud Union Jack flag was allowed to enter. Urban and rural alike, white New Yorkers prospered because of slavery and were immersed in it, even the ones who held no slaves themselves.

About a mile north of the tip of Manhattan Island, where the built-up area gave way to farmland and gentlemen's estates, a place called the African Burial Ground received an ever-growing number of bodies during the eighteenth century. New York law forbade black funerals at nighttime, when fellow slaves could gather to mourn, and it forbade honoring the deceased with African ceremonies. No headstones marked the lives these people had led, or offered silent solace to their survivors.

As the city expanded after the American Revolution, the burial ground was forgotten and built over, until many feet of soil and rubble covered it. Workmen digging the foundations for a federal construction project near the modern City Hall and Brooklyn Bridge found it again in 1991. Work stopped while historians and archeologists were called in and recognized what the builders had uncovered. Community outrage at simply continuing the building led to one corner of the much larger site becoming a national historical monument. Scientists at Howard University examined the bones. Upon them they found mute evidence of the beatings, injuries, poor diets, and early deaths that New York City slaves had endured. Four hundred and nineteen skeletons have been reburied at the historical site with ceremony and respect. Many more, presumably, still lie untouched nearby. A spiral path leads visitors into the outdoor memorial, built, as visitors learn, in the form of an African Ancestral Libation Chamber. Somebody who follows the spiral downward toward its center passes plaques identifying specific burials, each haunted by such a phrase as "female, age 16–20, with child, age 1–2" or "male, age 45–50." Here, finally, are the grave markers that these people's survivors could not put up in their own time.

What, then, of 1742, when more bodies than usual were interred, after a wave of executions that David Grim remembered many decades later? During the previous winter, which was fiercely cold, one fire after another had broken out across the largely wooden city. Blazes struck the fort at the lower end of Manhattan Island, the governor's house, private dwellings, a stable, a warehouse, scattered haystacks, and more. Smoldering coals at some of the fires suggested that somebody had set them deliberately. The ponds where firefighters drew water were frozen and any one of the fires could have set the whole city in flames. "Fire, fire, scorch, scorch, a little, damn it, bye and bye," a black man named Quack was heard to say as one fire broke out.[7] Had he set a fire himself? Was he applauding, or perhaps making a bitter prophecy? We cannot know for sure, because these are the only words of his that ever were recorded. Whatever his intention, Quack was among the slaves who burned at the stake.

Justice Daniel Horsmanden of New York's Supreme Court of Judicature launched an investigation. He tied together the suspicious fires, a few burglaries, and John Hughson's tavern near the Hudson River. Hughson's was a place where black New Yorkers, seafarers of many shades and languages, and poor New York whites drank and caroused. Supposedly they dined there lavishly, though it is difficult to imagine how most of Hughson's patrons could have afforded even a decent meal, let alone a feast, especially that bitterly cold winter. Supposedly they plotted to burn the city, take its women, and establish their own rule. Every city has such places, and both the authorities and the good folks usually stay away, exaggerating in their imaginations whatever goes on behind their doors. A tavern on Chalmers Alley in Charleston, South Carolina, known as "the Pink House" was much the same as Hughson's, and there were many others of the same sort. Unlike Hughson's tavern, the Pink House still stands, serving now as an art gallery.

In Horsmanden's mind, Hughson's tavern became the headquarters of a truly "hellish" plot, so he launched a campaign of arrests and trials. The great fear that Horsmanden fanned swept up slaves who did dirty work and slaves who wore fancy livery and powdered wigs while they served rich New Yorkers. All of them came before his court. So did Spanish-speaking prisoners of war, captured at sea and enslaved upon arrival in New York, who may or may not have been of African descent. A mysterious white outsider named John Ury, who said he was a Latin teacher but who Horsmanden thought was an undercover Catholic priest, was charged with preaching sedition. Mary Burton, who worked at Hughson's tavern, provided testimony that linked the thefts to the tavern. Other evidence came from hearsay attributed to a young Irish woman, Peggy Kerry. She frequented Hughson's and had borne a child by one of its black customers. Kerry went to the scaffold on June 12. On the same day, three slaves burned.

Was there a plot? Was there any connection between the robberies and the fires? Had a few blowhards boasted too much under the influence of winter ale and rum punch? Was it all just hysteria? Horsmanden's account is our main source about what went on in his court, and we cannot be sure about the testimony he heard. One New Englander drew an obvious comparison, with the disgraced Salem, Massachusetts, witchcraft affair of 1691. But unlike the accusers and judges in Salem, who relied on invisible "spectral evidence," there were worldly reasons in 1741 to take the notion of a plot seriously, because slave rebellions seemed to be breaking out across the western hemisphere.

Slaves rose up on the Caribbean island of Antigua in 1736. Three years later, in 1739, came the Stono Rebellion in South Carolina. "Maroon" communities of runaway slaves were holding whites at bay in the Great Dismal Swamp south of Chesapeake Bay, in isolated places scattered around the

Carolina Low Country, in Jamaica's Blue Mountains, and in Brazil. Some slaves were finding refuge in Indian country. Sailors and travelers brought news to New York of all these. John Ury probably was the Latin teacher that he claimed to be, not a seditious Catholic priest, and the Spanish-speaking captives who got caught up in the New York events may not have been African at all. But in 1741 the Catholic Mose community in Florida was no secret in the British colonies. Horsmanden certainly was wrong when he tried to use Ury as a classic "outside agitator," but he was close to the mark in his fearful realization that slaves often knew what was going on far away.

City people had direct memories as well. Older New Yorkers could recall that in 1708 slaves on Long Island had rebelled and murdered a family of seven. Four of them were executed "with all the torment possible."[8] In 1712 slaves in New York City set a fire and killed white men who came to put it out. The authorities executed nineteen, including three at the stake, one over a slow fire for the greatest possible torment, one by starvation, and one by having his living body torn apart.

Eighteenth-century New York City was just one place in the African Atlantic world. Ports all around the Atlantic basin were African too. Black men and women dwelt in British London, Plymouth, Bristol, Cardiff, Liverpool and Glasgow, in Dutch Amsterdam and Rotterdam, in French Le Havre, Brest, Nantes, Bordeaux, Spanish Bilbao and Seville, and in Portuguese Lisbon and Oporto. Somebody (black or white, slave or free) from any of these places could have felt more or less at home in port cities along Africa's west coast (Elmina, Cape Coast, Lagos, Luanda), in Brazil (Salvador, Recife), around the Caribbean (Bridgetown, Kingston, Cap Haïtien, Port-au-Prince, Havana), and in North America (Charleston, Norfolk, Baltimore, Newport, Boston, and Quebec). Black seafarers as well as white ones manned the vessels that carried Atlantic commerce, including commerce in slaves. Every major city that faced the eighteenth-century Atlantic was in some sense a slaving port.

Whatever European tongue the colonists spoke, Portuguese, Spanish, English, French, Dutch, or Danish, the whole American slave system developed on the edges of and under the protection of European empires. Lisbon, Madrid, London, Paris, Amsterdam, and Copenhagen were as caught up in African enslavement, the trans-Atlantic slave trade, and the wealth that slavery produced as were black enslavers in Africa, the white owners, captains, and crews of slave ships, and the masters of American plantations. European-style laws and treaties defined the terms of enslavement and set the powers that masters could exercise. European navies protected traders in coastal African ports and shippers at sea. European bankers and insurers financed the vessels that brought slaves across the Atlantic and that carried slave-grown sugar, coffee, rice, indigo, and tobacco to market. European armies protected American colonies from invasion and uprisings. Great European ports thrived because of their trade in slaves, and in the goods that slaves produced. Western Europe's cityscapes and countryside were dotted with the houses of slave traders and absentee slave masters who had made great fortunes. Successful masters who went "home" pushed their way into the European nobility and bourgeoisie. Without European demand for slave goods and without European protection for the whole institution, colonial western hemisphere slavery could not have developed, let alone have thrived.

Great Britain had more than a little hand in how its version of western hemisphere slavery took shape. Taking advantage of what its colonists already were doing, the Crown established the Royal African Company in 1672 and gave itself part-ownership. Until 1698 the company claimed a monopoly on British trade to Africa, including the growing trade in slaves. British diplomats in Madrid negotiated the *asiento* with the Spanish government, allowing British slave vessels and their cargoes into Spanish-American ports. In 1735 Parliament specified that British creditors could seize the slaves of colonial debtors, if the debtors fell into default. Early in the eighteenth century the Royal Navy put down piracy in the Caribbean, making it safe for British vessels, including slavers. For much of that century Portugal was a British client state, and British vessels dominated the enormous slave trade between Africa and Brazil. When Virginia tobacco arrived at Bristol or Glasgow, British customs collected a hefty import tax, even if the tobacco was to be reshipped elsewhere; in return, British farmers were banned from growing the crop.

The Crown gave up rejecting Acts of Parliament in 1714, but it claimed the power to veto colonial statutes. It did not veto the early colonial laws that created and governed colonial slavery, and it did veto later colonial laws that tried to tax the slave trade out of existence. With the support and protection of their government, British merchants in Liverpool, Bristol, and other slaving ports worked out their business plans. They counted on the Royal Navy to protect their ships and human cargoes at sea. Royal governors from Barbados to New Hampshire received instructions that London officials prepared with the plantation colonists foremost in their minds. The capital value of what slaves produced made its way into the main British economy. Even now, the names of several major British corporations (Barclays Bank, Lloyds Bank, Tate & Lyle Sugar) and cultural monuments (the Tate Gallery) mark the origins of their founders' fortunes in slavery and the slave trade. Britain's role in colonial American slavery is beyond doubt.

But British colonials, not the king or Parliament, made, wanted, and profited from the slavery that was all around them. "Rule, Britannia, Britannia
rule the waves, Britons never, never, never shall be slaves," go the words of
a rousing, patriotic British song written in 1739.[9] Colonial Britons sang it
too. Their legislative assemblies and the self-styled patriotic, upstanding men
who filled them were the guardians of colonial Britons' precious liberties,
including the liberty, or privilege, of holding slaves with the full protection
of positive, enacted colonial law.

British-American colonists wanted the slaves, purchased them, renamed
them, maimed, whipped, and killed them, separated them from one another,
and claimed the lives of their children. Colonial "interlopers" violated the
Royal African Company's seventeenth-century monopoly on the African
trade. After the monopoly ended, colonial shippers joined enthusiastically
in the open trade. Newport, Rhode Island, particularly, thrived as a slaving port. "Don't forget the Guinea voyage," colonial ship owners instructed
captains as they prepared to cross the Atlantic.[10] The width of the Atlantic
Ocean separated Britain's western-hemisphere "dominions," where slavery
was a fundamental fact of daily life, from Britain itself, where no law actually
recognized the right of one person to hold another person as property for life.

Slavery bound the whole colonized western hemisphere together, whatever the language, nationality, and religion of the Europeans. Western hemisphere slavery wove several separate strands into a distinctively American
pattern. One strand in that pattern was the sociological condition of slavery,
which meant the loss of all past and future, all property and family, and all
honor. For social purposes, a slave was dead. Slavery in this sense was age-
old and it has existed virtually world-wide at one point or another. A second
thread in the pattern was plantation economics, as some human beings
forced others to produce luxury or exotic crops for a booming world of commerce, consumption, and merchant capitalism. The only reward the produc-
ers would get was being allowed to live. This began as sugarcane cultivation
spread from the Middle East across the Mediterranean, then to the Atlantic
sugar islands. But it flourished in the western hemisphere.

Plantation slavery spread across Brazil, the whole Caribbean basin, the
Carolina and Georgia Low Country, the Chesapeake Bay region, and the
nineteenth-century American South as far as Texas. Slaves grew, harvested,
and processed sugar, coffee, tobacco, rice, indigo, and, eventually, cotton as
cash crops. Whatever the crop, plantations were business ventures in which
the owners set all the rules and paid their workers nothing other than bare
sustenance, under conditions that no free person would tolerate, and with no
hope for the workers of improvement or freedom. People invested in them

to make money from crops that had little or no local use, but that could bring great profits in markets far away. There was nothing comparable to the plantations in the enslavers' European mother countries, whether slavery existed in them (as in Spain or Portugal) or not (as in Britain, France, and the Netherlands). Plantations did not develop everywhere in the Americas, but plantation economics underpinned and shaped the entire colonial pan-American economy.

The third thread in American slavery's tapestry was the idea that "race" justified enslavement. The separate ideas that eventually fused into the concept of race existed as early as the time of Columbus, but the earliest enslavement of African and native people did not rest on them. Those ideas did not come together fully until after the American Revolution. Other studies have explored how the concept of race developed. This book will examine how black men and women confronted the idea and the practice of race as they struggled to hold and expand the partial freedom that they won in the United States during the Revolution. But, taken together, the age-old, world-spanning sociological fact of slavery, the early-modern economics of capitalist plantation production, and the ideology of racism fused in the western hemisphere into history's most prosperous and powerful form of enslavement, usually known as the slave-plantation complex. It developed most fully and most powerfully in the post-independence American South.

Perhaps ironically, where the human cost of slavery was worst, in terms of life expectancy and death rates, the enslaved people developed strong cultures, very distinct from what Europeans tried to impose on them. In both Brazil and the West Indies, slaves maintained African religious faiths, created their own dialects of the dominant tongue, and started to turn those dialects into separate languages. They shaped their own cuisines, both from the dismal foodstuffs that masters allotted and from what they were able to hunt, gather, grow, and find for themselves. They began to create the western hemisphere's unique, spontaneous, many-voiced contributions to world music. Brazilian and West Indies slaves vastly outnumbered the white people who exploited them, allowing them to build communities that were almost entirely their own. Africans continued to arrive among them, so that memories and knowledge of their origins remained constantly fresh.

Much the same happened in British America, but with variations. By the eve of the Revolution, South Carolina's slaves formed 70 percent of the province's total population, including the still lightly settled backcountry. In the coastal rice parishes the proportion reached nine in ten, the same level as in the sugar islands. During the malaria and yellow fever season, whites, who were vulnerable and free to flee, might disappear from the lowland plantation country altogether.

The closest North American analogue to the *patois* speech of the West Indies is Gullah, which took shape in the rice swamps of the Carolina lowlands and Sea Islands. Like West Indian patois, it could be unintelligible to any outsider. That was part of its point, because it allowed the people who spoke it to talk and plan and dream and let out their rage in relative safety. The slaves at Mulberry Plantation were among Gullah's makers. People like them used Gullah to keep alive their memories, to share the wisdom that it took to survive, and to pass what they learned on to their children. Some coastal Carolina people still speak Gullah, despite the displacement and dispersal of long-settled black communities by resorts and golf courses for the benefit of tourists and leisure corporations.

Rice slaves also were starting to develop the enormous, far-flung family patterns that have become an enduring part of African-American life. Brotherhood, sisterhood, cousinhood across many degrees of separation, and artificial kinship: all these were creating patterns that gave them obligations to one another, protection against their enemy-masters, and protection as well for their children if sale, inheritance, a gambling debt, bankruptcy, a wedding gift to a master's son or daughter, or simple misery for its own sake should rip them from one another.

In the rice fields, slaves worked most often by set tasks rather than in gangs under an overseer. Once the task was done, the slave could claim free time. Rice labor was intricate, and slaves who worked the crop had to cooperate, not for the master's sake but for their own. It also was dangerous, as the death rates for rice slaves suggest. Summer and winter alike, they worked surrounded by fetid water. For part of the growing cycle the rice crop was inundated, and until the first frosts came the fields offered perfect breeding grounds for the mosquitoes that carry yellow fever and malaria. They were home to alligators and snakes as well. In the bone-chilling winter, dikes, dams, and irrigation channels had to be dug and repaired.

Hardly ever can we hear colonial Carolina slaves' voices, either what they said or how they said it. The closest we can get is the reports of missionaries who tried to bring them to Christian salvation, once the colonists made sure in their laws that finding Christ would not end enslavement. Apparently not many of the slaves paid attention to the preaching, although the missionaries, who were Englishmen ordained into the Anglican Church, did mean well and did report what they saw. But even if slaves heeded the missionaries' messages, there would be no black call-and-response, no black spontaneity, in an orderly Anglican service. Court records offer little more. If it did come about that a slave was tried before a court of white men for murder, there would be testimony, and the courtroom testimony of the world's lowly people is often the best way to know what such people felt, believed, feared, and sometimes hoped. But few such trials occurred for slaves. The master's command was, literally, the supreme law of his own land, even extending to matters of life and death.

We can see a little bit more deeply into the lives of Chesapeake slaves. Like the succession of planters who dwelt in the great house at Mulberry, Chesapeake planters designed their mansions along the James, York, Rappahannock, and Potomac Rivers to be seen and admired, celebrating the wealth and the power of the family who dwelt within and especially of the man who ruled the plantation as his own small kingdom. Given any chance at all to build for themselves, tobacco slaves created dwellings not for a master's proud self-display, but rather around open spaces, for the community to share. Such was the case at Carter's Grove, built facing the James River in 1755 for Carter Burwell, grandson of King Carter. Careful excavation sponsored by Colonial Williamsburg resulted in a reconstruction of the quarter, on the original site, with tools and material that would have been used at the time. Until the estate returned to private hands, a visitor could explore the quarter and learn from knowledgeable, costumed interpreters how slaves had lived. Basic to what the interpreters taught was that in these quarters families and the community, not separate individuals, counted most.

Tobacco slaves faced a problem that sugar and rice slaves did not have to confront: being spread out and moved across large distances. A sugar plantation in the West Indies might occupy just a few hundred intensely cultivated, carefully tended acres. Rice production stayed put in the Carolina lowlands, where the flow and ebb of tides could be harnessed to flood and drain the fields as the crop required. But eighteenth-century Virginia and Maryland tobacco planting sprawled from the lowland tidewater across the hilly Piedmont to the foot of the Blue Ridge mountain range. A single great planter might have many separate holdings, separated by miles from one another. On each holding there might be several slave quarters like the one at Carter's Grove, each containing twenty to thirty people. All the way from the coastline to the foot of the mountains great families owned much of the good tobacco land. They could transfer slaves from one holding or one quarter to another, separating family members as surely as if somebody had been sold away. Being inherited, or given as a wedding gift, or taking a black child away to be a white child's companion meant separation as well.

The 40 percent of late eighteenth-century Virginians who were black drove the tobacco economy. They came to Virginia in a burst of imports that lasted from roughly 1680, when Virginia's rulers finally completed the shift from indentured white servitude to slavery, until about 1750, when the slave population began growing of itself. Initially, the planters had bought English servants' time rather than slaves' whole lives, because the servants were markedly cheaper. Virginia servitude was different from servitude in England, where the law, the church, a servant's family, and, if necessary, escape to London gave some protection. If a Virginia servant survived, servitude would end. But for as long as their indentures lasted, servants could be gambled away, inherited, bought and sold, "like a damn'd slave," as one described it.[11] A Virginia court could sentence a female servant who became pregnant to serve extra time as compensation to her master, even if the master was the father and the conception had come from a rape. But still these people were English and expected to be free. By the late seventeenth century few English men and women, no matter how desperate, were willing to go to Virginia, unless the alternative was to be hanged. By 1680 there was no doubt of Virginia Africans' slave status, and by then Virginia had a full set of slave laws to control them.

Slaves cost more than servants, both because of the higher costs of the slave trade and because there was no limit on their time of labor. But unlike servants, there was no need to grant them land at the point of freedom, because freedom never would come. Servant discontent was one reason why in 1676 Virginia broke into a chaotic civil war, called Bacon's Rebellion after its leader, Nathaniel Bacon. Bringing in more black people, as slaves, and driving a wedge of laws and privileges between them and poor whites might prevent another Bacon from emerging. About the same time that Virginia's rulers turned to slavery and cemented it into their laws, they also began to give up on long-held dreams of returning to England with piles of tobacco money. Instead, they would stay in Virginia and begin to build the Chesapeake great houses that signified that they were in their province to stay.

The Africans who came to eighteenth-century Virginia and Maryland found a situation that was grim, but that was different from Carolina or the West Indies. If they came from Africa rather than the West Indies, their Middle Passage might have been the worst of all, because it took the longest time. By the time a vessel arrived at a Chesapeake pier it might have called at several islands and in Carolina, though Virginia planters, like Carolinians, did order specific kinds of slaves for express delivery. One new Virginia slave in every four would not survive the first year, mostly because of respiratory disease in the cold Virginia winter.

Planters and traders gradually learned that if the new slaves arrived in springtime they had a better chance of survival than if they came in autumn or winter. Tobacco labor was not sugar growing, which was brutal from the first digging of trenches for new cane to the agony of twenty-four-hour days and seven-day weeks during sugar harvest and processing. It was not rice growing either. It did not require the wintertime cleaning of muddy ditches and building dikes, or the summertime work with rice plants, all the time deep in foul water, ridden with snakes and alligators and, during the summer's heat, with disease-bearing mosquitoes. Working tobacco did not mean treating indigo in vats of human urine. So, unlike the West Indies or Carolina, Virginia's slave population began to rise of its own accord. By the middle of the eighteenth century Virginia's planters no longer needed the slave trade, and they could begin to impose steep import taxes on new Africans. The planters who made Virginia's laws told themselves that they wanted to make the cost of the slave trade prohibitive, for humane reasons.

Living as they did, black Virginians and Marylanders faced a different situation and different challenges than slaves further south. No patois or Gullah emerged among them, because for those languages to develop there had to be dense communities, much larger than a Virginia tobacco quarter. Nor was there a great colonial-era rebellion in Virginia between Bacon's rising in 1676 and the outbreak of the Revolution in 1775.

Tobacco was not as difficult or dangerous a crop as West Indies and Brazilian sugar or Carolina rice. But the labor that it required never ceased. The plants grow on a fifteen-month cycle from seeding to harvest and they require a great deal of care. Planters prided themselves on their skill with the plants and ranked one another by the quality of their finished leaf and its price on the London market. But slaves did the work and they probably knew the plants better than did the masters. Mostly, they worked in gangs, not at individual tasks, and they learned to regulate the pace of work so that the fast and strong among them would not outpace the slow and the weak.

Unlike the Carolina lowlands, where most people were either of the great planter class or slaves, much of what Virginia slaves did, neighboring poor whites did as well. Of necessity, rice had to be a rich man's crop, because of the cost of the hydraulics and large slave forces that the crop required. So did sugar, because of the intensity of the labor and the cost of the refining machinery. But all that tobacco required was land, plants, simple tools, a curing barn, and labor. In the Chesapeake, white plain folk abounded, particularly inland from the main waterways. Almost all Virginians and very many Marylanders were caught up in tobacco production, white or black, free or slave, rich, middling, or poor. In many ways, poor Chesapeake white people and slaves came to be like one another, whether we consider their dwellings, their food, their clothing, or their health. If we could hear their speech they probably would sound much the same as one another, melding together different British terms and accents with African words and tones into a Virginia form of the English language.

But many things in their lives told black Virginians and Marylanders that they and poor whites were different from one another. Black women worked in the fields, and taxes were due on their value. In the eyes of Virginia lawmakers each slave woman was living, productive property. Part of what she produced was more living, productive property, meaning her children, whoever fathered them, including the master. Like any other property, she could be taxed. A married white woman could not be taxed because, at law, her personality and her property merged with those of her husband. No white women, married or single, rich or poor, were allowed to do field work, as much a marker of the emerging racial distinction as was denying black people the right to firearms.

A small Virginia farmer would defer to a great planter. Such men dominated his world as militia colonels, judges, vestrymen of the established church, and delegates to the annual meeting of the House of Burgesses in Williamsburg. But he probably could vote, and he and his kind could unseat a burgess if the man got too arrogant or just proved incompetent. A poor white Virginian could rent a slave at planting or harvest time. He and the planter might stand on common ground when they met to drink after the militia muster, on court day, at the annual election, or at a horse race or a cock fight. Slaves could and did regard poor whites with contempt, but it was the poor whites who rode patrol at night, policing and protecting the planters' world, and they had power to punish any slave they caught. Such men might own no slaves themselves or only a few, but almost certainly they wanted them. White Virginians and black ones made the Chesapeake world together, but by no means was that world one of harmony.

The records and diaries that Virginia planters kept show what their slaves endured. Consider two cases. One is William Byrd II (1677–1744), who typified the Virginia planter class as it settled down to rule its province early in the eighteenth century. The other is George Washington, before he emerged as a national American hero. Writing to a noble British friend, Byrd likened himself to "one of the patriarchs of old," and described how he gave benevolent direction to his "people" at his Westover plantation on the James River.[12] But Byrd peppered his journal, which he wrote in code and kept under lock and key, with casual accounts of the violence his "people" had to endure. Byrd's wife caused "little Jenny to be burned with a hot iron" and "Prue to be whipped violently notwithstanding I desired not, which provoked me to have Anika whipped likewise. . . . Eugene was whipped for running away. . . . In the afternoon I beat Jenny for throwing water on the couch. . . . Eugene was whipped again for pissing in bed and Jenny for concealing it. . . . Eugene pissed abed again for which I made him drink a pint of piss," and on and on and on.[13] What Byrd so casually did to Jenny, Prue, Eugene, and Anika tells more about life at Westover and at places like it than the patriarchal benevolence that he saw when he looked in his mirror.

Washington's diary is much less revealing than Byrd's. For the most part it is a bare record of weather and growing conditions for his crops. But his business records are revealing. In 1769 Washington found himself involved in the breakup of Bernard Moore's estate. Moore was in debt to the Custis family, which included Martha Washington and her two children. The chosen method for dealing with Moore's business failure was to hold a lottery of all that he possessed. The organizers, Washington among them, divided all the property, including the slaves, into parcels. They priced tickets on each parcel at 10 pounds each. One of the parcels included "Kate, and a young child, Judy," and a separate parcel was made up of "A Negro girl, Aggy, and boy, Nat, children of Kate."[14] Aggy's and Nat's separation from their mother made no difference. Settling Moore's property meant getting the best possible return against the debt that he owed for his creditors, including Washington's stepson and stepdaughter. The law required Washington, as their guardian, to act in those children's interest, without regard to Kate, Judy, Aggy, or Nat.

About the middle of the eighteenth century, as planter culture was taking its mature form and as Virginia's need for the slave trade was ending, an element crept into Virginia life that threatened the racial separation the planters had so carefully crafted. This was not outright anti-slavery but rather evangelical Christianity. Planter Anglicanism was ceremonial and its church services celebrated the planter class as much as they worshipped God. If black people took part at all, it was in separate galleries, above the main congregation. Enthusiastic, spirit-rapt Baptists, Methodists, and New-Light Presbyterians were different. They owed nothing to the Church of England hierarchy, which reached across the ocean to the bishop of London and ultimately to the king, who was head of the church. Instead, the evangelicals chose their ministers from among themselves. Often they worshipped outdoors, forming circles of sisters and brethren. They welcomed black men and women on equal terms, sometimes singling them out to preach. Evangelical "chapel folk" in Britain shared their spirit. They too rejected the ceremony and trappings of the established church. But worshipping in a circle was very much an African rather than a European way to praise and to pray.

Nobody wrote down the words of these people's sermons. Nobody could have captured the body language of an evangelical preacher, possibly black, who was seized by the spirit. We cannot know whether anybody spoke out directly against slavery during evangelical worship. But these congregations were communities of equality. All their members understood that they were equal sinners before their often-angry but also merciful Lord. For a white male, joining such a congregation meant giving up the rituals of Virginia manhood, including the conviviality of a drinking party after the militia muster or on election day, of horse racing, or of betting on a cockfight at the crossroads tavern. For black Southerners of both sexes, it meant dealing with white people as equal brothers and sisters. Small wonder that planters, sheriffs, and Anglican ministers sometimes rode right into outdoor meetings on their quarter horses and thoroughbreds, flailing their whips at white and black evangelicals alike.

This, in outline, was slavery in colonial America. Slavery was nothing new in world history when Columbus crossed the Atlantic Ocean at the end of the fifteenth century. By the time that slavery emerged in seventeenth-century British America, it was nothing new in the colonized western hemisphere, either. One way or another, almost every civilization and culture in the entire world had practiced it by the time American colonization began. Africans had no monopoly at all on being open to enslavement; it could happen to anybody, and people of all sorts enslaved others. Only in northwestern Europe, including Britain, France, and the Netherlands, did it not exist during the age of colonization, but that did not stop British, French, and Dutch colonists from creating slavery wherever they settled. As western hemisphere slavery developed, it fused together social degradation, plantation production, and the beginnings of the idea of race. Together with the Spanish mines in Mexico and Peru (where black and Native American slaves also labored), the slave plantations of Brazil, the Caribbean, and the southern mainland British colonies became the beating economic heart of the entire European colonizing venture, at an enormous cost in human suffering and death. By the middle of the eighteenth century slavery was everywhere that the Europeans claimed and settled, including the settlements of proud, freeborn, liberty-loving colonial Britons.

Enslaved people resisted, every way they could. They rebelled, but rebellion after rebellion ended in bloody defeat. They created their own cultures. Their masters tried to keep them ignorant, but they had many ways to learn about the world around them. Almost everywhere they looked in their world, there was slavery, and slavery's pan-American form, stretching from the valley of the St. Lawrence to the valley of the Rio de la Plata, seemed immeasurably strong. Slaves could become free, though in most of the British colonies that was extremely difficult to do. There were black people all over the colonized western hemisphere, and, whether their masters spoke French, English, Dutch, Danish, Spanish, or Portuguese, the presumption was that they were slaves.

In 1763, when Britain defeated France in their great struggle for American and world domination, nobody would have thought that a bare thirteen years later, in 1776, the proud, patriotic British subjects who dwelt in the North American colonies would abandon their British identity, overthrow their allegiance to a distant king, establish a republic, and take command of their own world. Nobody would have thought, either, that the whole principle of human slavery could be challenged and that slavery's destruction was about to begin. Slavery's world destruction did begin in the American revolutionary era. Black North Americans took a major role in how that happened. But the Revolution also opened the way for the strongest slave regime in world history to assemble itself, entirely on its own terms, across the American South.

Notes

1. Winthrop D. Jordan, *White Over Black: American Attitudes Toward the Negro, 1550–1812* (Chapel Hill: University of North Carolina Press, 1968), 73.

2. Massachusetts Body of Liberties (1641), paragraph 91, history.hanover.edu/texts/masslib.html, accessed March 5, 2011.

3. Morgan, *American Slavery, American Freedom*, 329.

4. Quoted in Ira Berlin, *Many Thousands Gone: The First Two Centuries of Slavery in North America* (Cambridge, MA: Harvard University Press, 1998), 112.

5. Charles Sackett Sydnor, *Slavery in Mississippi* (New York: D. Appleton Century, 1933), 72.

6. Toni Morrison, *Beloved* (New York: Signet, 1991 [orig. pub. 1987]), 72.

7. Jill Lepore, *New York Burning: Liberty, Slavery, and Conspiracy in Eighteenth-Century Manhattan* (New York: Knopf, 2005), 61.

8. Jordan, *White Over Black*, 116.

9. www.fordham.edu/halsall/mod/rulebritannia.html, accessed April 16, 2011.

10. Virginia Bever Platt, "And Don't Forget the Guinea Voyage": The Slave Trade of Aaron Lopez of Newport," *William and Mary Quarterly*, 3rd ser., 32 (1975): 601–18.

11. Edmund S. Morgan, *American Slavery, American Freedom: The Ordeal of Colonial Virginia* (New York: Norton, 1975), 128.

12. Rhys Isaac, *The Transformation of Virginia, 1740–1790* (Chapel Hill: University of North Carolina Press, 1982), 39–40.

13. All Byrd quotations from *The Secret Diary of William Byrd of Westover, 1709–1712*, ed. Louis B. Wright and Marion Tinling (Richmond: Dietz Press, 1941).

14. Henry Wiencek, *An Imperfect God: George Washington, His Slaves, and the Creation of America* (New York: Farrar, Straus & Giroux, 2003), 179–80.

CHAPTER TWO

~

"The Same Principle Lives in Us"

Black People and the Revolutionary Crisis

"In every human Breast, God has implanted a Principle, which we call Love of Freedom; it is impatient of Oppression, and pants for Deliverance, and by the leave of our modern Egyptians I will assert that the same Principle lives in us."

—Phillis Wheatley to Reverend Samson Occum, February 11, 1774

It took two revolutions to destroy slavery in the United States. The first is the subject here. The second is what Americans usually call the Civil War. In April 1861, as the United States was falling apart and that second revolution loomed, black people north and south, free and enslaved, knew that the fundamental issue was them. White Northerners could prate about preserving the Union at any cost and white Southerners about abstract constitutional issues and states' rights. But few people of any sort were fooled. Black Americans' great task in the early years of that war, 1861 and 1862, was to force the central issue into the open, and get into the fight. When they did, after the Emancipation Proclamation on January 1, 1863, there was no question for them about which side to choose. About one hundred seventy thousand black men donned the Union's blue uniform as soon as they were able. A bare handful put on Confederate gray, and only at the very last minute with the promise of freedom as the lure.

Four score and seven years earlier, when the simmering problems of the British Empire boiled into armed conflict in eastern Massachusetts and the first American Revolution broke out, black people were not the central problem. Neither they nor their white counterparts had started the crisis that tore the British Empire apart between 1763 and 1776. The British did that, by meddling with an imperial system that had worked, and by insisting that they could bind colonials "in all cases whatsoever."[1] But from the start black people joined in, pushing whites to recognize them as part of the problem and perhaps as a necessary part of the solution as well. Unlike the Civil War, it was by no means clear during the Revolution which side was best to choose, so black people, like whites and Native Americans, divided. Nonetheless they involved themselves in almost all the great memorable events of the era, except the Continental Congress and the Constitutional Convention. Yet what America had done to them, and the question of their future, haunted even those memorable gatherings.

Neither fools nor ignorant, black men and women understood that even the earliest protests about British taxes offered them opportunities such as the colonial order never had presented. They realized that the ruling race was deaf to the implications of its own outcries about rights, privileges, and liberty, including its extraordinary claim that the British were bent on colonial "enslavement," and they criticized such language relentlessly. They grabbed every chance to speak, write, and act that the Revolution presented, challenging slavery mightily as they did. They found white allies in many places, some acting from principle, some out of necessity, but all acting in ways that benefited the race, whether whites intended that result or not.

Perhaps more than any, black people's words and actions changed what might have been a mere struggle for one people to separate the political band that had connected them with another into a revolution that transformed all it touched. They did not destroy American slavery. Even with stronger white support, even had George Washington, Benjamin Franklin, and Thomas Jefferson lent their full prestige, even had masters been paid off with land seized from its rightful Indian owners, that task probably was impossible at the time. But by the Revolution's end slavery had become a problem that Americans and Europeans could not ignore. In 1760 slavery existed everywhere in colonial America. As of 1800 it was dead in most of New England, under slow though ultimately lethal fire in the rest of the old Northern states, banned from expanding into the huge zone between the Ohio River and the Great Lakes, and shaken throughout the plantation South.

During the Revolution thousands of former slaves freed themselves and departed the United States. Communities of free black Americans emerged in both the North and the South. Within them, people could talk and make plans, in places that were their own. They could make their minds known to the larger world, speaking and writing in ways that the colonial order simply had not allowed. Though free, they did not abandon their enslaved fellows. The odds against them were huge, but they forced open a space for themselves in American society.

What they helped to ignite spread to Canada, to fashionable opinion in France and Britain, and to the great explosion that destroyed slavery in Ste. Domingue (Haiti) between 1791 and 1794. It reached back to Africa and southward to the new republics of Spanish America. Slavery lasted in the British West Indies until Acts of Parliament destroyed it between 1834 and 1838. The revolutionary French did decree an end to slavery in their colonies in 1791 and the great revolution that transformed slave Ste. Domingue into free Haiti followed. But under Emperor Napoleon Bonaparte they tried to defeat the Haitians. The restored Bourbon monarchy reinstated and preserved it in their other Caribbean islands, Guadeloupe and Martinique, where it lasted until 1848. At that point slavery was still slowly dying in Peru and Argentina. It persisted in Brazil and Cuba nearly to the twentieth century. But what black people achieved during and as a result of the American Revolution helped to begin slavery's long, drawn-out demise in the whole Atlantic world, including its violent destruction in the United States between 1861 and 1865.

Black people's experience of the American Revolution overlapped with whites', but the two were not the same. For white colonial people who chose independence, the great achievements were abandoning the British identity that had defined them, destroying the British power that had ruled them, creating a new identity as proud Americans, establishing the terms of their own liberty, and giving themselves the power to rule their world, under the United States Constitution. Black people who found freedom during the era did it on both sides, under Britain's Union Jack flag as much as under the American Stars and Stripes. On both sides they found bitterness and disappointment, as well as liberation. Britain and the United States ended the African slave trade within a year of each other, in 1807 and 1808 respectively. But in America the domestic slave trade replaced it, taking hundreds of thousands of women, children, and men from the old slave states to Tennessee, Kentucky, Alabama, Mississippi, Louisiana, Missouri, Arkansas, and Texas. As those people moved west to the Gulf Coast and the lower Mississippi Valley, they intersected with a slave society that was already flourishing when the United States acquired Louisiana from France in 1803 and Florida from Spain in 1819.

There is much more to the story of black people's American Revolution than the familiar martyrdom of black/Native American seafarer Crispus Attucks on Boston's King Street on March 5, 1770. Attucks got caught up in a protest by white Bostonians against the occupation of their town by British troops, sent there for the sake of protecting Britain's tax collectors from Bostonians' scorn and abuse. The protest turned nasty, the troops panicked, and they opened fire. Attucks was among the five who died from their musket balls. We remember him, rightly, but his story is only a beginning.

Consider the simple fact that we do know his name, and something of his tale. For colonial America, we can know a lot in the abstract about slavery and the people who endured it, but hardly anything about real black people, with faces, names, and histories. By the Revolution's end it is different. We know that John Adams, defending the British soldiers who fired that night against the charge of murder, lumped Attucks together with other malcontents as "a motley rabble of saucy boys, negroes and molattoes, Irish teagues and outlandish jack tars."[2] Attucks appeared to Adams "to have undertaken to be the hero of the night."[3] But Adams did know who Attucks was, did place him among angry people that men like Adams could not control, and did credit Attucks with leadership. We cannot know much about what Attucks looked like. He may have been tall. Was he well built? Thin? Light or dark skinned? But we can see the actual faces of some of his revolutionary-era fellows, thanks to painters who took them seriously. We can know some of their names. Full biographies are possible for a few, taking us deep into each subject's life and world. We can know their minds.

Enslaved colonial women and men had ways to communicate over great distances. Historian Sterling Stuckey calls it "the Word" and astute historical novelist Lawrence Hill has his fictional Carolina slaves describe it as "the fishnet." But, of necessity, such communication was secret, passed from person to person. John Adams learned from a worried Georgian in September, 1775, that word could travel hundreds of miles in a week or two. Secret, whispered sharing of things no white person should hear persisted as long as slavery itself. But by the Revolution's end there was another way. White men and women of letters spoke of their membership in a large, international "republic of letters." Black people began to create a large republic of knowledge, letters, and open speech that was their own.

The new possibilities opened one by one. As protests about liberty mounted during the imperial crisis, the time began to seem ripe for speaking out in petitions to the authorities. Then came war, which meant the chance, or the need, to choose a side, in the hope of freedom. When the war of independence was over, "reversing sail" to Africa began to seem a realistic prospect to some, rather than the hopeless fantasy that it had been under the old order. Still others realized that America had to be their home, despite all its wrongs, including the facts that slavery had survived the revolution, that the African slave trade flourished under the Stars and Stripes until 1808, and that, for all the changes that had taken place, most of their fellows remained in slavery's thrall.

By the third quarter of the eighteenth century, newspaper articles, pamphlets, and printed sermons were opening cracks in slavery's high, thick walls. As early as 1700, Boston's Samuel Sewall published *The Selling of Joseph*. "Originally and naturally," there was "no such thing as slavery" and "these Ethiopians . . . are the Sons and Daughters of the first Adam . . . and the Offspring of God; They ought to be treated with a respect agreeable."[4] Between Sewall and the outbreak of the imperial crisis six decades later, a literate black person might have read protests against slavery by Francis Le Jau (1712), John Hepburn (1715), Ralph Sandiford (1729), Elihu Coleman (1733), Benjamin Lay (1737), John Woolman (1754), and Anthony Benezet (1763), among others.

Sewall was a Massachusetts Puritan and Le Jau an Anglican missionary in South Carolina. Hepburn, Sandiford, Coleman, Lay, Woolman, and Benezet all were Quakers in Pennsylvania or New Jersey. The doctrine of the Friends, as Quakers called themselves, that every single human possesses an inner light direct from the Holy Spirit had always rendered slavery problematic for them. Unlike most of the extreme Protestants who had emerged during the Reformation, they had, for the most part, made their peace with the ways of the eighteenth-century world. Around the Atlantic basin Quakers owned ships that brought slaves from Africa. They profited from plantations where slaves labored. They traded the sugar, rice, indigo, and tobacco that slaves produced. But thanks to pressure from such Friends as Lay, a former merchant in Barbados who took to dwelling in a cave near Philadelphia and prostrating himself in the winter snow outside Quaker meetinghouses, all in order to protest slavery, and from Woolman and Benezet, American and British Quakers moved toward opposition to slavery after 1750. In 1774 the Philadelphia Yearly Meeting made separating entirely from slavery a matter of discipline.

How might a black person who could read have responded? Consider a few instances. Benjamin Banneker was born free in Maryland in 1731. Though he never joined the Friends, he attended their meetings for worship throughout his life, which means that he would have known what was going on in their circles. Banneker certainly knew about Lay's, Woolman's, and Benezet's efforts to return the Quakers to their original intensity of belief and action, which had faded since their founding during England's seventeenth-century revolution. In 1764 he might have learned from the newspapers, which he read regularly, that Boston lawyer James Otis was taking the argument about slavery out of the realm of religion and into the politics of protest, linking it to the colonial cause. Otis was one of the earliest colonials to see that Britain's new tax policies threatened what colonials called their rights and liberties. He thought deeply and he drew the protest's full implications. Everybody, Otis wrote, is freeborn, black and white alike. None of the justifications for enslavement of black people could withstand questioning. Everybody involved in enslavement was a tyrant.

Four years later, in 1768, Banneker might have read in a Maryland paper that, in neighboring Virginia's House of Burgesses, newly elected member Thomas Jefferson had helped introduce a bill to allow masters to free slaves if they chose, instead of requiring a special act. Banneker certainly knew that whites were waking up to the horrors of the African slave trade. Even Virginia's burgesses turned against it, passing a bill in 1772 to tax it out of existence. In all probability, Banneker learned a year or so afterwards that the king had rejected the bill, on the advice of his Board of Trade.

Banneker was a solitary man who dwelt mostly within his own powerful mind. Did he actually read Otis, or learn what the Virginia burgesses had done? We cannot know, but he did emerge as an anti-slavery spokesman. He spent his whole life on the edge of plantation country and he, or somebody like him, was bound to share what he learned with the people in the tobacco fields. Somebody, certainly, was telling slaves what was going on outside their supposedly closed plantation worlds.

African-born Phillis Wheatley could read too. She had been in Boston for about three years when Otis first linked slavery to the American cause, but she was only ten at the time and probably missed it. Captured into slavery early in her girlhood, she was lucky, in a sense, because she ended up in the capital of Massachusetts rather than on a plantation. Clearly, she possessed an immense talent for language. She learned English fast, and at fourteen she published the first of the poems that eventually made her famous on both sides of the Atlantic. Books were part of her life and she might well have read *Some Historical Account of Guinea* after the Philadelphian Anthony Benezet published it in 1771. Nobody who read Benezet's book could dismiss Wheatley's birth land as a benighted place of darkness, paganism, cannibalism, and savagery.

Benezet did his homework. He studied maps, travelers' accounts, ancient records, Arab sources, and Muslim writings. He learned about (in his terms) Jalof, Fuli, and Mandingo people, and about the Kingdoms of Rio Sestro, Whidah, Benin, and Kongo. He informed his readers about Islam south of the Sahara and about early African conversions to Catholicism. He knew that some Muslim Africans could read Arabic. Benezet wrote about African towns, cities, and markets. In his pages one could learn about how Africans refined, smelted, and used iron, how they farmed food crops and herded animals, and how they wove cloth and dressed themselves. He knew that Africans had their own history before any Europeans appeared along the coast to disturb them. He learned how different sorts of Africans administered justice among themselves. Nobody who read him could accept stereotypes about a degraded, backward Africa whose enslaved children had been lucky to escape to the so-called benevolence of Christian masters.

What Benezet wrote had consequences on both sides of the Atlantic. In the same year that Benezet published his book, 1771, the Englishman Granville Sharp, who read, admired, and used it, got wind of the plight of James Somerset, whose master, Charles Steuart, had returned from Boston to England. Somerset had escaped into London's black community but Steuart's agents had tracked him down and recaptured him. Now Steuart held Somerset on board the *Ann and Mary*, waiting in the Pool of London before it departed for the West Indies, where the short, bitter life of a sugar slave awaited him as punishment. Sharp set out to aid him, and to test the law of slavery within England. That meant confronting England's legal establishment, the people who made and enforced the law.

James Somerset was no simple, passive victim. Steuart had brought him to England from Boston, but the enslaved Somerset had dwelt in Virginia and traveled widely in the colonies. Steuart was a customs official, charged with collecting the deeply unpopular taxes and enforcing the equally unpopular laws that Britain was imposing on colonial commerce. While Steuart traveled on the Crown's business, Somerset went about business of his own. He spent time in Philadelphia, where a network that linked anti-slavery Quakers to black men and women operated quietly but effectively, aiding individual slaves who sought their personal freedom but working as well with the goal of ending slavery itself. Quakers Benjamin Lay, John Woolman, and Anthony Benezet were not quiet: all of them expressed their opposition to slavery in very public ways. The immediate agenda was within the Quaker community. Many Friends in Philadelphia held slaves on a small scale and other Quakers in Britain, the southern mainland colonies, and the West Indies helped the plantation economy to run. Progress could be slow; Quaker masters who did come to agree that slavery was wrong could require their slaves to purchase their freedom with earnings from extra work, rather than simply setting the slaves free. Nonetheless, Somerset had good reason to have encountered the Quaker/black anti-slavery network.

By 1770 that network stretched across the Atlantic, linking people in the colonies both to British Friends and to the black British community. Somerset tried to disappear into the black community when he escaped from Steuart. When Steuart recaptured him, the black community learned about it quickly and tried to help him. The best way was to turn to the law. As the case brought on Somerset's behalf made its way toward a legal decision it generated wide publicity. Enemies of slavery realized that more was at stake than one man's probable exile to the West Indies. The case offered a chance to strike against slavery. Some in London called it "the Great Case of the Negroes."[5] But winning it did not promise to be easy.

The sort of powerful, prosperous eighteenth-century Englishmen who became members of Parliament, county high sheriffs, and Crown Court judges recognized the slave trade's importance to Britain's economy. They knew that Parliament permitted and protected it and that most people in the economically important colonies south of Virginia wanted slaves. They realized that taxes paid on Virginia tobacco imports at Bristol, Liverpool, or Glasgow lessened the tax burden on Britons, and that British merchants rather than colonial planters profited from sending the American tobacco on to the lucrative French market. Some of them were absentee West Indies planters who dwelt in England and who had entered the British elite, marrying their sons and daughters into the titled aristocracy. Known as the "West Indies Interest," they formed a powerful group in Parliament. Britain had no actual law of slavery, although informal custom kept many of the country's fifteen thousand black men and women in what amounted to slave conditions. A widely known legal opinion that dated from 1729 held that slaves brought into the country could claim no rights in an English court.

But Sharp had the money to hire London's best lawyers. He got a writ of *habeas corpus* from England's highest tribunal, the Court of King's Bench, requiring that Somerset's captors appear before a judge and justify why they were holding him as a captive. If they could not do so, Somerset would go free. William Murray, who bore the noble title Baron Mansfield and was Lord Chief Justice of England, presided at the hearing and granted the writ.

He did it reluctantly. Like most men of his kind, Lord Mansfield possessed a profoundly conservative temperament. He despised the whole American protest movement against parliamentary taxation, which was well underway by the time Somerset's captors appeared before him. He did not believe in using his court to address moral, social, and political problems. That was Parliament's business, not his. He stated in court that "setting 14,000 or 15,000 men [held in slavery in Britain] at once loose by a solemn opinion, is very disagreeable in the effects it threatens."[6] Mansfield was not hostile to black people. A young black girl named Dido, age seven at the time, was growing up as a member of his own family. But he tried to avoid pronouncing on the matter, inviting the parties to make a quiet compromise and set Somerset free without a ruling. However, neither would do it, forcing Mansfield to confront the problem directly. He knew what he was going to do, and he did not like it. He virtually invited Parliament to step in on behalf of slaveholders within England and overturn his ruling.

But, as a good judge, Mansfield believed that "the law must rule us." Both parties insisted on judgment, so, he said, "let justice be done whatever the consequence." He found that whatever the case might be in British America, where slaves had virtually no rights, in England any person, including a supposed slave, could claim access to the King's justice. Steuart and the ship's captain had been unable to justify holding Somerset against his will. "The state of slavery," Mansfield held, "is so odious" that it required "positive law" to exist. There was no such law in England so "whatever inconveniences, therefore, may follow from the decision, I cannot say this case is allowed or approved by the law of England and therefore the black must be discharged."

Mansfield's finding did not actually abolish slavery in England. The Lord Chief Justice merely held that a black person there had the same rights as any other subject to appear in court and claim the law's protection. No private person could hold another person against that person's will. Colonial "positive law" did legalize slavery and deny all rights to somebody like Somerset. But the colonial law of slavery did not reach Great Britain and English courts would not apply it. From *Somerset* onward, persons held as slaves in England could go to court and obtain their freedom.

Colonial slaveholders had reason to shudder when they learned what Mansfield had decreed. The entire American movement against British policy rested on the argument that authorities in Britain, such as Mansfield, were interfering with American rights, and Mansfield himself was known to despise the American cause. He was careful not to extend his ruling to the colonies, probably realizing that even if he did it could not be enforced. Nonetheless, a New York City newspaper expected that the decision would bring "greater ferment . . . than the Stamp Act" of 1765, which had provoked the American protests.[7] American slaves learned about it too. The *Virginia Gazette* reported in 1774 that an escaped slave could be expected to try to reach Britain "from knowledge he had . . . of *Somerset's* case."[8] When Dinah Nevil sued for the freedom of herself and her children in a Pennsylvania court in 1773, the matter seemed to offer the possibility of extending the Somerset ruling to America; Nevil's Quaker backers certainly hoped that would be the case.

As Otis thundered, as Benezet wrote, as Somerset escaped, as Sharp took Somerset's struggle to court, and as Mansfield pondered the case, enslaved Boston poet Phillis Wheatley realized that the question of slavery was opening up. It took her awhile to see. She wrote in one poem that:

> Twas mercy brought me from my *Pagan* land,
> Taught my benighted soul to understand
> That there's a God, that there's a *Saviour* too.[9]

But when she addressed the Earl of Dartmouth, appointed in 1772 as secretary of state for the colonies, her tone changed:

> I, young in life, by seeming cruel fate
> Was snatched from *Afric's* fancied happy seat . . .
> Such, such my case. And can I then but pray
> Others may never feel tyrannic sway.[10]

Possibly Wheatley already knew that Lord Dartmouth was sympathetic to the plight of enslaved black people in the colonies. In 1764 he had recommended John Newton, the former slave trader who wrote "Amazing Grace" and eventually entered the English campaign against slavery, for the Anglican ministry. The poem she wrote for Dartmouth reveals the carefully controlled but unmistakable voice of her personal outrage, beyond any white colonial talk about taxation, representation, and the powers of Parliament. Susannah Wheatley, whose husband John bought her when she arrived in Boston, realized quickly that the young African woman possessed genuine genius in her aptitude for language. She and her daughter encouraged Wheatley to read widely and to write. But she did not set the poet free, probably because her husband would not allow it.

In 1773 Wheatley went to England as a celebrity, where she met Lord Dartmouth, the Earl of Lincoln (who called on her), Benjamin Franklin, a fellow poet whom she identified as Mrs. Carter, anti-slavery campaigner Granville Sharpe, and Brooke Watson, future Lord Mayor of London. She exchanged letters with the Countess of Huntingdon, to whom she dedicated the 1773 London edition of her *Poems on Various Subjects*. Both Dartmouth and Watson presented her with handsome gifts. She bought books and toured the capital's sights. Under Massachusetts law she still remained a slave, but she certainly knew about *Somerset* and that all she had to do to be free was go to court.

Arrangements even were made for her to read her poetry for King George, but she returned to Boston instead to take care of her sick mistress, who clearly had treated her as a human being with great talent (despite not free-ing her), and with whom she apparently had a strong bond. In 1775, when she wrote a poem to George Washington, he sent her a personal reply, ad-dressing her respectfully as "Miss Phillis," and invited her to call on him, which she did. But back in Massachusetts she was a slave until 1778, when the death of her master led to her freedom. She knew how deeply her own history drew on pain beyond any that a white colonial was likely to endure. Not only black and enslaved, but a woman, she did see implications in the American movement that only a very few white colonial protestors against British taxation could grasp.

Quite probably Wheatley learned at some point what Boston rebel leader James Otis had had to say about slavery as early as 1764, when she was only ten. She certainly knew who Otis was and most likely met him. Others of Otis's sort, drawn from "the most respectable Characters in *Boston*," signed a published attestation in 1773 that Wheatley's poetry was her own, after doubts were cast upon it.[11] But perceptive as he was, Otis had looked at the bitter fact of American slavery from the outside. Wheatley saw it from within. Despite her fame, her high contacts, and her eventually gaining free-dom, when she became a free woman after her mistress died she had to turn to laundry work and cleaning to support herself. Worn out early, she died in 1784 at the age of thirty-one.

As Wheatley developed from a precocious, talented child to a famous writer she joined an anti-slavery network that spread across the Atlantic Ocean and spanned the deep gulf that slavery had gouged between black and white people. Granville Sharp approached Lord Mansfield's High Court on Somerset's behalf because black Londoners alerted him to Somerset's plight. He and Benezet opened an extended correspondence. Benezet wrote to Quaker slave trader Moses Brown in Rhode Island, helping to convince Brown to change his ways. In Virginia slaveholding revolutionary leader Patrick Henry read Anthony Benezet, honored "the Quakers for their noble effort to abolish Slavery," asked "would any one believe that I am master of Slaves, of my own purchase," and admitted that "I cannot justify it."[12] Non-Quaker Philadelphia physician and revolutionary Benjamin Rush wrote to both Sharp and Benezet. Wheatley wrote to him, to the Count-ess of Huntingdon, and to Native American minister Samson Occum, and she exchanged letters with American naval hero John Paul Jones. Black mathematician Benjamin Banneker included some of Wheatley's poems in his almanac. White ministers John Allen, Samuel Hopkins, Ezra Stiles, Levi Hart, and Nathaniel Niles worried about slavery in their Sunday sermons. White poets John Trumbull and Philip Freneau mocked it. So, late in 1775, did Englishman Thomas Paine, newly arrived in Philadelphia, just before he published his great revolutionary pamphlet *Common Sense.*

Clearly, a moment had arrived to challenge slavery itself. On January 6, 1773, a slave called simply Felix submitted a "humble PETITION" to the rulers of Massachusetts, including both its royal governor and its elected legislators. Others, apparently, had joined him but had declined to sign the document. Felix wanted his freedom, but he was apprehensive. Rather than invoke and challenge the white revolutionaries' rhetoric, Felix and his un-named associates tried to play on their emotions: "We have no Property! We have no Wives! No Children!" They pleaded "that your EXCELLENCY [the governor] and Honours [the assemblymen] . . . would be pleased to take [our] unhappy state . . . under your wise and just Consideration." They demanded nothing, asking for "such Relief only, which by no Possibility can ever be productive of the least Wrong or Injury to our Masters."[13]

Quite probably, Felix was Felix Holbrook, who joined Peter Bestes, Sambo Freeman, and Chester Joie in a much stronger statement only a few months later. By then, they had found their shared voice, with no ritual trembling or humble language. Somebody among them had been studying the history and law of slavery, and they knew that under Spanish slave law self-purchase was possible. They wanted the same right for themselves. It was a clever move: Holbrook, Bestes, Freeman, and Joie certainly knew that, to English and colonial-English people who valued their freedom, Spain stood for tyranny. They had no illusions that their oppressors liked them. If freedom should come, they would submit to "such regulations and laws, as may be made rela-tive to us" but only "until we leave the province." That, they informed their readers, "we determine to do as soon as we can from our joint labours procure money to transport themselves to some part of the coast of *Africa,* where we propose a settlement."[14]

Here, clearly, is the African voice of longing to reverse sail and return. They sought escape not just from slavery but America itself. But they had been watching the colonial protests. They knew that Boston's Committee of Correspondence was laboring mightily to rouse all the people of Mas-sachusetts to resist Britain. So they signed their own address "by order of their Committee." Like slaves in Charles Town, South Carolina, who cried "liberty" as early as the Stamp Act protests of 1765, these people were do-ing much more than just imitate the whites who surrounded and oppressed them. Actually enslaved, rather than threatened by supposed enslavement, they were turning the enslavers' language and organization against the en-slavers.

In May, 1774, a great "number of Blackes" in Massachusetts sent a hand-written petition to the new royal governor, Major General Thomas Gage. They spelled badly, but they had mastered the language of the white revolutionaries. They knew that they possessed a natural right to freedom. Never had they "forfeited this Blessing" by "compact or agreement." Naked, grasping power, the same demon that haunted the language of white revolutionaries had dragged them from their plentiful and populous African homelands. But they did not see their future in Africa. Rather than returning, they wanted unoccupied public land, so they could build their own settlement. They, or their ancestors, had come from Africa, but they were American and they intended to stay in the country they knew.[15]

In August, as British political authority was falling apart across Massachusetts, a slave named Caesar Sarter took on the whole question. The printer of *The Essex Journal*, which circulated throughout northern New England, gave his essay on slavery the top position on page one. Sarter was African-born, so, like Phillis Wheatley, he knew both freedom and enslavement first-hand. He deferred very slightly to his white readers when he asked them to "attend to the request of a poor African." But his rage was obvious. White colonists' "charter rights" were in danger, but their worries did not compare to his own "miserable slavery, in a different part of the globe" from where he had been born. Sarter did not need Anthony Benezet to know about Africa. He remembered it, and though some might think "we are happier here than there, and will not allow us the privilege of judging for ourselves [but] every man is the best judge of his own happiness." "Would you desire the preservation of your own liberty?" he asked. If so, then "as a first step, let the oppressed Africans be liberated; then, and not till then, may you . . . look to Heaven for a blessing on your endeavours to knock the shackles with which your task masters are hampering you, from your own feet."[16]

By 1774 it was becoming clear both that a time had arrived for choosing one of two sides and that black people were exploring their possibilities with the British. Abigail Adams heard about the petition to Governor Gage while her husband John was in Philadelphia at the First Continental Congress. She described it to him as a conspiracy. She feared the petitioners had told Gage, who was British commander-in-chief in America as well as royal governor of Massachusetts, that they would fight for him should it come to war, which clearly was going to happen. If they had said so to the governor, they were not alone. In February, 1775, while townsfolk were collecting gunpowder and musket balls to store at Concord, Massachusetts, patriot authorities in New York arrested two black men in Ulster County, New York, for collecting arms too, in order to recover their own freedom. After the first arrest, the authorities arrested nearly twenty more. White revolutionaries arrested still more in the town of Jamaica, on New York's Long Island, in Westchester County, north of New York City, and in Dorchester County, Maryland.

These slaves had good reason to think that their chances were better with the British. News of the Somerset case had crossed the Atlantic and spread widely. White colonials, not distant Britons, held them in slavery. The whole British Empire was coming apart, and as it ruptured things became possible that had been unthinkable in the ordinary course of human events. Except for Boston, where Gage had stationed five thousand troops and based the Royal Navy's American squadron, British authority collapsed in Massachusetts over the summer and early autumn of 1774. It was weakening everywhere else. Power began to drain from the old colonial legislatures and Crown courts toward revolutionary committees and congresses and it looked more and more certain that war would come, soon. When news spread in April, 1775, that war actually had broken out in Massachusetts, slaves in Williamsburg, Virginia, knew that there was no point in seeking their freedom from the likes of Patrick Henry or George Washington. They turned instead to John Murray, Earl of Dunmore, who was to be Virginia's final royal governor.

Dunmore had come to America to make his own fortune by taking fees, making illegal land grants, and perhaps receiving outright bribes. All those had been possible in New York, his first American posting. So when the British Crown transferred him to Virginia he damned his new assignment in a drunken tirade at a farewell party. In 1774 he provoked a frontier war with Shawnee Indians over western land that they regarded as their own. But whatever his faults, Dunmore had reason to be appalled at white Virginians' continual rhetoric of liberty when it was obvious that their whole way of life rested upon slavery. When the express riders arrived in Williamsburg a few days after the battle of Lexington with the news of war, a few slaves approached Dunmore immediately. They would serve him and the Crown, if he would give them freedom. He sent them away. But they either had planted a seed in his mind or fertilized one that already was there.

The moment of independence meant having to choose a side. Was a person with the Americans? Or with the British? Choosing the one or the other drove fatal wedges among Americans of virtually every sort. It separated Benjamin Franklin and his loyalist son William, who had become royal governor of New Jersey. New York lawyers John Jay and Peter Van Schaack, friends since college, argued the matter back and forth until they went their separate ways, Jay to leadership in the Revolution and the young republic,

Van Schaack to unhappy exile in London. Farmers in New York's Hudson Valley retreated to the hills and debated the issue intensely, not knowing that a spy was among them and that every word they uttered reached the revolutionary committee in Albany. Husbands and wives, parents and children, sisters and brothers became enemies. Iroquois Indians argued about it, while both the British and the revolutionaries sought to enlist them. In 1777 the "Great League of Peace and Power" that had served them well for nearly three centuries failed under the strain and they collapsed into war, as much against one another as against the British (for the Oneida and the Tuscarora) or against the Americans (for the rest). As they consolidated their new power, the revolutionaries established political police, such as New York's "Commissioners for Detecting and Defeating Conspiracies."

Through it all, black people could have held back. Nobody would have blamed them for doing whatever their masters, whether loyalist or revolutionary, required them to do. Submission was supposed to be their lot, in return for the protection a master could give. But now fate had given them a moment when they found themselves free to choose.

On November 7, 1775, Lord Dunmore finally took up the offer that Williamsburg slaves had presented to him in April, announcing in the king's name that "all indented Servants, Negroes, or others (appertaining to Rebels)" would be "free that are able and willing to bear Arms." He still possessed the king's commission as governor of Virginia. But angry rebels had driven him out of Williamsburg and he actually governed nothing more than a few ships floating in Chesapeake Bay. Dunmore probably knew that what he said to white Virginians ("I do require every Person capable of bearing Arms to resort to His Majesty's STANDARD or be looked upon as Traitors") was mere bluster.[17] For black people who stood a chance of reaching him, however, Dunmore offered a moment in which they could decide what they wanted to do.

The Scottish earl had done what rebel slave owners had thought beyond contemplation, and they responded quickly. Thirteen days after his proclamation, one of Virginia's most notable leaders responded with a proclamation in the name of the revolutionary Committee of Safety. Constant and close attention to whatever slaves said and whatever they did was necessary. So were constant patrols. The proclamation's author was Patrick Henry, who disliked slavery and read Benezet, and who six months earlier, according to wide reports, had cried "Give me liberty or give me death" to his fellow Virginians.

Virginians possessed close to two hundred thousand slaves when Dunmore proclaimed freedom to rebels' slaves who would join him. Very probably

By his Excellency the Right Honourable JOHN Earl of DUNMORE, his

Majesty's Lieutenant and Governour-General of the Colony and Dominion of

Virginia, and Vice-Admiral of the same:

A PROCLAMATION.

AS I have ever entertained Hopes that an Accommodation might have taken Place between Great Britain and this Colony, without being compelled, by my Duty, to this most disagreeable, but now absolutely necessary Step, rendered so by a Body of armed Men, unlawfully assembled, firing on his Majesty's Tenders, and the Formation of an Army, and that Army now on their March to attack his Majesty's Troops, and destroy the well-disposed Subjects of this Colony: To defeat such treasonable Purposes, and that all such Traitors, and their Abettors, may be brought to Justice, and that the Peace and good Order of this Colony may be again restored, which the ordinary Course of the civil Law is unable to effect, I have thought fit to issue this my Proclamation, hereby declaring, that until the aforesaid good Purposes can be obtained, I do, in Virtue of the Power and Authority to me given, by his Majesty, determine to execute martial Law, and cause the same to be executed throughout this Colony; and to the End that Peace and good Order may the sooner be restored, I do require every Person capable of bearing Arms, to resort to his Majesty's STAN-DARD, or be looked upon as Traitors to his Majesty's Crown and Government, and thereby become liable to the Penalty the Law inflicts upon such Offences, such as Forfeiture of Life, Confiscation of Lands, &c. &c. And I do hereby farther declare all indented Servants, Negroes, or others, (appertaining to Rebels) free, that are able and willing to bear Arms, they joining his Majesty's Troops, as soon as may be, for the more speedily reducing this Colony to a proper Sense of their Duty, to his Majesty's Crown and Dignity. I do farther order, and require, all his Majesty's liege Subjects to retain their Quitrents, or any other Taxes due, or that may become due, in their own Custody, till such Time as Peace may be again restored to this at present most unhappy Country, or demanded of them for their former salutary Purposes, by Officers properly authorized to receive the same.

GIVEN under my Hand, on Board the Ship William, off Norfolk,
the 7th Day of November, in the 16th Year of his Majesty's
Reign.

DUNMORE.

GOD SAVE THE KING.

SIR,

AS the Committee of Safety is not sitting, I take the Liberty to enclose you a Copy of the Proclamation issued by Lord Dunmore; the Design and Tendency of which, you will observe, is fatal to the publick Safety. An early and unremitting Attention to the Government of the SLAVES may, I hope, counteract this dangerous Attempt. Constant, and well directed Patrols, seem indispensably necessary. I doubt not of every possible Exertion, in your Power, for the publick Good; and have the Honour to be, Sir,

Your most obedient and very humble Servant,

P. HENRY.

HEAD QUARTERS, WILLIAMSBURG,
November 20, 1775.

Image 2.1a and 2.1b. Lord Dunmore issued his proclamation of freedom for slaves "appertaining to rebels" (left) for strictly military reasons, but it marked a breach in slavery's hold. Patrick Henry's response (right) shows how much the proclamation worried rebellious white Virginians.

Sources: (left) By his Excellency the Right Honourable John Earl of Dunmore, his Majesty's Lieutenant and Governour-General of the Colony and Dominion of Virginia, and Vice-Admiral of the same: A proclamation [declaring martial law, and to cause the same to be executed] (A 1775.V55a). Tracy W. McGregor Library of American History, Special Collections, University of Virginia Library. (right) Courtesy of the Library of Congress, Broadside Collection

every single Virginia slave who was old enough to understand learned about it. For most of them, mere distance made accepting the offer an impossible dream. Even for slaves who were in range, reaching the governor's little fleet was difficult and dangerous. White Virginians kept careful watch on their own slave quarters. They patrolled the roads and the back ways. They watched the shoreline, and they guarded boat landings.

Despite all the rebels' precautions, about eight hundred black Virginians managed to reach Dunmore, the largest single escape from slavery in the whole history of British North America to that point. Formed into "Lord Dunmore's Ethiopian Regiment," they bore badges that read "Liberty to Slaves." They fought bravely against the American rebels at Norfolk and Great Bridge. Smallpox cut freedom very short for most of Lord Dunmore's black soldiers. Without inoculation, they fell before the great epidemic that swept across most of North America, from the Atlantic Coast to the Rocky Mountains and from Mexico to the Arctic, between 1775 and 1782. The tight, close quarters of Dunmore's small fleet could not have offered better conditions for the virus to spread, so he did what he probably had to do, abandoning victims to die on an island in the bay. About the same time that Dunmore was rallying his force South Carolina rebel leaders hanged a free black Charles Town harbor pilot named Thomas Jeremiah simply because they suspected that he was planning to aid a British invasion.

The British had a war to win, and throughout the long conflict they welcomed black men who would enlist. Slaves in Georgia and South Carolina possessed rich local knowledge of the watery byways around Savannah and Charles Town and they were willing to share it with the right people. Savannah fell to the British in 1779 and Charles Town a year later because black guides assisted the British invaders. A French fleet and American Army that tried to recapture Savannah got no such aid, and the mission failed. Black men joined loyalist guerilla bands that harassed the Continental Army and that plagued patriots. A black man known informally as Colonel Ty led a mixed black and white group that raided in Maryland, Delaware, and New Jersey. The colonel seems to have begun his military career as one of Lord Dunmore's "Ethiopians."

In 1779 the third of King George's commanders-in-chief in America, Sir Henry Clinton, made what Dunmore had begun into a general British policy, and broadened its terms. Clinton already had a whole unit called the Black Pioneers under his command. Now he would welcome all slaves of rebels if they crossed the British lines, promising them leave to pursue any "lawful occupation" they wanted to follow. He would welcome women as well as men. It was a promise of protection, not outright freedom, but it amounted to the same thing. Effectively, Clinton's order annulled the colonial "positive law" that allowed enslavement, if a person could reach the British lines. Black people responded strongly. The best measure is that roughly fifteen thousand black men and women who had freed themselves by rallying to the Union Jack departed with the British when they evacuated Savannah, Charles Town, and New York City in 1783.

From Lord Mansfield deciding that James Somerset would "go free" in 1772 to Sir Henry Clinton welcoming all slaves of rebels in 1779, British leaders were weakening slavery as an institution and establishing a reputation that many black people would remember and honor. Many slaves believed that the king was on their side. But Britain did not commit itself to outright anti-slavery. Apparently George III had no sympathy for slaves at all; he certainly thought that ending the African slave trade was foolish when Parliament did so in 1807. Whatever the king thought, policy makers in his cabinet and generals in the field counted on the support of white loyalists, many of them slave owners. They hoped for much of the war to win slave-holding rebels back to allegiance. As it became clear that they could not win the mainland war, they turned their energies to protecting their island colonies in the West Indies, including their enormously valuable sugar plantations. Neither Dunmore's proclamation of freedom for the slaves of rebels who would fight for the king nor Clinton's offer to protect any slave who reached his lines had any effect in the Caribbean at all.

There came one moment of absolute British disgrace, at the very end of the land war. In 1781 Lord Charles Cornwallis set out northward from Charles Town with a large army, including black soldiers and black civilian followers. His hope for winning the mainland war was to rally loyalists and pacify the South. As he moved through the two Carolinas and into Virginia, more and more black people joined him, including slaves from Thomas Jefferson's Monticello. They attached themselves to a force led by the traitorous American general Benedict Arnold while Jefferson, who was governor of Virginia at the time, fled into the woods.

Cornwallis's troops were superb. They had no trouble beating rebel forces, but the rebels fell back to fight again and white loyalists did not rally as the noble earl had hoped. The general found himself facing the classic problem of any British commander in America who ventured away from navigable water: supplies. As his stores dwindled, he headed for Yorktown, on the York River, to wait for seaborne relief. But a French fleet defeated the British vessels that were on their way to his rescue, and Washington quickly led a combined French and American force to lay siege to the trapped British army. To disguise his intentions, Washington counted on a black secret agent in

New York City to spread a report that the American troops were about to besiege the occupied town, rather than heading south to catch Cornwallis. As the trap closed and Cornwallis's stores ran out, he abandoned the black people who had come to him, sending them out of the British lines to where the rebels awaited them. No thought of mercy or continuing freedom was on the rebels' minds.

But after betraying his black supporters for the sake of the supplies they would consume, Cornwallis realized that he would have to surrender. He gave up on October 19, 1781, and the mainland phase of the war was effectively over. The British Parliament voted to stop supplying the war effort and to end hostilities. British forces withdrew to the three port cities they held, Savannah, Charles Town, and New York. Peace negotiations opened in Paris, and in 1783 the final treaty of peace was signed and ratified. Buried deep in Article 7, the treaty promised a further British betrayal: "His Britannic Majesty shall with all convenient speed, and without causing any destruction, or carrying away any Negroes or other property of the American inhabitants, withdraw all his armies, garrisons, and fleets from the said United States."[18] Among the negotiators was Henry Laurens of South Carolina, who had been one of the largest American slave traders before the Revolutionary War.

When word of the clause reached the black communities in the three occupied ports, a fully justified wave of fear swept through them. After all they had done and endured, reenslavement seemed to await them. Former masters began appearing to reclaim escapees and demanded that the British authorities help them. American authorities made it completely clear that they wanted the clause to be honored. George Washington himself put pressure on the final British commander, Sir Guy Carleton, to hand all black people back, so they could be returned to slavery.

Like Lord Mansfield, Carleton was an honorable man, and he found a way out, at least on behalf of most of the refugees. He deemed that all former slaves who had been inside the British lines for more than a year and who had served the British faithfully had earned the king's protection, and he offered them passage to elsewhere in the remaining British Empire. British officers arranging the withdrawal from New York City started a record that they called "The Book of Negroes." They recorded some four thousand three hundred men, women, and children who got passports and boarded outbound transports. Perhaps ten thousand more sailed to safety from Savannah and Charles Town. Some certainly remembered the rumors that circulated after Somerset's case that the king had a book of freedom. Exodus from the land of "our modern Egyptians," as Phillis Wheatley had described white colonials to the Native American minister Samson Occum, had come.[19] The revolutionary pamphleteer Thomas Paine had called George III "the hardened, sullen tempered Pharaoh of England"[20] in 1776. To the former slaves who left with the departing troops seven long years later, the distant monarch must have seemed more like Moses.

The great exodus of late 1783 did not lead to any promised land. The people who left scattered widely. Some went to the West Indies, where they faced the same danger of being reenslaved that haunted all free black people, whether in the Caribbean or in the new United States. Others joined the small community of black Britons, mostly in London. A very few became part of the early British ventures in distant Australia. Taken as a whole, they formed yet another scattering of black people across the globe, this time not from Africa by the slave trade but rather by their own liberation into the late eighteenth-century Atlantic world.

The largest single group went to Nova Scotia in Canada, encouraged by the honorable part that the British had taken in the face of American demands for their return. They sailed with promises that they would be given land, tools, seeds, animals, and implements. They would have the supplies they needed until they could establish themselves as free farmers. Like the many white loyalist exiles, they would create a triumphant new British colonial venture that would put the rebel former colonies to shame.

It did not work out, for many reasons. British officials proved slow to measure the heavily wooded land into individual grants. The promised supplies turned out to be poor, often consisting of aging, half-rotten leftovers from military stores. White exiled loyalists and demobilized former soldiers treated the black refugees with contempt or outright hostility. The settlement at Shelburne, at the southern tip of Nova Scotia, can serve as an example. The former slaves who disembarked there never did join the main settlement. Instead, they established Birchtown, named for the general who had signed many of their passports. It became, for a time, the largest free black community in North America, but it was a place of thrown-together shacks, set back three miles across the woods from the main town. Exposed to the open North Atlantic, the settlement's climate was cold and its growing season was short. The soil proved poor and thin. Most of the settlers had come from the Southern colonies and neither the climate nor the possible crops suited them. Demobilized soldiers in Shelburne, who also wanted land and who competed with the former slaves for work, descended on Birchtown in 1784 and sacked it.

After long years of sheer endurance, one of the settlers, Thomas Peters, made his way to London in 1792 to seek something better, not just for himself but for his people. There he connected with England's anti-slavery movement, including Granville Sharp and the brothers Thomas and John Clarkson. Their main campaign was to end Britain's slave trade, but they wanted black people to be able to show what they could do. They and their supporters had launched a project in 1787 to establish a free black community in Sierra Leone, and Peters convinced them that his people would be perfect settlers. John Clarkson, a young naval officer, returned to Nova Scotia with Peters to recruit volunteers. Some of the settlers there proved skeptical. They already had seen British promises of land, supplies, and a start toward a new life fail once. The war was over and in Nova Scotia they at least had no need to fear oncoming Americans bent on recapturing them. They were free and nobody could make them go. So, given the choice, they stayed where they were and Anglophone Canada's black community began to emerge among them. Slavery as an institution finally ended in Canada in 1834, when Parliament abolished it throughout the British Empire.

But more than a thousand of the Nova Scotia settlers took up the chance to go to Sierra Leone in 1792, establishing Freetown when they arrived. Some, like Peters, were African-born. Though reaching their actual homes was impossible, they were finally reversing the ocean-spanning arc of evil and pain that had begun when they or their forebears were captured for the slave trade. As in Nova Scotia, they did not find all they wanted. John Clarkson strove mightily to have the promises made to them honored, but the Sierra Leone Company that sponsored the venture proved paternalistic, believing it could run the settlers' lives for them. The settlers divided bitterly among themselves. They had to deal there with West African conditions, vastly different from the cold of Nova Scotia, but different from New York, Virginia, and Carolina as well. They were safe from reenslavement, but they could see the slaving ships that sailed past Freetown, bound for the West Indies and reeking of the misery inside. The settlers' African neighbors, with whom they had no choice but to deal, were taking part in the trade. But the settlers' lives were their own and they had left their long American nightmare behind. Like their fellows who stayed in Canada as proud British subjects, these repatriated Africans had claimed their freedom. They did so because of the American Revolution, though not within the new nation, conceived in liberty and dedicated to the proposition that all men are created equal, that the Revolution had brought forth.

Drittes Regiment Garde.
Chef. Se. Hochfürstliche Durchlaucht der Landgraf

Image 2.2a and 2.2b.   Black men served with honor on both sides during the Revolutionary War, as European observers noted. Anne S. K. Brown Military Collection, Brown University Library

Black men and women chose the American side as well as the British. Phillis Wheatley honored Lord Dartmouth with her verses in 1772, but three years later she wrote her ode to Washington (in which she did not mention slavery directly). Perhaps the general found it disturbing to write his polite reply to "Miss Phillis"; it is hard to imagine a Virginia planter addressing any slave in such terms. But she did accept his invitation to visit, and he proved equally polite as her host. As Wheatley was writing her poems, other black women working at country Massachusetts taverns were spotting and reporting British spies simply from their haughty demeanor.

When Washington arrived to take command of the ragtag Continental Army besieging occupied Boston early in July, 1775, he was astonished to find black men among his troops. Some were free. Others aimed to win their freedom by serving in place of their masters. As a Virginia planter, Washington was just as astonished at how his white New England officers and men treated one another as equals; he would have "condescended" to the plain folk at home. He needed the white soldiers. But he thought he could do without black troops, so in November he issued a general order to dismiss them.

George Washington was a man who learned from experience, and who changed his ways when he had to. He learned quickly that he needed soldiers of any color. He rescinded the order in December and black New Englanders continued to serve. Very probably, such men saved him and his troops at the one point in the whole war when the British could have captured him, destroyed the army, and ended the war on their terms. It came during his futile attempt to defend New York City late in the summer of 1776, when smart British strategy and Washington's own inexperience let most of his troops get trapped in Brooklyn Heights, across the East River from Manhattan. All that the British had to do was cut them off by sending warships up the river.

On the night of August 29, a biracial unit of black and white Rhode Island troops rescued both Washington and his army from the imminent catastrophe. A northerly wind and fog kept the British ships down-harbor, and, while the East River remained clear, troops from two Rhode Island regiments commandeered and manned every vessel that could float, ferrying the army across to a brief moment of safety in Manhattan before they had to retreat again. Most of the Rhode Islanders were experienced mariners, and very many of them were black, part of the black seafarers' world that spanned the Atlantic.

Washington would not scorn black troops again. On the contrary, when the moment finally came five years later to launch the assault on Cornwallis at Yorktown, Washington assigned a place in the lead, which was the position of honor, to a unit recruited at his suggestion from Rhode Island slaves and known as "The Black Regiment." Black men served in many other units of both the militia and the Continental Army, many of them in the regular army for the whole duration of the war. Some already were free; others were slaves, mostly serving in place of their masters in return for a promise of freedom, but sometimes in personal rebellion against masters who had chosen loyalism. Most of them probably were Northerners, but Delaware, Maryland, and Virginia allowed recruitment as well. Like Lord Dunmore's "Ethiopians," and Colonel Ty's guerillas, their goal was their own freedom, both personally and for their people. Washington became open to the idea of general black recruitment, understanding that, as with the Rhode Islanders, freedom would be the reward for slaves who served. But he stopped short of publicly endorsing a proposal for freeing slaves in the Carolinas and Georgia in return for service, put to him by one of his aides-de-camp, South Carolina's Lieutenant-Colonel John Laurens. Though the son of a major slave trader and planter, Laurens wanted slavery to end, and he saw military service as the best way to weaken it. But hardly any other white Carolinians or Georgians agreed, and the proposal died in Congress. Laurens himself died in a small skirmish, as one of the war's very last casualties.

Other black units besides Rhode Island's regiment served on the revolutionary side. Captain David Humphreys commanded one, a company drawn from Connecticut. Most likely Humphreys' troops, like other black soldiers, were a mixture of free men and men still in slavery. After the war Humphreys became a close friend, frequent guest, and protégé of Washington, in what was as close to a father-son relationship as Washington ever had. Did they discuss Humphreys' experiences during one or another of the former captain's visits to Mount Vernon? Quite possibly, though the circumspect Washington, aware that his letters probably would be opened and read, would not have committed anything on the subject to writing. Washington certainly was working toward his late-life realization that there ought to be no permanent place for slavery in the republic he was helping to found.

Little information survives about another black unit, who called themselves the "Bucks of America." All we really know about them is that Boston revolutionary leader John Hancock presented them with a flag, signing it with the same famous signature that he inscribed as president of the Continental Congress on the Declaration of Independence. The flag still exists. As part of French support, a unit called the Volunteer Chasseurs (cavalry) came to the Americans' aid from Ste. Domingue, which was still more than a decade from its own revolution against slavery. More than five hundred of its thirty-nine hundred members were black or mixed race. They probably were already free. The unit took part in the futile French-American attempt in 1779 to retake Savannah. Even had they connected with Georgia or Carolina slaves, these French-speaking black soldiers would have had a hard time communicating. Being free themselves, they might well have treated the black loyalists with scorn. But rice slavery in Georgia would have looked very much like sugar slavery in Ste. Domingue. The black Chasseurs returned home after the war, and some of them bided their time. Several emerged as leaders during the great revolution that destroyed Haitian slavery in the 1790s. One who had been in Georgia, Martial Besse, would rise to the rank of general during the French Revolution. Another, Henri Christophe, would for awhile claim the title of king of independent Haiti.

There is no American equivalent of the "Book of Negroes" that British officials kept during the embarkation. But we do have soldiers' stories. Some are bare outlines. Others told their tales late in life to federal commissioners, in the hope of receiving the pensions they had been promised when they enlisted. Connecticut's Jehu Grant, who finally requested his reward in 1832, described in his submission how he had escaped from a loyalist New England master so that he would not have to serve in the British forces. The commissioners turned him down two years later, ironically on the ground that, as an escaped slave at the time of his service, he had no claim. Others fared almost as bitterly. Austin Dabney of Georgia, an artilleryman who won his freedom by serving and who took a severe wound, finally received a land grant from the state in 1819 to honor his service. Local whites in Macon protested against the grant. Most of them had not been born when Dabney was fighting for the freedom they enjoyed.

But Dabney did stay in Georgia as a free man, telling his tales of the Revolution as he aged. Former black soldier Agrippa Hall stayed in Stockbridge, Massachusetts, reminiscing about how he had served as personal aide to two generals, John Paterson and the Polish volunteer Tadeusz Kosciuszko. He and Kosciuszko rejoiced to see each other when the Pole returned to America in 1797. The Marquis de Lafayette rejoiced the same way in 1824 with former slave James Armistead Lafayette. The American had spied in Lord Cornwallis's camp during the final siege at Yorktown, to the astonishment of British officers when they saw him among the victors after the surrender. Freedom presented the chance to claim his own identity, as opposed to whatever he had been called in slavery, and he honored Lafayette by taking the French nobleman's name.

Altogether about five thousand black men served in the American forces. More, probably, served under the British. But one difference is striking. The British did arm black volunteers and enroll them in the ranks. Pictures survive from both sides of black men in full uniform. But Sir Henry Clinton's

Pioneers, the only formal British unit other than Lord Dunmore's Ethiopian Regiment identified as black, carried spades and shovels, not muskets. Their task was not to fight. It was to dig ditches and latrine trenches and to raise defensive earthworks. There was nothing in the British army comparable to the black Rhode Island regiment that Washington deployed to begin the final assault at Yorktown. The people who fought under the Union Jack and who departed with the British in 1783 were grasping the chance that history had given them to strike at slavery in their own lives. But the people who joined the American army, or who stayed when they could have left, were making a riskier bet for higher stakes. Their wager was that they could build lives of their own in the only land they really knew, and strike at the institution of slavery within the emerging American republic.

Notes

1. "An act for the better securing the dependency of his majesty's dominions in America upon the crown and parliament of Great Britain," March 18, 1766, avalon .law.yale.edu/18th_century/declaratory_act_1766.asp, accessed April 17, 2011.

2. Benjamin L. Carp, *Defiance of the Patriots: The Boston Tea Party and the Making of America* (New Haven: Yale University Press, 2010), 143.

3. Sidney Kaplan and Emma Nogrady Kaplan, *The Black Presence in the Era of the American Revolution* (Amherst: University of Massachusetts Press, 1989), 8.

4. Sewall, *The Selling of Joseph* (Boston: Bartholomew Green and John Allen, 1700), 3.

5. Kirsten Sword, "Remembering Dinah Nevil: Strategic Deceptions in Eighteenth-Century Antislavery," *Journal of American History*, September 2010, 326.

6. All *Somerset* case quotations from 20 *Howell's State Trials* 1, 79–82, and 98 *English Law Reports*, 499–510.

7. *New York Journal*, August 27, 1772, quoted Steven M. Wise, *Though the Heavens May Fall: The Landmark Trial That Led to the End of Human Slavery* (Cambridge, MA: Da Capo Press, 2005), 199–200.

8. *Williamsburg Virginia Gazette*, June 30, 1774, quoted Wise, *Though the Heavens May Fall*, 200.

9. Wheatley, "On Being Brought from Africa to America," *Poems on Various Subjects, Religious and Moral* (London: A. Bell, 1773), 18.

10. Wheatley, "To The Right Honourable William, Earl Of Dartmouth, His Majesty's Principal Secretary Of The State For North-America, &c.," *Poems on Various Subjects, Religious and Moral* (London: A. Bell, 1773), 73–75.

11. Thomas Hutchinson et al., "To the Publick," *The Poems of Phillis Wheatley*, ed. Julian D. Mason, Jr. (Chapel Hill: University of North Carolina Press, 1966), 48.

12. David Brion Davis, *The Problem of Slavery in the Age of Revolution, 1770–1823* (New York: Oxford University Press, 1976), 196.

13. *The appendix: or, Some observations on the expediency of the petition of the Africans, living in Boston, &c. lately presented to the General Assembly of this province. To which is annexed, the petition referred to. Likewise, thoughts on slavery. With a useful extract from the Massachusetts spy, of January 28, 1773, by way of an address to the members of the assembly.* By a lover of constitutional liberty. Worcester, MA: American Antiquarian Society, Early American Imprints, Series 1, no. 12651.

14. Kaplan and Kaplan, *Black Presence*, 14.

15. Kaplan and Kaplan, *Black Presence*, 13–14.

16. Roger Bruns, ed., *Am I Not a Man and a Brother: The Antislavery Crusade of Revolutionary America, 1688–1788* (New York: Chelsea House, 1977), 337–40.

17. Kaplan and Kaplan, *Black Presence*, 74.

18. The Definitive Treaty of Peace, 1783, avalon.law.yale.edu/18th_century/paris.asp, accessed April 17, 2011.

19. Wheatley to Occum, February 9, 1774, *Massachusetts Gazette*, March 24, 1774.

20. Thomas Paine, *Rights of Man, Common Sense, and Other Political Writings*, ed. Mark Philp (New York: Oxford University Press, 1995), 28.

CHAPTER THREE

~

"The Fruition of Those Blessings"

Black People in the Emerging Republic

"I have abundantly tasted of the fruition of those blessings which proceed from that free and unequalled liberty with which you are favoured."

—Benjamin Banneker to Thomas Jefferson, 1791

On October 20, 1774, the First Continental Congress, meeting in Philadelphia, took a major step on the question of slavery. The Congress had
gathered to work out a common American position in response to the strong
punishments that Britain had inflicted on Boston for the town's destruction
of a large amount of valuable East India Company tea the previous December. Speaking for Americans from Georgia to New Hampshire, Congress
responded that Boston's problems were everybody's problems. Words would
not be enough, so Congress adopted a total boycott of overseas commerce,
to Britain and everywhere else.

The second article of this "Continental Association" declared that "We
will neither import nor purchase, any slave imported after the first day of
December next; after which time, we will wholly discontinue the slave trade,
and will neither be concerned in it ourselves, nor will we hire our vessels, nor
sell our commodities or manufactures to those who are concerned in it."[1] The
boycott was absolute and it applied everywhere, to Savannah and Charles
Town (as it still was called) as well as to New York and Boston. Some of
the colonial legislatures, particularly the House of Burgesses in Virginia, had
tried to tax the slave trade out of existence, only to have the distant British
Crown veto the tax. But the king could not veto anything the Congress did.

Lord Mansfield's decision in the *Somerset* case had been important. Enslaved people rightly took it as a sign that they could hope for freedom on the British side. But Congress had given a sign that there was hope on the American side. Moreover, it was taking a public stand on behalf of the entire American people. Banning the trade was the strongest action against slavery that Americans undertook as a whole until the Thirteenth Amendment to the Constitution abolished slavery altogether in 1865.

Perhaps young James Forten had that signal in mind seven years later, in 1781, when he got the chance to choose the certainty of freedom with the British or to take his chances in America. He had been born free in Philadelphia, where Congress met, and, though he was only a child in 1774, he was old enough to learn what was going on around him. Forten yearned for the sea, so in 1781, when he became old enough, he signed on to an American privateer, a vessel licensed to prey on enemy shipping as if it were part of the navy. The first voyage went well, but on the second a Royal Navy warship captured his vessel. Because Forten was black and on the rebel side, he faced the prospect of West Indies enslavement, but the captain's son, who was on board, struck up a friendship with him over a game of marbles. The captain made the Philadelphian his son's companion. The black American young man and the white English boy grew close, and the captain offered to sponsor Forten in London. Forten turned the offer down. America was his country, so he went as a prisoner of war to the notorious *Jersey* prison ship, moored in Wallabout Bay on Long Island. Like every prisoner there, he faced hard suffering, though it was better than West Indies enslavement, from which there would have been no escape. Even though the main fighting ended at Yorktown just about the time Forten first sailed, he was not released until the official end of hostilities two years later. When he finally arrived home, his family had given him up for dead.

Forten certainly had other reasons for turning down the British captain, in addition to what Congress had decreed in 1774. He had chosen to sail on the privateer; perhaps he felt a seafarer's loyalty to his shipmates. As a Philadelphian, Forten certainly knew about the debates among the Quakers. He could have read the anti-slavery pamphlet that the Englishman Thomas Paine (who came from a Quaker background) published late in 1775, just prior to Paine's great assault on monarchy and call for independence in his pamphlet *Common Sense*. When he signed on, Pennsylvania's law for gradually ending slavery had been in effect for a year. It was true both that a slaveholder commanded the American army and it was true that another slaveholder had written the fine words of the Declaration of Independence about all men being created equal and having unalienable rights. But by late 1781, when Forten was captured, George Washington had written politely to Phillis Wheatley, found how much he needed black troops, and given them the position of honor in the final assault on Lord Cornwallis at Yorktown, leading the attack. Cornwallis, for his part, had betrayed the black Southerners who had rallied to him in the hope of winning their own freedom. Slavery was becoming a real, troubling issue, and liberation was beginning to seem possible. But the problem did not fit neatly with any other issues of the revolutionary era. To understand the American side, we have to start with the Declaration of Independence, proclaiming as it did that "all men are created equal" and that "life, liberty, and the pursuit of happiness" are every man's birthright.

The Declaration's great contribution to the history of slavery's destruction came in just four words, "all men are created equal." Perhaps without realizing it fully, their author, Thomas Jefferson, was picking up and expanding on a point that Lord Mansfield had made by implication in his *Somerset* decision. For Mansfield, slavery was "odious." But in his up-and-down world of kings, nobles, gentry, and commoners, "positive" enacted law still could give slavery protection. What positive law could not give was moral justification, meaning rightfulness. The implications of Jefferson's words ("created equal . . . unalienable rights . . . life, liberty, and the pursuit of happiness") are much larger. If equality is the fundamental human condition, slavery cannot be justified. Any law that protected slavery was inherently wrong, with the clear implication that it had to be rejected, on principle. Jefferson was a lawyer and he may have seen that implication. Other people in his world, both black and white, certainly did see it, and they acted on it. Jefferson's draft of the Declaration tried to go further, with what he meant to be a ringing denunciation of slavery. John Adams read Jefferson's words and liked the passage. However the Continental Congress cut the whole denunciation during four intense days of editing, while Jefferson writhed in his seat. All the rest of his life he blamed the delegates from South Carolina and Georgia for the cut. But given what Jefferson actually wrote, Congress probably was right. The problem had been raised and would not go away, but what Jefferson wrote in that passage revealed immediately how difficult resolving it was going to prove.

Jefferson's attempt to place the slavery question in the Declaration came at the end of the document's extended middle section, which took the form of a courtroom indictment. In the words of the Declaration itself, his goal in that section was to "prove" to a "candid world" that King George's reign presented "a long history of abuses and usurpations, all having in direct object the establishment of an absolute tyranny over these states." Acting as a prosecuting attorney, Jefferson arranged his evidence from the seemingly trivial to the very serious. In outline form, he was telling a story that made sense of the breakdown of relations between Britain and the colonists.

Jefferson had no absolute proof of the king's intentions. Like many a courtroom lawyer, he presented a circumstantial case, inviting readers and listeners to follow his logic toward the conclusion he had drawn, which was that the king's time was over. He wrote masterfully, almost musically. Every one of his charges was spare and hard. He was following a good writer's rule of showing what he meant the reader to see, rather than just telling. Follow my evidence and logic, he was saying as he submitted these "facts" to "a candid world," and you will agree with my charge that the king's purpose was to impose tyranny. As far as Americans were concerned, George III had to be deposed.

Jefferson intended the slavery matter to be the final charge, and, when he reached it, his language changed. Here is the passage with its original typography. Despite its length, or perhaps even because of its length (since all the other charges are very concise), it bears close reading:

> he has waged cruel war against human nature itself, violating it's most sacred rights of life & liberty in the persons of a distant people who never offended him, captivating & carrying them into slavery in another hemisphere, or to incur miserable death in their transportation thither. this piratical warfare, the opprobrium of *infidel* powers, is the warfare of the CHRISTIAN king of Great Britain. determined to keep open a market where MEN should be bought & sold, he has prostituted his negative for suppressing every legislative attempt to prohibit or to restrain this execrable commerce: and that this assemblage of horrors might want no fact of distinguished die, he is now exciting those very people to rise in arms among us, and to purchase that liberty of which he has deprived them, & murdering the people upon whom he also obtruded them; thus paying off former crimes committed against the *liberties* of one people, with crimes which he urges them to commit against the *lives of another*.[2]

Consider the words that Jefferson chose. Cruel war, people who never offended, miserable death, opprobrium, infidel, CHRISTIAN, MEN, prostituted, execrable, assemblage of horrors, murdering, crimes and crimes again: this intense emotion is not Jefferson at his best. Nor did he help his case by writing much of the charge as one long, confusing, run-on sentence. Jefferson wrote eloquently and powerfully about slavery many times in his long life ("I tremble for my country when I reflect that God is just," "we have the wolf by the ears," "a fire bell in the night"[3]). But he forced the language here. He fell back on the typographical trick of capital letters to make one of his points. Then, as now, heavy capitalization meant shouting, and in any dispute shouting signifies that persuasion has failed. Taken simply as a piece of writing, words that an author has put together in order to make an effect, the whole passage contrasts strikingly with the sharp, precise language that preceded it. What the passage actually said is just as problematic.

Until Jefferson reached the slavery issue, he had been citing one action after another of "the present king" and adding them up into a pattern. But when he tried to blame George III for slavery he was on shaky ground, twice over. First, he charged that the king (actually meaning the king's predecessors) had imposed slaves on white colonists against their own desire. That was simply bad history. The Crown had fostered and protected the slave trade, but colonials wanted the slaves and kept buying them. Coming from a land where there was no legal slavery, colonial British Americans from Barbados to New Hampshire had created it among themselves, on their own terms, to benefit themselves. The Royal African Company, in which the Crown held stock, had had a monopoly on trading slaves in the seventeenth century. But that ended in 1698, and many American merchants in both Northern ports and Southern ones had grown wealthy by trading slaves. Some of them sat with Jefferson in the Continental Congress.

Jefferson was on slightly better ground when he accused the king (through the king's servants) of urging the slaves to rise: he had Lord Dunmore in mind. But given that the Americans were in armed rebellion when Dunmore issued his slavery-shaking proclamation of November, 1775, that Dunmore's sworn duty was to maintain the king's peace, and that Dunmore was offering freedom to real slaves of rebels who would assist him in putting the rebellion down, the logic was poor, at best. Dropping the specific language about slavery, Congress reduced the matter to a vague charge that the king had "excited domestic insurrections among us." That could have applied to the white loyalist mayor of New York City who organized a plot to kidnap Washington just as readily as to Dunmore forming his Ethiopian Regiment.

The main body of Jefferson's charges against the king does ring with a consistent, deeply felt belief on Jefferson's part. This was that George III had forfeited his right to rule in America and needed to be deposed. He made the case strongly. Somebody reading his indictment of the king might or might not agree, but the line of argument was clear, until Jefferson reached the slavery problem, when both his language and his logic failed him. The Master of Monticello was bothered deeply by slavery, even though it made his whole life possible. He remained troubled until he died. By trying to blame the king, he was dealing with his own conscience. But he also was trying to put slavery on the revolutionary agenda, which was exactly the same task that black Americans confronted. Other people in the white revolutionary community were making a better job of it than he.

Absolutely foremost among them were the founders of Vermont, which tore itself free of New York in 1777, after years of guerilla resistance to New York authority by Ethan Allen and his fellow Green Mountain Boys. Like everybody who opted for independence, the Vermonters had to create a new government, on terms that suited themselves. They adopted a very simple democracy, borrowing almost word for word from the democratic state constitution that Pennsylvania created in 1776. But the Vermonters went one step further, proclaiming as the very first item on their Declaration of Rights that "no male person, born in this country, or brought from over sea, ought to be holden by law, to serve any person, as a servant, slave or apprentice, after he arrives to the age of twenty-one Years, nor female, in like manner, after she arrives to the age of eighteen years, unless they are bound by their own consent."[4]

What the Vermonters proclaimed was momentous in the growing assault on slavery. Lord Mansfield had simply pronounced that James Somerset "must go free," dodging the possibility of declaring that slavery was entirely dead in his England and even suggesting that Parliament pass a law to overrule him. Lord Dunmore had offered freedom to slaves "appertaining to rebels" who would fight, but not to all slaves. Jefferson tried to blame both slavery and slaves' resistance on the king. The Vermonters showed no hesitancy and no confusion. Their ban was immediate and they intended it to be absolute. The United States census of 1790 did record sixteen slaves in the state, but that was a clerical error. The people to whom it referred were free. The Vermonters would not take part in the slave trade. They would not accept that enslavement under "positive law" elsewhere meant enslavement among them. No male in their state over twenty-one and no female over eighteen could be bound except "by their own consent."

The numbers involved were tiny. In 1790 the United States census recorded 255 free black people in Vermont. Nonetheless, for the very first time in the whole history of the colonized western hemisphere, there was a place where every adult man and woman was presumed free, no exceptions. Vermont remained a separate republic until 1791, when slaveholding New York finally abandoned its claim that Vermont was only a "pretended state" and that the Vermonters were really New York's "revolted subjects." Congress admitted it as a state, bringing it under the Constitution. Until then, any fugitive slave who reached its borders could have claimed the same "Freedom Principle" that held in mainland France, or could have sought freedom in a Vermont court just as the Somerset ruling allowed in England. None, apparently, did. But one Protestant minister under consideration for a Vermont pulpit wanted to bring a female slave from Connecticut, noting that he had a legitimate bill of sale. Ethan Allen responded that, even if the bill were from God Almighty, the woman would become free if the minister brought her to Vermont.

Other white people acted too. In 1780 Pennsylvania adopted an act for getting rid of slavery, by freeing all children born thereafter when they reached age twenty-eight. Full of self-congratulations, the Pennsylvanians gave thanks that "We . . . are enabled this Day to add one more Step to universal Civilization by removing as much as possible the Sorrows of those, who have lived in undeserved Bondage."[5] But under the act the owners of Pennsylvania slaves would not lose what they already had, because it freed nobody born prior to its passage. Nobody escaping from slavery elsewhere would become free by getting to Pennsylvania. Slavery began to diminish in the state, but it lingered for decades. In 1782 Virginia passed a law allowing masters to free slaves without seeking special permission. Some released the slaves they owned, most often just one or two. But "King" Carter's grandson, Robert Carter III, freed all of his 452 people in 1791, and took what steps he could to set them up in a new life. He was not alone. At independence there had been a bare handful of free black people in Virginia and neighboring Maryland. According to the United States census there were 20,909 in 1790. Their number reached 64,497 in 1810.

New York made a false start in 1785, five years after Pennsylvania adopted its gradual emancipation law. It too proposed to end slavery slowly, but the bill that passed its legislature denied former slaves legal equality with whites. The state's peculiar "council of revision" rejected the bill, not, the council said, to protect slavery but rather to prevent the creation of a permanent inferior free class. New York finally started gradual emancipation in 1799, and freed its last slaves on July 4, 1827. New Jersey was even slower. Under the terms of its emancipation act of 1804 there were still some three hundred slaves in the state in 1850. A handful remained in the year Abraham Lincoln won the presidency.

The late-Roman church father Augustine of Hippo once recorded how he had prayed before his full conversion to Christianity for chastity, "but not yet." He might have spoken on the subject of slavery for a great many white revolutionary Americans. They had come to dislike slavery. They wanted somehow to get rid of it, but "not yet" and, for the most part, without any loss to themselves. To really understand the difference that the American Revolution made to slavery and to black people, we must look to what they did for themselves as they considered the possibilities that the Revolution

presented and, in the words of many an eighteenth-century official proclamation, "governed themselves accordingly."

As white colonial British subjects began transforming themselves into
American citizens, the black people among them were quick to call them
out for their fine language about tyranny and enslavement. As early as April
1773, the circular letter that black Massachusetts men named Peter Bestes,
Sambo Freeman, Felix Holbrook, and Chester Joie published in Massachusetts borrowed the white revolutionaries' techniques ("by order of their
Committee"), and called on them to live up to their emerging rhetoric of
revolution ("We expect great things from men who have made such a noble
stand against the designs of their *fellow-men* to enslave them"). At the end of
1776, a "Great Number of Negroes" expressed "their astonishment that it has
never bin considered" that "every principle from which America has acted"
pointed toward their own "freedom which is the naturel right of all men." In
Connecticut, two men identified only as Prime and Prince pointed out the
inconsistency "with the present Claims of the United States, to hold so many
Thousand . . . in perpetual slavery." Twenty New Hampshire slaves sought
their freedom in 1779, both because they had been "born free" in Africa and
"for the sake of justice, humanity, and the rights of mankind."[6] Pennsylvania's
gradual manumission law was weak. New Jersey writer John Cooper criticized
it sharply, asking whether "if we keep our present slaves in bondage, and only
enact laws that their posterity shall be free . . . . it would be plainly telling
our slaves, we will not do justice unto you, but our posterity shall do justice
unto your posterity."[7] A year after it took effect, masters tried to amend it by
extending the date for registering slaves and thus keeping them in bondage.
If not registered, they would go free. Black Pennsylvanians responded with an
outraged petition. "The grand question of slavery or liberty is too important
for us to be silent," they told the assembly. "It is the momentous passion of
our lives; if we are silent this day, we may be silent forever."[8]

Slavery ended abruptly in Massachusetts in 1783, because black people
pushed for it. In 1780, the state had adopted its revolutionary state constitution, ending six years without a formal, legally established government.
Primarily the work of John Adams, the constitution opened with a "Declaration of the Rights of the Inhabitants of the Commonwealth." The wording
was important: "inhabitants" could be taken to cover everybody within the
commonwealth's boundaries. The very first words read "All men are born
free and equal, and have certain natural, essential, and unalienable rights;
among which may be reckoned the right of enjoying and defending their
lives and liberties."[9]

In 1781 two slavery cases began to make their way through the courts. The first, in far-western Berkshire County, pitted "Brom, a Negro Man & Bett a Negro Woman" against landowner and merchant John Ashley, who had acquired Bett long previously as a wedding gift from his father-in-law. Bett, or Mum Bett, was the prime mover of the case. As she told the story much later, she tried to stop Ashley's wife when the mistress assaulted Bett's sister. The enraged mistress injured Bett instead. Bett fled and sought the help of a young lawyer, Theodore Sedgwick, who would go on to a distinguished career as a United States senator. Tapping Reeve of Connecticut, founder of the first law school in the United States, joined Sedgwick in arguing the case. According to her nineteenth-century biographer Harriet Martineau, she told Sedgwick that she had heard Ashley and others discussing the language of the state constitution, "thought long about it, and resolved she would try whether she did not come in among them," since "she was not a dumb beast."[10]

The trial record is spare. Ashley's position was that Brom and Bett were his "legal Negro servants," meaning slaves. Therefore they had no standing in court, exactly the argument that James Somerset's master had made before Lord Mansfield a decade earlier. Sedgwick and Reeve responded that the two "are not, nor are either of them, nor were they, or either of them . . . the Negro servants or servants of him aforesaid John Ashley during their lives,"[11] and invoked the first article in the commonwealth's newly adopted Declaration of Rights. The jury found for Bett, who promptly renamed herself Elizabeth Freeman, and for Brom, who disappeared from the record. As a free woman she went to work for Sedgwick's family, living with them until her death in 1829. Though some historians dispute the matter, the great leader in the twentieth-century struggle for black equality W. E. B. Du Bois maintained that she was his great-grandmother. Historical markers in Pittsfield County, where she claimed her freedom and Du Bois grew up, honor them both.

The other case also began in 1781, when Quock (or Quok) Walker escaped from enslavement to Nathaniel Jennison. He sought refuge with the family of his parents' former owner, who apparently had promised freedom to him, but Jennison recaptured him and beat him for his attempt to leave. Like Elizabeth Freeman, Walker went to court, charging assault and battery against his captor. Altogether the case was tried three times. One lower court jury found for Walker and another found against him. Finally the Commonwealth of Massachusetts took up Walker's cause, prosecuting Jennison for assault. That case reached the Supreme Judicial Court in 1783, where Chief Justice William Cushing presided.

Image 3.1. Susan Sedgwick's watercolor shows Elizabeth Freeman nearly three decades after Freeman emancipated herself, with the legal aid of Sedgwick's father. Freeman's self-possessed dignity is apparent. Massachusetts Historical Society, Boston, MA, USA / Bridgeman Art Library

Like Lord Mansfield, Cushing was a man of fundamentally conservative mind. Four years after the Quok Walker case, he presided at the trials of leaders of the farmers' tax protest called Shays' Rebellion. He sentenced the rebellion's leaders to death, and his anger at them still burns through the written record of the trial. But, like Mansfield, he valued the law and to him the matter of slavery in Massachusetts was clear. Slavery was incompatible with Massachusetts being a republic of free citizens. That ended the matter. Cushing went much further than Mansfield, grasping the chance to extend the issue before him from one person's plight to the condition of all Massachusetts slaves. About three thousand people gained immediate freedom. Now there were two places on the western side of the Atlantic, Vermont and Massachusetts, where slavery was dead. But Cushing's jurisdiction stopped at the borders of Massachusetts. There was no reason for courts in other states to honor his decision, and none did.

The theme of this book is not what white Americans did, tried to do, or failed to do. It is how black people in revolutionary America used the opportunities that their time presented to them. But we cannot escape the problem posed by Thomas Jefferson. That is not for Jefferson's own sake, but rather because all Americans who have tried to deal with the meaning of the Revolution have had to deal with him. More than any other among the great figures of his era, Jefferson, his words, and his actions have loomed over the American Republic and over all of the Republic's people ever since.

This is not the place to ask whether Jefferson was an authentic enemy of slavery. That he disliked it is clear. That he contributed to its demise also is clear. His assertion in the Declaration of Independence that "all men are created equal" was not "self-evident" at all. It flew in the face of how most of humanity organized and understood itself. It also undercut slavery's fundamental rationale. In a world of tribes, one tribe might enslave another. In a world that takes inequality for granted, somebody will have to be at the bottom. But, if equality is the fundamental human condition, it required real mental contortions to justify the right of some people to hold others down by force. In that sense, Jefferson gave the Republic (starting with himself) both a huge aspiration and an equally huge problem.

Nor is this the place to consider his long, unquestionably sexual relationship with his slave Sally Hemings. It began at some point between 1787, when she arrived at the age of fourteen in Paris, where he was serving as American minister, and their departure for Virginia in 1789. It lasted until his death, on July 4, 1826, and became a public scandal when a newspaperman broke it in 1803, during Jefferson's first term as president. John Adams described what he learned as "a natural and almost inevitable consequence of a foul contagion in the human character, Negro slavery," and added that "there was not a planter in Virginia who could not reckon among his slaves a number of his children."[12] Whether the relationship was coerced, loving, or simply a matter of practical agreement between two very unequal people is beside the immediate point. Historian Annette Gordon-Reed has explored elsewhere the deeply human questions that the relationship posed and that its memory still poses.

Those questions do bear on the subject here, in the sense that, as with Phillis Wheatley, the revolutionary era gave both Sally Hemings and her brother James a chance to make a fateful choice. Jefferson had brought the Hemingses to Paris during his time as American minister to the court of Louis XVI, James in 1784 to master the art of French cooking and Sally as companion to his daughter. When the time came to return from London, Wheatley could have invoked the *Somerset* decision by going to any Crown court. The two Virginians could have claimed France's "Freedom Principle" the same way. But both Wheatley and the Hemingses chose to return to America, which meant returning to slavery. Wheatley knew she had a good mistress, who had brought out her talent for writing, and she knew as well that the mistress was very ill. The Hemingses took a chance that Jefferson would treat them well. They did realize that, if they chose freedom in France, Jefferson had the power to take out his anger on their relatives at Monticello. Jefferson freed James in 1796. He allowed two of his children with Sally to go free and disappear into the white world in 1822, which their light skin enabled them to do. He freed the other children by his will in 1826 and Sally left Monticello with them, living as a free woman in Charlottesville until she died in 1835. The other members of the extended Hemings family remained in slavery and were dispersed when Jefferson's executors sold Monticello by auction in 1831, in order to pay his enormous debts.

We need not linger over why Jefferson did not free his slaves, save for James and Sally Hemings and a few members of her and Jefferson's own family. George Washington was able to free his entire slave force in his will because he had managed his affairs well, and in his old age he was free of debt. Unlike Washington, Jefferson was an appallingly bad business manager. He carefully noted every expenditure he ever made in his account book, but he never bothered to work out his balance. He never hesitated either to buy anything he wanted on credit. Jefferson could not have freed his slaves because he did not have clear title to them. Other people had claims on all of Thomas Jefferson's property, land, slaves, personal belongings, and even the house at Monticello, as long as Jefferson's debts remained unpaid, and those debts never stopped growing.

Nor is it even necessary to come to general terms with Thomas Jefferson, whether the terms should be to honor him for his high ideals, to forgive him for his weaknesses, to be compassionate for his dilemmas, or to damn him as a hypocrite. In all of his complexities he still haunts the American Republic, and he probably will for as long as the Republic endures. But it is necessary to watch him wrestle with the problem of slavery. He did so very publicly, and the way he did it helped to set the problems that the black Americans who are the real subjects here would have to face. They would say as much themselves.

Jefferson's attempt to bring the issue of slavery into the Declaration of Independence illustrates his problem. Jefferson could not handle emotion. His best prose is logical, thoughtful, and usually cool, rather than warm. His careful, closely reasoned indictment in the Declaration of "the present king of Great Britain" contrasts strikingly with Thomas Paine's flat-out assault six months earlier in *Common Sense* on "the hardened, sullen tempered Pharaoh of England," whose ancestor William the Conqueror had been nothing more than a "French Bastard landing with an armed banditti."[13] Paine understood how to do take-no-prisoners polemical writing and he was comfortable with it. Jefferson did not understand such writing, and he never did it well. That is why his effort to blame the king both for introducing slavery and for encouraging slaves to rise fell flat. Its overdone language betrayed his problems with slavery, which were real enough, and nothing more.

Jefferson returned to the issue in 1781 when at the request of a French friend he began writing his only book, *Notes on the State of Virginia*. It appeared in French in 1786, in a bad English translation from the French in London in 1787, and in Jefferson's own English prose in Philadelphia in 1788. For the most part the book is its author's love song to Virginia and to everything about it. He described landscapes, rivers, mountains, mines, natural wonders, birds and animals, plants and trees, crops, public life, and politics. Jefferson never crossed the Blue Ridge, though it lies not far west of Monticello, but in his imagination Virginia's grand prospects reached as far as New Orleans, El Paso, and even Mexico City. He thought it would be easy for Virginia's commerce to dominate the Ohio and Mississippi Valleys, despite the Appalachian ridges that separated it from them. Though he was a great planter for whom others labored, he wanted Virginia's future to be with "those who labor in the earth . . . the chosen people of God."

Jefferson's prose as he described his Virginia was calm, and his descriptions were precise, until he turned to slavery, in his chapter on the commonwealth's laws. He noted several provisions for revising the laws at the time. Perhaps he missed the deep, bitter irony in one proposal, "to make slaves distributable among the next of kin, as other moveables," simply not seeing that dividing them to suit the needs of the heirs in a master's family meant breaking their own families. But at the end of his short list of proposed revisions, he came to a proposal (his own) "to emancipate all slaves born after the passing of the act." As with his draft of the Declaration, as soon as he touched slavery directly, he began to lose control.

Jefferson wanted slavery gone, but he wanted black people gone too. The memories of slavery, on both sides, were one reason. He had been born to mastery, and he understood how absolute dominion over another human being damaged any person who possessed it. He understood too that, if freedom came, the former slaves would bear huge grievances and good reason to retaliate against the former masters. His short, powerful indictment of the damage slavery did to masters and slaves alike in *Notes on Virginia* came from his own experience, and John Adams told him it was "worth diamonds."[14] But having made those astute comments about the effects of slavery on master and slave alike, he turned to another theme altogether, nature. In pages that are very painful to read now, especially given their authorship, he trotted out every argument of his day that seemed to justify black inferiority. Those points made, he used supposed black inferiority as a reason why black people (even, presumably, his own children with Sally Hemings, though he never spoke or wrote about them) could have no place in his republic.

Jefferson possessed a huge library, and very probably he had a copy of Anthony Benezet's exploration of African historical and social reality, as opposed to slave traders' and slaveholders' myths. But if he had read Benezet, as Patrick Henry certainly did, it had no influence on his thought. Jefferson had found the answer to his own dilemma. In some sense all men are created equal, and black people did deserve freedom. But nature had made them so different from whites that they would have to go, somewhere. In a word, racism trumped equality.

In merely practical terms, any plan to free and then expel all slaves in just Virginia, let alone the whole United States, was hopeless. Jefferson himself, as secretary of state, certified the census that the federal government took in 1790. It recorded 694,280 slaves and 59,150 free black people. That total of 753,430 people was 25 percent larger than the whole number whom the African slave trade brought to the British colonies and the young United States. Returning them to Africa, or taking them to Cuba or Guatemala, or to somewhere unspecified, would have required every ship on the Atlantic, assuming they were willing to go.

But Jefferson did think they would have to go, and he deployed every ill thing he could think of to say why that was so. His racist stereotypes seem endless as one wades through them. Black women did not have white women's beauty and therefore they did not have white women's feelings. Black people were more ardent sexually, but it was "more an eager desire, than a tender delicate mixture of sentiment and sensation." They had "a strong and disagreeable odor," ignoring the point that Jefferson could bathe and perfume himself but that neither bath nor scent awaited a slave returning from the fields. They had rhythm, but "whether they will be equal to the composition of a more extensive run of melody, or of complicated harmony, is yet to be proved." "Never," Jefferson thought, "did I find that a black had uttered a thought above the level of a plain narration, never seen even an elementary trait of painting or sculpture." He had read Phillis Wheatley and he dismissed "the compositions published under her name" as "beneath the dignity of criticism." Conjuring up white America's long nightmare of fantasies about black male sexuality, he noted "their own judgment in favor of the whites, declared by their preference of them, as uniformly as is the preference of the Oranootan [the great African apes, gorillas and chimpanzees] for the black women over those of his own species." Closing the argument he suggested "as a suspicion only, that the blacks, whether originally a distinct race, or made distinct by time and circumstances, are inferior to the whites in the endowments both of body and mind."

The passage makes very dismal reading, not least because Jefferson's supposed reluctance ("as a suspicion only") to draw his conclusion ("the blacks . . . are inferior to the whites in the endowments both of body and mind") is mere façade: he believed everything hostile to black people that he could find. Some of what he wrote was just commonplace belief in his day, such as the total falsehood that the great African apes mated with black women (with its obvious implication about the danger posed to white women in America by black men). Some of it has made its way into the enduring fears that still dwell in white America.[15]

So far in advance of his time in some ways, Jefferson merely held mainstream opinion in others. Jefferson had written his book for one friend's eyes. He wanted it held back from publication, fearing that what he had to say about slavery would bring criticism upon him from his fellow white Virginians. He did not reckon at all with the consequences of what he said about black people, whom he could not imagine including among Virginians at all. Nor could he imagine that such people would read what he had to say about slavery and about themselves and respond, some in polite tones, others with unconcealed anger, still others with an appreciation that, despite it all, what he had to say about human equality and unalienable rights counted most.

Over the six years that separated Jefferson's first draft of his *Notes on Virginia* from his final published version, Americans took part in a great national discussion. They considered themselves both as they hoped they were and as they were proving to be; they contemplated their past and the lessons it taught; most important, they pondered their future as an independent, republican people. All sorts of men and women joined in the discussion, many of them the sort who never would have taken part in high politics under the old colonial order. Black people made themselves part of that discussion, such as the Philadelphians who asserted that their "all was at stake" when other Pennsylvanians set out in 1781 to repeal their state's gradual emancipation law, passed only a year earlier. They knew how easily lost the gains that they were making might prove to be. They recognized that one loss, one retreat, from their fragile, limited, but real gains was sure to lead to another, and that to a third and then a fourth.

The final result of the great national discussion was the United States Constitution. Fifty-five notable white men gathered in Philadelphia during the summer of 1787 and drafted it in secrecy. Over the year that followed, people from Georgia to New Hampshire took part in a long, intense, very public debate about whether to accept what the Convention had wrought. Finally, the Constitution's friends won and the new government took effect in the spring of 1789. The Constitution's supporters, Federalists as they called themselves, gained the day thanks both to very sophisticated arguments, most notably James Madison's, Alexander Hamilton's and John Jay's *Federalist* essays, and to smart, hard politics.

No black Americans sat in the federal convention, or in the state-level conventions that decided one by one whether to vote the new constitution up or down. Some may have voted in the elections for the state conventions, but there is no sign that they had any impact. Exactly one group of free black men, in Providence, Rhode Island, is known to have taken a stance, toasting the new constitution when they celebrated July 4, 1788. It was a brave act, because Rhode Island was a heavily anti-Federalist state. It had not sent delegates to the Philadelphia convention the previous year and it did not accept the Constitution and join the union until 1790, the last of the founding states to do so.

As the state conventions ratified the Constitution, giving practical meaning to its opening assertion that "We the People of the United States . . . do ordain and establish this Constitution," "federal processions" wound through the streets of town upon town in celebration. They culminated in a huge march of Philadelphians on July 4, 1788. The marching groups had much to celebrate. They had taken part in a great achievement and with the Constitution their revolution had reached its political settlement. They celebrated themselves, who they were, what they had done, and what they could do. Tradesmen of all sorts, clergy, professors and students in the colleges, lawyers and judges, and many more marched in separate groups, each group's place in the parade assigned by lot rather than by supposed social rank. There were free black people in all the towns where such processions took place. But not a single black contingent joined the marchers.

It might seem that what had just happened, as the people of the United States of America gave themselves an identity and the power to run their world, had nothing to do with them. Whether that was true, whether this was a white people's constitution only, would be a subject of hot argument during the seventy-three years that separated this great founding moment and the Republic's dissolution and collapse into civil war in 1861. Black people did take a very active part in that argument.

During the movement for the Constitution, its writing, and its ratification, "the people" were setting the rules of their new political society. Those rules established the terms by which some men would acquire political power, use it, be continued in it, and be deprived of it. Black people in America had very little part in setting those fundamental rules. But like white women, who were free but without political power, and like native people whom the triumphant United States kept pushing back, black people, whether free or still enslaved, had to act within the framework that the Constitution set up. So we must look to the document. The "grand question of slavery" was just as present in the Constitution as in Jefferson's draft of the Declaration, but not in the same way. The differences between the document of 1776 and the document of 1787, each of them debated and voted upon in the very same chamber in Philadelphia's Independence Hall, speak to the changes that eleven years of upheaval had made. Black Americans haunted the Constitution. They haunted the small elite gathering that wrote it. They haunted "the people" as they ratified it. What the Framers proposed and "the people" ratified would haunt black Americans as well.

The task that confronted the Framers in 1787 was to create power where none existed. The United States could not pay its debts, could not honor its treaty commitments, and could not, it seemed, govern itself. James Madison, the Constitution's main author, made the matter plain to his own mind when he jotted down his thoughts on the "Vices of the Political System of the United States" in April, 1787, just before the federal convention assembled. Madison was diagnosing what he thought were America's ills. The Constitution would be his and the other Framers' prescription for those ills.

Like his friend Thomas Jefferson, Madison did not like slavery. Again like Jefferson, he lived all his life with what the labor of his own slaves made possible, at Montpelier, his family's Virginia plantation. Madison was cooler of mind than Jefferson. He never rose to Jefferson's rhetorical heights, on slavery or anything else. But he was much more analytical. He had spent the years following the war of independence in deep study of the history and theory of republics from ancient Rome and Greece onward. Almost all of them ultimately had failed, allowing tyrants from Julius Caesar in Rome to Oliver Cromwell in seventeenth-century England to step in and supposedly save the republic's people from their own follies. Madison feared that possibility, and he saw a huge problem among Americans that might lead to such a takeover. He framed his analysis in terms of what he called "republican theory."

According to "republican theory," "right and power being both vested in the majority, are held to be synonymous [sic]." In other words, whatever the majority decided was bound to be right. But that implied that the majority's members would be selfless and public-spirited. They would think in terms of the public good, not in terms of what they wanted for themselves. In a good republic there would be no "special interests" of any sort. In practice, that was simply not so, because "whenever therefore an apparent interest or common passion unites a majority what is to restrain them from unjust violations of the rights and interests of the minority, or of individuals?" In other words, people were bound to be selfish and short-sighted. In one short sentence, Madison also noted, "Where slavery exists the republican Theory becomes still more fallacious."[16] Madison's words in that sentence were flat, but his insight was profound. The interests of masters and the interests of slaves simply could not be reconciled. In a republic, citizens might consent to be ruled by the majority. But slavery existed only because some human beings were in a position to force their absolute will upon others. The problem Madison raised in that one short sentence would very nearly prove fatal to the republic that he and his fellow founders were bringing forth.

With that said, Madison turned to the practical task of creating the federal government. The slavery problem forced its way into the debates about the Constitution in at least four ways. First, the Framers were embarrassed by slavery. They simply did not want to use the word. So they turned to euphemisms, ways to speak of it without actually naming it. Persons "held to service in one state, under the laws thereof," (Article IV, Section 2) meant slaves. "Such persons as any of the states now existing shall think proper to admit" (Article I, Section 9) meant Africans on their way to slavery in this new land of the free.

Second, slavery alone among American economic interests would get special treatment. Since independence, revolutionary Americans had been wrestling with the problem of equality. Most of their first attempts to create power, in the original state constitutions, recognized inequality by setting property requirements for voting and holding office. The federal constitution does not do so, at all. In this sense it was acknowledging the political equality of all free men. It set out to create legal equality in the realm of economics as well. It established the terms and rules for a common market that stretched from Georgia to New Hampshire and it forbade the states to give economic privileges to their own people or to their own local interests. Massachusetts could not favor its seafarers or fishers. New Jersey could not favor its iron manufacturers. Pennsylvanians could not favor their wheat farmers. All citizen could participate in the new common market; none would have special privileges within it.

But slavery was a huge, glaring exception, starting with apportioning power. Seven of the founding thirteen states, Pennsylvania, New Jersey, New York, Connecticut, Rhode Island, Massachusetts, and New Hampshire, had ended slavery, were starting to end it, or seemed likely to end it. The six remaining, Delaware, Maryland, Virginia, North Carolina, South Carolina, and Georgia, would remain slave states until the Civil War. In immediate terms, freedom would outweigh slavery in the United States Senate, where all states had two members. But that would not last long. It seemed very likely that the western parts of Virginia and North Carolina would seek separate statehood, giving the slave states parity in the new United States Senate if not outright control of it. From then until California entered the union in 1850, the slave states had the power in the Senate to block anything that they wanted to block.

The second way the Constitution apportioned power was in the House of Representatives, set up to represent "the people" according to their numbers. Southern delegates to the Convention wanted slaves to count fully in determining how many representatives a state would have. Some Northerners objected. The compromise that resulted allowed slaves to be counted in three-fifths of their actual numbers. They would add members to their state's delegation, but the masters, not they, would choose those members.

Slavery alone would have special weight in choosing the only truly national officers, the president and vice president. The Framers did not expect "the people" to choose their national leaders directly. Instead, state legislatures would pick presidential electors, each state having as many as it had members of the House of Representatives and the Senate. Again, the three-fifths rule would operate, so that slave states would have extra weight. That helps explain why eight of the first twelve presidents were slaveholders. The slave South's excessive power did not change as one state after another began choosing its electors by popular vote. Any white Virginian or Georgian, where slaves were counted as three-fifths of free people for purposes of political representation, still enjoyed more weight in the Electoral College choice than any New Yorker or Pennsylvanian.

The Constitution protected slavery in practical terms as well. Though the Northern states were gradually abolishing slavery, there would be no American equivalent for France's "freedom principle" or the rule that *Somerset* established in England. In those places, an escaping slave could find freedom, secured by the courts from the law of slavery elsewhere. But under the so-called fugitive slave clause in Article IV no person "held to service or labour in one state, under the laws thereof, escaping into another, shall, in consequence of any law or regulation therein, be discharged from such service or labour, but shall be delivered up on claim of the party to whom such service or labour may be due." The language was deliberately obscure. The Framers did not want to put the word slavery into their document. But their intention, which was that the laws of the remaining slave states would trump the laws of the emerging free states, was clear. Nor was this the only instance. The first Continental Congress had banned the slave trade entirely in 1775. But, according to Article I of the Constitution, "The migration or importation of such persons as any of the states now existing shall think proper to admit, shall not be prohibited by the Congress prior to the year 1808."

The Framers were turning back on two high points of anti-slavery from the independence period of the mid-1770s. One was the complete ban on the African slave trade that the First Continental Congress adopted in 1774. The other was the high, universal language of human equality and unalienable rights, including life, liberty, and the pursuit of happiness, that Thomas Jefferson wrote into the Declaration of Independence. Instead of a ban on the trade, there would be an extension of the time when it was allowed. Rather than universal rights, the preamble of the Constitution promised to secure "the blessings of liberty" to "ourselves and our posterity." Whether such blessings included the "liberty" of holding slaves and whether the black people who had aided in winning the struggle for independence figured among "ourselves and our posterity" was left open for others to resolve.

How the Convention made these arrangements is not the subject here. Other books discuss what went on very well. It is worth noting that in James Madison's opinion the moment when the Convention seemed in greatest danger of breaking up, and thus failing, came during its debates about giving slavery special representation by counting the slaves as full people, even though for legal purposes they were property, with no political voices or rights at all. Like the language of avoidance ("persons held to service"), that hot argument was a clear sign of how both the issue of slavery, as an institution, and the place of black people, still overwhelmingly held in slavery, presented problems for the United States that they never had presented in the colonial order, when slavery had been near-universal.

The fact that slavery had begun to break up in the Northern states was one such problem. Slavery was turning from a general fact into the South's increasingly "peculiar" institution, even prior to Connecticut Yankee Eli Whitney's invention of the cotton gin in 1793. Forbidding a "person held to service or labor in one state, under the laws thereof" to claim freedom under the laws of another state did recognize that freedom was emerging. The recognition, however, was backhanded. The fugitive slave clause reversed Lord Mansfield's dictum that "positive law" was necessary to establish "so odious" an institution as slavery. The Constitution did not establish a national "positive law" permitting slavery. But it did allow the laws that established slavery in the states where it remained to trump the positive law of other states that were getting rid of it. The new central government would be on the side of the slave states and the masters.

People who took part in the great national discussion about adopting the Constitution between the autumn of 1787 and summer of 1788 took notice. Maryland delegate Luther Martin, often dismissed by historians as an erratic drunk who did little to aid the Convention's labors, objected strongly to the slavery provisions at the Convention's end. Echoing what James Madison had written privately about slavery and "republican theory," he declared publicly that slavery and "the genius of republicanism" could not coexist. He saw no reason why Americans should not stop the African slave trade immediately rather than allow it to run for twenty more long years.

Many of the Constitution's foes, who found themselves stuck with the negative label "Anti-Federalists," raised the slavery issue as they argued against ratification. Hugh Hughes of New York remembered the old disputes early in the protest period about whether distant Americans, who had no votes, could be "virtually" represented in the distant British Parliament, even though the interests of colonists and Britons clashed. He saw clearly that the three-fifths clause rested on the same falsehood, which was that somehow masters could speak for their slaves and gain political power by doing it. Some opponents of the Constitution speculated that the Federalists actually were out to "enslave" their fellow citizens, just as the British supposedly had been out to enslave the colonists. John Neal of Massachusetts saw where that argument led: "Americans *deserved* to be enslaved if they agreed to a compact that legalized the slave trade."[17]

All of this was the talk of white citizens. Supporting the Constitution or opposing it, Federalist or Anti-Federalist, Southern or Northern, whether worried about slavery enough to speak out (like Luther Martin, Hugh Hughes, and John Neal), worried but keeping silent (like James Madison), or not worried at all (as was the case with very many), everybody who took part was also taking part in American political society as the Revolution had shaped it. They were settling the rules of their own governance, among themselves, for themselves, and for their posterity.

Slave and free alike, the black people all around them watched. Very probably they talked among themselves, but they said very, very little out loud during the struggle over the Constitution. They were not simple by-standers, however. They had been almost totally irrelevant to the issues that had torn the British Empire apart. They were not irrelevant at all to the issues that surrounded the creation of the American Republic, as the Con-stitution showed within its text and as the debates about whether or not to accept it made clear. Black people had indeed turned themselves into part of the problem, on a national scale, and the problem they posed simply would not go away, until finally it tore the Republic to shreds. But while white Americans were working out the terms of their citizenship, black Americans faced a different challenge.

The talented, self-taught free black mathematician of Maryland Benjamin Banneker caught the point perfectly in 1791, when he wrote to Secretary of State Thomas Jefferson. With Jefferson's approval, Banneker had been hired to aid in laying out the new federal capital at Washington. At some point he read Jefferson's *Notes on Virginia*, with its long, tortured argument that black people were simply and naturally inferior to whites. Banneker recog-nized that he was taking "a liberty which seemed to me scarcely allowable" in addressing somebody in Jefferson's "distinguished and dignified station." This was liberty in its antique sense of a daring act, because Banneker knew that he belonged to a "race of beings who have long labored under the abuse and censure of the world." But Banneker used "liberty" in its modern, American sense as well. He was a free man, "not under that state of tyran-nical thralldom, and inhuman captivity, to which too many of my brethren are doomed." He had "abundantly tasted . . . of [the] blessings . . . that free and equal liberty with which you [Jefferson] are favored." Banneker certainly realized he was paraphrasing both Jefferson's own language in the Declara-

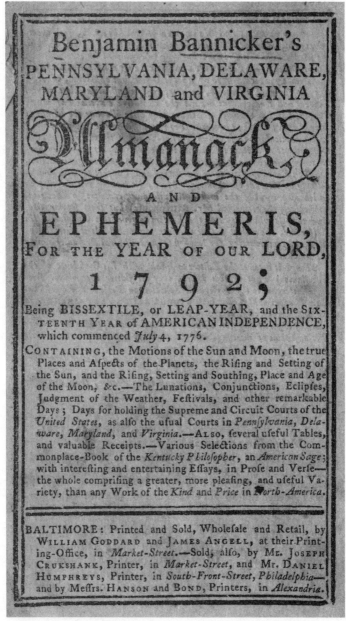

Benjamin Bannicker's

PENNSYLVANIA, DELAWARE,
MARYLAND and VIRGINIA

Almanack

AND

EPHEMERIS,

FOR THE YEAR OF OUR LORD,

1792;

Being BISSEXTILE, or LEAP-YEAR, and the SIX-
TEENTH YEAR of AMERICAN INDEPENDENCE,
which commenced *July* 4, 1776.

CONTAINING, the Motions of the Sun and Moon, the true
Places and Aspects of the Planets, the Rising and Setting of
the Sun, and the Rising, Setting and Southing, Place and Age
of the Moon, &c.—The Lunations, Conjunctions, Eclipses,
Judgment of the Weather, Festivals, and other remarkable
Days ; Days for holding the Supreme and Circuit Courts of the
United States, as also the usual Courts in *Pennsylvania, Delaware, Maryland,* and *Virginia.*—ALSO, several useful Tables,
and valuable Receipts.—Various Selections from the Com-
monplace-Book of the *Kentucky Philosopher*, an *American Sage*;
with interesting and entertaining Essays, in Prose and Verse—
the whole comprising a greater, more pleasing, and useful Variety, than any Work of the *Kind* and *Price* in *North-America.*

BALTIMORE: Printed and Sold, Wholesale and Retail, by
WILLIAM GODDARD and JAMES ANGELL, at their Print-
ing-Office, in *Market-Street.*—Sold, also, by Mr. JOSEPH
CRUKSHANK, Printer, in *Market-Street,* and Mr. DANIEL
HUMPHREYS, Printer, in *South-Front-Street, Philadelphia*—
and by Messrs. HANSON and BOND, Printers, in *Alexandria.*

Image 3.2. As an almanac maker, Benjamin Banneker had to carry
out extensive, complicated calculations to predict the movements of
the sun, moon, planets, and stars. As a black spokesman, he challenged
Thomas Jefferson directly and forcefully. ©American Antiquarian Society

tion of Independence and the Constitution's language about securing "the blessings of liberty to ourselves and our posterity."

Banneker confronted Jefferson directly, with the Virginian's own words. There had been a time, Banneker wrote, when the Master of Monticello had affirmed to the world the equality of all men and their endowment with unalienable rights including life, liberty, and seeking their own happiness. But now the Virginian himself was "guilty of that most criminal act, which you professedly detested in others." Banneker had read all the ugly, demonstrably false things that Jefferson had written about black people. It was time for Jefferson, and his people, "to wean yourselves from those narrow prejudices."

Banneker spoke for his "brethren"; he also spoke directly for himself. He had read Jefferson's double dismissal of Phillis Wheatley's poetry in terms both of its authorship (not her poems but rather "the compositions published under her name") and its merit ("below the dignity of criticism"). He wanted there to be no doubt in Jefferson's mind that his work was his own. So Banneker sent Jefferson a copy of the extremely detailed calculations he had done for the almanac that he was about to publish. He pointed out that "this calculation is the production of my arduous study." Like the ever-curious Jefferson, he had "long had unbounded desires to become acquainted with the secrets of nature." Realizing that Jefferson, like himself, was an eternal student, Banneker knew that he "need not recount to you the many difficulties and disadvantages which I have had to encounter."[18]

Banneker was offering himself to Jefferson as a fellow member of what their time called "the republic of letters," a network of thinking men and women that crossed all boundaries of political nations and of intellectual discipline. Jefferson responded politely, and he sent the almanac to the French Academy of Sciences, as evidence "against the doubts which have been entertained" about black people (not least by Jefferson himself). Banneker may have been pleased with the polite tone of Jefferson's response. But he probably would not have been surprised, just saddened, had he been able to know that, writing to an American friend, Jefferson voiced his suspicion that Banneker had white help on his mathematical calculations. As for Banneker's eloquent, ironic letter, it revealed to Jefferson nothing more than "a mind of very common nature indeed."[19]

Perhaps Banneker realized that his "brethren," rather than the likes of Jefferson, were the people to whom he needed to speak. By the time of his death, in 1806, a black community of letters, as well as of neighborhoods, families, organizations, churches, and businesses, held together by frustrations, hopes, and plans, was well on its way to assembling itself across the United States. Denied, for the most part, membership in the Republic's political society, with its public life of voting, holding office, and making policy, the black community was creating a civil society on its own terms, in ways that had not at all been possible under old colonial order. Its participants reached out to possible white allies, but they reached more deeply into and among themselves, slave and free alike, taking the fullest advantage that they could both of the opportunities that the American Revolution had opened for them, and of the spaces within American life that they had forced open during the Republic's founding time.

Notes

1. Journals of the Continental Congress—The Articles of Association; October 20, 1774, avalon.law.yale.edu/18th_century/contcong_10-20-74.asp, accessed March 10, 2011.

2. The Declaration of Independence, Merrill D. Peterson, ed., *The Portable Thomas Jefferson*, (New York: Penguin, 1977), 235–41.

3. Jefferson, *Notes on the State of Virginia*, ed. David Waldstreicher (Boston: Bedford St. Martin's, 2002 [orig. pub. 1787), Query XVIII, 195); Jefferson to John Holmes, April 22, 1820, *The Portable Thomas Jefferson*, 567–69.

4. Constitution of Vermont—July 8, 1777, avalon.law.yale.edu/18th_century/vt01.asp, accessed March 10, 2011.

5. "An Act for the Gradual Abolition of Slavery," 1 March, 1780, Roger Bruns, ed., *Am I Not a Man and a Brother: The Antislavery Crusade of Revolutionary America, 1688-1788* (New York: Chelsea House, 1688–1788), 446–50.

6. All quotations from Kaplan and Kaplan, *Black Presence*, 26–31.

7. John Cooper, "To the Publick," *New Jersey Journal*, September 20, 1780, repr. in Bruns, *Am I Not a Man and a Brother*, 456–59.

8. "To the Honourable the Representatives of the Freemen of the State of Pennsylvania," *Freeman's Journal*, September 21, 1781, repr. Kaplan and Kaplan, *Black Presence*, 31.

9. J. R. Pole, ed., *The Revolution in America, 1754–1788* (London: Macmillan, 1970), 480.

10. Harriet Martineau, *Retrospect of Western Travel* (London: Saunders and Ottley, 1838), I, 104–5.

11. www.mumbet.com/index.php/index.php/77-articles/mumbet/50-court, accessed March 10, 2011.

12. Adams quoted in Joseph J. Ellis, *American Sphinx: The Character of Thomas Jefferson* (New York: Vintage, 1998), 259.

13. Thomas Paine, *Common Sense*, ed. Thomas P. Slaughter (Boston: Bedford St. Martins, 2001 [orig. pub. 1776]), 83, 94.

14. Adams quoted in David Brion Davis, *The Problem of Slavery in the Age of Revolution, 1770–1823* (New York: Oxford University Press, 1976), 178.

15. All Jefferson quotations from Jefferson, *Notes on the State of Virginia*, ed. Waldstreicher, 176–80.

16. James Madison, "Vices of the Political System of the United States," press-pubs.uchicago.edu/founders/documents/v1ch5s16.html, accessed March 10, 2011.

17. David Waldstreicher, *Slavery's Constitution: From Revolution to Ratification* (New York: Hill & Wang, 2009), 122–23.

18. *Copy of a letter from Benjamin Banneker to the secretary of state, with his answer* (Philadelphia: Daniel Lawrence, 1792).

19. Kaplan and Kaplan, *Black Presence*, 144–47.

CHAPTER FOUR

~

"Now Our Mother Country"

Black Americans and the Unfinished Revolution

"This land which we have watered with our tears and our blood is now our mother country and we are well satisfied to stay."

—Richard Allen, 1827

Imagine the United States in 1826, half a century after Congress declared independence. The last members of the revolutionary generation, black, white, and native, female and male, patriot and loyalist, were recounting their long-ago memories to anybody who would listen, and preparing to fade into history. As they passed, they left behind a world vastly different from the one into which all of them had been born.

The differences were as great for black people as for anybody else. Consider one simple contrast between the colonial era and the early republic. Africans and their descendants in the colonial world were not simply victims, and we can watch them making their own history, within what life allowed. But we know hardly any of them face-to-face. We hear only a few of their spoken words: thus "Fire, fire, scorch, scorch, a little, damn it, bye and bye," just before the New York City conspiracy trials of 1741. We have almost nothing that they wrote. They appear in many a painting, but always as subordinates, in the background, never as subjects in their own right. There are careful pen-portraits of people who escaped, but masters published these to aid in recapture, not to mark the escaped person as worth knowing. A few of their names clearly were African: Cuffee (Kofi), Cudjoe, Quashee, or perhaps Phillis. But in slavery's circumstances such names signified degradation, not their bearers' African past. Most of the names the enslavers forced upon them were diminutive (Billy rather than William), or fit for a goddess (Venus) but insulting to a slave. For all but a very few we cannot know even as much as the haunting modern-day markers ("male, age 25–30") reveal at New York's African Burial Ground.

The great project of the captors had been to wipe enslaved people off history's record. Whether they were captured or born into slavery, their very names signified that they were to possess neither a past nor a future, only slavery's eternal, hopeless present. When it seemed in 1775 that the free black Charles Town harbor pilot Thomas Jeremiah did have a vision of what might be, and that he would aid the British in order to bring his vision about, white Carolinians did not just hang him, after a summary trial. They burned his body (or forced their slaves to do it), as if to remove him completely from the earth and from memory. The year was 1775, not 1741. Somehow Jeremiah had found a niche and turned himself into a well-respected, prosperous figure on the Charles Town waterfront. He left records enough to reconstruct his life, his ordeal at the hands of the revolutionary authorities, and his death. Still, we have no idea what he looked like.

Half a century later the picture had changed. By then the American historical record abounded with black men and women whose full names we know. We can see some of their faces and read what some of them wrote. Black people of the revolutionary generation were presenting the United States with their own agenda for its future. They did not begin African-American history. That had started when their first captive ancestors arrived. But their generation inscribed a new chapter, in which they changed the direction of both their own history and the history of the country.

They could not have brought slavery down in 1776 or in 1826, certainly not alone and not even with the allies they had. Thanks to the Revolution many black people turned themselves from slaves into free individuals, but the structure of public power excluded them almost completely from political society, meaning the public rituals of voting, seeking office, and making policy. Freedom did give a very significant number of black men and women the chance to create their own civil society, outside formal politics. Within what they built, they kept the Revolution's anti-slavery thrust alive while most of white America ignored, forgot, or simply denied it. They debated among themselves about what best to do. They found allies, and they also confronted enormous hostility, North as well as South. From the start, they knew that they were taking part in world-shaking events of which their parents and grandparents in colonial America could only have dreamed. But the vast majority of their brothers and sisters remained enslaved, within a

Southern world where slavery prospered, spread fast, and waxed rather than waned in its power.

By 1826 a few black people had become trans-Atlantic celebrities. When Phillis Wheatley visited England before independence, she mingled with the sort whom the English call "the Great and the Good." A British anti-slavery campaigner wrote that if she "was *designed for slavery* . . . the greater part of the inhabitants of Britain must lose their claim to freedom." Her poems appeared in a French edition and the philosopher Voltaire described her as "a Negress who writes very good English verse."[1] His fellow French thinker and writer Abbé Henri Gregoire included Wheatley in a volume honoring fourteen "Negroes and Mulattoes Distinguished by their Talents and their Writings," and reprinted three of her poems. The Marquis de Barbé-Marbois, who inspired Jefferson to write his *Notes on Virginia*, professed astonishment at her work. Writers in Germany admired her. American adventurer Gilbert Imlay wrote in 1792 of his outright shame at reading Jefferson's dismissal of her in his *Notes on Virginia*. President Samuel Stanhope Smith of the College of New Jersey (now Princeton University) asked in 1810 how many Southern planters "could have written poems equal to" hers.[2]

United States Senator James McHenry published a short biography of Benjamin Banneker, calling him "a striking contradiction" to the common notion that black people were "naturally inferior to the whites and unsusceptible of attainments in arts and sciences." McHenry cited the British thinker David Hume as holding that opinion, but clearly he had Thomas Jefferson in mind. McHenry was a Federalist, scoring a party political point against a Democratic-Republican president, but he also admired Banneker for Banneker's sake. Abbé Gregoire gave Banneker a place in his book about distinguished black people, noting with obvious delight that because of Banneker's scientific work even Jefferson seemed to have retracted what he had written about black intellect in *Notes on Virginia*.[3]

In the United States free black people began creating their own institutions, starting with the most basic of all, their families. American-style slavery meant that there was absolutely no security between husbands and wives, or parents and children. But a free couple could marry legally, which meant gaining some state protection for their rights in relation to each other and their children. Nonetheless, they still faced great difficulties. Snooping public officials could pry into their lives, and perhaps snatch a child into forced "apprenticeship." The ill-paid work most black men could get was often so dangerous and difficult that it shortened their life spans, leading to early widowhood for many black women. But nobody could buy or sell these people, inherit them, force another partner on a man or woman against their will, or give or gamble them away. A black woman might hire herself out for domestic work, or even wet-nursing. But nobody could demand that she neglect her own baby on pain of a whipping in order to breast-feed another woman's child.

Freedom meant the chance to believe and to worship as people chose, starting in the South. Distinctive black Christianity had begun to emerge among such churches as Methodist and Baptist during the colonial period, in mixed congregations. Caught up in the spirit, a black church member might preach. Now separate black churches started to take form and black men started to become ordained, recognized ministers, often against strong opposition. As with the whole slavery question during the era, the churches came into being in both the North and the South, and among people who chose both sides in the large conflict between Britain and the colonies.

Black Baptist David George established the first separate black congregation in America at Silver Bluff, South Carolina, in 1774, joined in his ministry by Virginia-born George Liele. Both of them fled America with the departing British in 1783. Andrew Bryant founded another black Baptist congregation in Savannah in 1788. Black itinerant minister John Chavis preached the Presbyterian gospel to mixed congregations across Maryland, Virginia, and North Carolina. Carolina-born John Morrant spent time as a captive with Cherokee and Creek Indians, served in the Royal Navy, established a black Methodist congregation in Nova Scotia, and finally brought his preaching to New England. Black Congregationalist Lemuel Haynes, who had been a revolutionary soldier, served a mostly white Calvinist church in Rutland, Vermont, for decades after independence.

The story of Philadelphia's Mother Bethel African Methodist Episcopal Church shows how distinctively black American Protestant Christianity began, and where it led. Originally its members called it the African Church in Philadelphia. The name Mother Bethel came later. The ground at the intersection of Sixth and Lombard Streets where the church building stands is the oldest continuously black-owned property in the United States and the church's present building is the fourth on the site. Docent tours show visitors how the structure's architecture and the precious objects displayed in its museum present one of the great stories in black American history. The church is a few blocks' walk from Independence Hall, where the Continental Congress declared independence in 1776 and where the federal convention wrote the United States Constitution in 1787. Each building is a place of historic beginning, where people confronted the problems that the past had given to them and set the terms for living in an uncertain future.

Richard Allen, who established Mother Bethel in 1791, started his historic life journey as a slave, working extra so he could raise the money to buy freedom for himself and his family after his master converted to Methodism and accepted the Methodists' anti-slavery testimony. Part of the work Allen did was as a blacksmith. He also joined the Methodists and in 1786 he launched a successful early-morning black service at predominantly white St. George's Methodist Church. The church forced Allen and his friend Absalom Jones out in 1787 when they refused during a service to move from white pews to a gallery reserved for black people. By this point Allen had a strong, proud sense of himself. White bishop Francis Asbury, who led the Methodist movement in post-revolutionary America, invited Allen to join him on a preaching tour into plantation country. Allen knew the humiliation he would have to endure and declined the offer.

Allen already had it in mind to establish a distinctively black church, and in 1787 he bought the land where Mother Bethel stands. He finally founded his own congregation on Methodist principles four years later, purchasing a former blacksmith shop to use as the church's first sanctuary. Many white Methodists opposed the venture, partly from belief that black people could not run their own lives and affairs, partly from a desire to maintain control and supervision. But some notable white people gave it their support, including President George Washington and Bishop Asbury. In 1816 the African Methodist Episcopal Church finally established itself as a separate denomination, with Allen as its first bishop. Honoring Allen's origins, Mother Bethel's present-day sanctuary is horseshoe-shaped. The pillars that support the upper gallery stand, proportionally, where a horseshoe's nails would be driven into the animal's hoof. The AME seal centers on a blacksmith's anvil. The museum displays church furniture that Allen made with his own hands, including his pulpit. He was not a tall man, so its platform is raised.

Unlike Allen, Absalom Jones left the Methodists, accepting ordination in the Episcopalian Church and founding the black Episcopalian Church of St. Thomas in 1792. Its original site was virtually next door to Allen's congregation, and the two continued to work together until Jones died in 1818. In 1793, when yellow fever swept through the city, they led black Philadelphians in a very brave act of public service, stepping in to aid the sick and bury the dead while anybody with enough money to flee the epidemic got out of town. Few black people had such means, and a mistaken belief circulated that they were less likely than white people to get the disease. The task was dangerous, because black people were no more immune to the disease than anybody else. It meant dealing with putrid, decaying, infectious corpses.

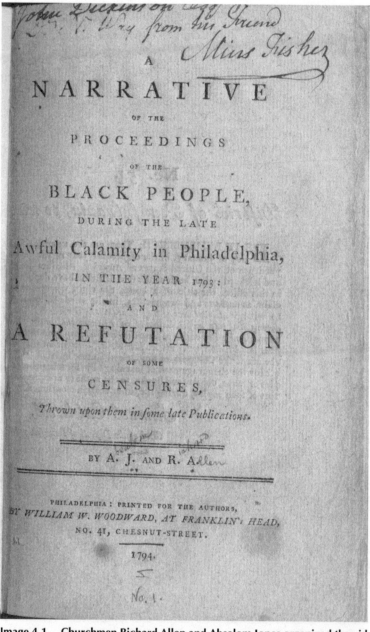

Image 4.1.   Churchmen Richard Allen and Absalom Jones organized the aid the Black Philadelphians provided during their city's yellow fever epidemic of 1793. In this pamphlet they protested forcefully against allegations of profiteering by white editor Matthew Carey. Courtesy of the Library of Congress

Many of the people whom Allen and Jones led in the effort paid with their lives for giving their service.

Nonetheless, in bitter thanks for the risk the black care-givers had taken, white printer Matthew Carey accused some of them of profiting from Philadelphians' agony, and even of looting the dead. Allen and Jones knew that free people did not have to tolerate such abuse, and they published a strong reply. Under the slave regime they would not have dared to challenge a white man that way, but in the new order nobody denied their right to do it.

Carey's pamphlet showed the direction the country was taking: straight toward excluding black people from respect for anything they might accomplish and, ultimately, from the new republic's blessings of liberty. On July 4, 1805, a racist mob drove black Philadelphians out of an Independence Day celebration. But Mother Bethel's members were teaching themselves how to control their own society, on their own terms. Among the displays in the museum at Mother Bethel is a wooden box for church elections. Instead of the usual slots for paper ballots, it has round holes in the top, so that congregants, many of whom could not read, could cast their votes with colored marbles. Literate or not, they were deciding issues that mattered. As much as any paper ballot, the box marks how American democracy struggled its way into existence, as people learned how to rule themselves, including how to disagree.

Allen, Jones, George, Liele, Morrant, and their like: such men and the people who joined them in prayer and church-building were establishing more than places to worship. They were creating black America's first separate, distinctive, public institutions. They were teaching themselves how to meet their own needs, deal with their own disputes, cooperate across whatever divided them, and cope with the hostile white communities all around them—how to act as citizens in a republic that did not respect their claim to full citizenship. They established burial societies to honor the end of somebody's life, mutual welfare societies to pool and loan members' money, and schools to teach children to read, write, and count. From 1827 to 1829 black Americans could read the black-owned and black-published newspaper *Freedom's Journal*, the first of its kind in the world.

In Boston a free leather worker named Prince Hall established a black lodge of Freemasons in March 1775, when British troops were in control of the town just before the outbreak of the Revolutionary War. He and his fellows were claiming their place in a much larger world. For males of their era, Freemasonry offered international brotherhood, goodwill, and cooperation for the sake of human betterment. George Washington, Benjamin Franklin, the Marquis de La Fayette, the Mohawk Indian leader Joseph Brant/

Thayendanegea, Voltaire, the composer Wolfgang Amadeus Mozart (who took on the theme of slavery in one of his operas), and King Frederick the Great of Prussia all belonged to Masonic lodges. Washington took his oath as president on a bible that was used in Masonic rituals. The great seal of the United States displays Masonic images, including the mysterious eye sitting atop a pyramid on the seal's reverse side.

Hall and his fellow Masons were claiming a place in Freemasonry's world of knowledge, fellowship, and enlightenment. But they could not get a charter from any American lodge. So, in a superb piece of historical irony, they received their Masonic recognition on March 6, 1775, from a lodge of British officers, who by that time were hated by most Bostonians. The Revolutionary War broke out six weeks later, when some of those officers led a force out of occupied Boston to capture American supplies and leaders at the town of Concord. Hall nonetheless went on to serve as a revolutionary soldier.

Black entrepreneurs began to go into business and some of them prospered. James Forten, who had turned down a Royal Navy captain's offer to sponsor him in London, returned to Philadelphia, where he learned the difficult trade of sail-making. When the master sail maker who taught Forten his skills retired, Forten took over the business and eventually became its owner. He employed both black and white apprentices and journeymen, and he prospered on the high reputation his sails acquired. He became a wealthy, respected man. But he did not vote, knowing what awaited him if he showed up at an election. Paul Cuffee, who began his public life by refusing to pay taxes because he could not vote, slowly built a shipping company out of a venture that he started with a single fishing boat. African-born Amos Fortune bought his freedom in 1770 after half a century of slavery in Massachusetts, moved to the New Hampshire town of Jaffrey, and established a business tanning cattle hides into leather for shoes, boots, and saddles. He was one of the founders of the town library in 1796.

On both sides of the Atlantic, Black writers began to tell slavery's story as they had known it. Ministers David George and John Morrant both published their accounts in London. Quobna Ottobah Cugoano issued his *Thoughts and Sentiments on the Evil and Wicked Traffic of the Slavery and Commerce of the Human Species* there in 1787, the same year as the American constitutional convention. Cugoano was not the first writer who wrote about and condemned the slave trade, but his predecessors had been white. They were outraged about slavery, but from the outside. Cugoano knew it from within. Two years later Olaudah Equiano published his *Interesting Narrative*, which became the best-known piece of black writing of its time. It took Equiano's story from Africa (though he may actually have been born in

South Carolina) to eventual freedom in England. Adventures along the way carried him to the Caribbean and South Carolina, into battle with the Royal Navy, and back to America, all while he remained enslaved. As a free man he visited Portugal, where he debated theology with a Catholic priest, and Turkey, where he learned about Islam.

Exiles George and Morrant, black Britons Cugoano and Equiano, Americans Banneker and Wheatley, poets Jupiter Hammon and Francis Williams, memoir-writers Briton Hammon, James Gronniosaw, Ignatius Sancho, Boston King, and Venture Smith: these people created the genre of black English-language literature. Wheatley read widely, and with sophisticated appreciation. She developed her distinctively American themes on models that she drew not from white American poets (who generally were poor) but rather from the great writers of seventeenth- and eighteenth-century England, including John Milton and especially Alexander Pope.

Equiano, Gronniosaw, and Smith drew on the familiar literary genre of captivity narratives, which took a person into an unfamiliar world, revealed that world in its complexity, and showed how the narrator changed as she began to find herself at home in it. The genre's patterns were set in Mary Rowlandson's great account of her time with hostile Wampanoag Indians during King Philip's War in New England in 1675 and 1676. Black writers reversed the genre's conventions. The strange, uncanny world into which they led their readers was not their Africa or the world of Native Americans. It was their readers' own England and America. The adaptation required for the narrator to survive was not to the ways of so-called savages; it was to the often savage ways of English and American men and women toward their slaves.

Equiano gave his readers a tale of adventure at sea as well. His service in the Royal Navy took him to two of the great battles of the Seven Years' War, one at Quiberon on the coast of Brittany and the other at Louisbourg in the Gulf of St. Lawrence. What he described was the very stuff of mid-eighteenth-century Anglo-American patriotism. "Rule Britannia, Britannia Rule the Waves, Britons never, never, never shall be slaves" went the words of a patriotic song written in 1739. But during his time in the Royal Navy, Equiano was a slave. He expected freedom in return for his service, but at the war's end his master, a naval officer, sold him. Equiano had trusted the officer, admired him, and in some ways identified with him, much, perhaps, as Wheatley identified strongly enough with her Boston mistress to return rather than stay in London when she had the choice.

Equiano's new enslavement took him to a sailor's berth on a slave ship that sailed between the Caribbean and Georgia. Sold again, to a Quaker,

Equiano got the chance to work his way out of slavery, and he returned to England. He met his wartime master and expected to be greeted warmly. The man's coldness showed how little he, Equiano, really had counted. But Equiano did believe in Britain. Decades later, as he brought his book to its end, he was promoting free British trade with Africa, certain that unlike the slave trade it would benefit both Britons and Africans.

In one of Phillis Wheatley's earliest poems she marveled that "*Negroes*, black as *Cain*, may be refin'd and join th' angelic train." But in the very first poem of her published collection she considered the African-born Roman poet Terence: "why this partial grace, to one alone of Afric's sable race, from age to age, transmitting thus his name with the first glory in the rolls of fame."[4] She added that she would "snatch a laurel" of glory herself. Flirting in print with an unnamed army officer, she evoked the image of an idyllic Africa, nothing like the barbaric, pagan land from which enslavement by Christians supposedly had rescued her. Perhaps the strongest sign of her growing consciousness of herself as a black writer comes in a piece that seems completely conventional on the surface. Wheatley had seen some pictures at an exhibition, and she wrote to the artist, gushing about the beauty that she found in his paintings. She was addressing "S.M. a young *African* painter, on seeing his works." In him she recognized a fellow member of a black artistic and intellectual community that was just beginning to emerge. She knew the most important thing a troubled person can know, that she was not alone.[5]

Indeed she was not. In his one published poem the revolutionary soldier and future Congregational minister Lemuel Haynes wrote about "the Battle of Lexington." His language, like Wheatley's, seems conventional, until the final couplets:

> Twice happy they who thus resign
> Into the peacefull Grave,
> Much better those in Death Consign
> Than a Surviving Slave.
> This Motto may adorn their Tombs
> (Let Tyrants come and view)
> "*We rather seek these silent Rooms*
> *Than live as slaves to you.*"[6]

Liberty or death: Patrick Henry used the same language. But Haynes published the poem as "Lemuel a young Mollato." Who was the "you" in his final line? The red-coated British? Or white America?

Artists immortalized the faces of many of these men and women on canvas, because their faces were worth remembering. Working in London, transplanted Bostonian John Singleton Copley carefully studied an anonymous black male model before placing the man's image in the background of his great canvas, Brook Watson and the Shark (1778, based on an event in 1749). The separate study, at the Detroit Museum of Art, is worth viewing in its own right. Rembrandt Peale created a dignified portrait of Absalom Jones in 1811, as the minister was entering old age. His father Charles Wilson Peale, who had painted the earliest portrait of George Washington, portrayed free Maryland Muslim Yarrow Mamout as a wise old man in 1819. AME Church founder Richard Allen posed for an unknown artist as early as 1783 and New Yorker Peter Williams did so about 1815. Susan Sedgwick, daughter of the lawyer who aided Elizabeth Freeman to end her enslavement, crafted a simple but compelling watercolor of Freeman in 1811. Images survive of Phillis Wheatley and Benjamin Banneker. The Wheatley portrait, which is a rough print in its present state, probably is derived from a painting by Scipio Moorhead, the black artist whose pictures moved her to poetry when she saw them. Save in Copley's Brook Watson, none of these figures is peripheral to somebody else. Each is the main subject. Each painting, including Copley's anonymous model for Head of a Negro, shows somebody with a story to tell, and, except for that model, we know their stories.

Beyond the famous ones who left behind public records, portraits, and writings, there were thousands of others who left at least the names that they had chosen for themselves. British clerks in New York recorded four thousand such names in the "Book of Negroes" as they prepared for evacuation in 1783. Many more survive in American church, town, tax, militia, war veterans', and court records, for their descendents and historians to find. Burial monuments honor some of their individual lives, most of all the tomb at Mother Bethel, which holds the bodies of Richard Allen, his second wife Sarah, and successor AME bishop Morris Brown.

The colonial era, when almost all black men and women in America had been slaves, produced nothing like such buildings, images, artifacts, and records. During and after the Revolution free black Americans joined in a huge burst of creativity that swept across the young United States. The burst started with the republican political institutions that Americans created to govern themselves between 1776, when they overthrew their king, and the years 1787 and 1788, when the Framers wrote the Constitution and "the people" accepted it. Americans turned woodland into farming country (forgetting who had rightfully owned it) and they established new cities. New

York started to emerge as a world capital. People built roads and canals to link themselves to one another. They founded schools and colleges. Inventors created machines, authors wrote books, and painters crafted distinctively American art. Political parties emerged, pitting citizens against one another for office and power, but also bringing order and direction to America's chaotic public life. The whole country seemed to be a runaway success, and, despite all the odds against them, some black people seemed to be part of that success, as the new republican America took shape.

But, as if in imitation of the monarchical British Empire that it replaced, the new republican American empire bound together a zone where slavery either did not exist or was dying and a zone where slavery flourished. What separated these zones was not the width of an ocean but just a line drawn across the North American map. The revolutionary era had weakened and partially destroyed slavery, but in the South it survived the revolutionary years and then flourished anew, thanks to the cotton gin. Cotton production underpinned much of America's post-revolutionary success and thanks to it slavery entrenched itself in the Republic's political and economic system. The "West Indies interest" had been powerful in Parliament, but could not control it. But from George Washington's time until Abraham Lincoln's, Southerners dominated American public life, including the presidency, the Supreme Court, and Congress. Trade in colonial tobacco, rice, and sugar had been important to the eighteenth-century British mercantile economy. Commerce in cotton underpinned the whole industrial economy of the young United States. Completing American slavery's destruction would require a huge effort, beyond any other in the struggle to end it throughout the Americas that the era of the American Revolution began.

By 1826 cotton culture had been booming across the South for three decades. It, too, was a product of the revolutionary generation's explosive energy, beginning with Connecticut Yankee Eli Whitney's discovery in 1793 of an easy, efficient way to clean the lint of short-staple cotton from its entangling seeds. Cotton was not a wholly new crop. Native Americans, Africans, and South Asian Indians all had grown it. So did colonial-era planters on the Sea Islands along the coast of South Carolina and Georgia. But Whitney's gin allowed highly profitable short-staple cotton cultivation all across the Deep South, where other varieties would not grow. Very quickly, the United States became the leading cotton producer on the planet, serving a market that knew no limit. Planters needed ever more land, and they needed ever more slaves to work that land. The supply of both land and slaves seemed endless. The federal government supplied the land, by driving off its Cherokee, Creek, and Choctaw owners, no matter what effort they made to adapt to white ways. The domestic slave trade, driven by the rapidly growing populations of the east coast states, supplied the labor. No longer universal, slavery had become the South's "peculiar institution," and it prospered.

But slavery's tentacles reached into the northeastern manufacturing states, whose factories turned raw Southern cotton into finished yarn and cloth, whose ships carried goods to and from Southern markets, and whose banks and insurance companies handled Southern capital. They extended to the free states of the Midwest that traded their goods down the Mississippi River to New Orleans. They stretched across the Atlantic, where British mills took far more of the ever-increasing cotton crop than the infant factories of the northeastern states possibly could handle. The white South was decades away from forming the fully self-conscious, unashamed, near-nation that struck for its independence in the name of defending slavery in 1861. But it defended its interests every time slavery was challenged, and it did so ferociously in 1819 and 1820 over the question of admitting Missouri to the Union as a slave state. An aging Thomas Jefferson likened the uproar to a "firebell in the night," adding that "we have the wolf by the ear, and we can neither hold him, nor safely let him go. Justice is in one scale, and self-preservation in the other."[7]

The embers of Jefferson's youthful anti-slavery sentiments still glowed. His "self-evident" proclamation in the Declaration of Independence that "all men are created equal" posed a fundamental challenge to the whole rationale of slavery at the very moment that the United States emerged into world history. He had a hand in containing its westward expansion by his part in the series of Northwest Ordinances that the Confederation Congress passed in the years 1784, 1785, and 1787, which forbade slavery to develop in what is now Ohio, Indiana, Michigan, Illinois, and Wisconsin. But he did not try to stop its expansion into Kentucky, Tennessee, and the Mississippi Territory, telling himself that if slavery became "diluted" there it would wither away. He won the presidency in 1800 because of the added weight that the three-fifths clause of the Constitution gave to Southerners in the Electoral College. Except for signing the act that ended the African slave trade in 1808, Jefferson did nothing as president to stop slavery's expansion. On the contrary, he encouraged it, by supporting the planters who began turning much of southern Indian Country into the cotton kingdom, by buying slave-holding Louisiana in 1803 and not ending slavery there at the moment of purchase, and by outright hostility to the newly independent black nation in Haiti.

By 1825 James Madison clearly felt the same, accepting the presidency of the American Colonization Society. The society was organized for the purpose of returning former American slaves to Africa, in Liberia. The actual effect of achieving its goal would have been to remove the free black American population from all contact with the millions of slaves who would remain. In the society's view, as in the view of most white Americans by then, the black people who had carved out their own lives, begun to organize their own communities, and in some cases won fame, all thanks to a Revolution that they had supported rather than fled, had no place in the American future.

Thus the problem of slavery in post-revolutionary America yields many separate answers. One, at the level of ideas, is that slavery indeed became a problem, rather than a simple fact. A second, in worldly reality, is that slavery broke apart in the North and cracked open in the South, allowing free black communities to emerge. But by 1826 the white South's now-peculiar institution enjoyed enormous strength, thanks to the energy that the Revolution had set loose. Eli Whitney's cotton gin, the brainchild of an inventive Connecticut Yankee, made the cotton kingdom possible. As cotton culture spread westward across Alabama and Mississippi, it fused with Caribbean-style sugar slavery that already was flourishing in Louisiana. Both the fact that slavery did turn into a problem and the fact that the white slave South prospered and grew on a far larger scale than during the colonial era were part of the Revolution's heritage. Let us turn to the people for whom the Revolution did not bring freedom at all.

Congress outlawed the African slave trade in 1808, as soon as the Constitution allowed. During the trade's final legal years, South Carolina, Georgia, Florida, and Louisiana brought in all the Africans they could obtain. According to the closest student of this last phase of the African trade to North America, about 171,000 new slaves entered the United States from Africa between 1783 and 1810. These formed nearly half of all entrants to the United States during those years, and they accounted for more than a quarter of the entire African migration to North America, from the very beginning. As 1808 drew near, slave ships lined up for dock space in Charleston Harbor and the corpses of slaves who died on board while the ships waited washed up on the Carolina shore.

Centuries earlier, when Bartolomé de Las Casas urged King Charles of Spain to ban enslavement of Native Americans, he had told colonial Spaniards not to worry: there was an endless supply of Africans. When the African trade closed, there seemed to be an equally endless supply of American-born slaves. Soul by soul, driven overland in chains, sold and sold again along the way, and carried coastwise aboard ships designed just for the job, they journeyed from the Chesapeake and the Carolinas to Tennessee, Kentucky, Alabama, Mississippi, and onward to Missouri, Louisiana, Arkansas, and Texas. This was not the Middle Passage. These people spoke English. They knew what was happening. But it was wrenching enough. Like their African ancestors, they were being ripped away from what they knew and forced into lifelong labor far away so that somebody else could pursue happiness.

For them, it might seem as if nothing had changed since colonial times, when slavery had been a western-hemisphere fact. But they had ears to listen, eyes to read (despite the laws that forbade them learning how), and brains to ponder their fate and consider what they could do to change it. Consider first how they shared what they knew and how they knew it. Call their secret links to one another the fishnet, the grapevine, or the bush telegraph, they had ways to share information over very long distances, including what they could glean from the white world that surrounded them. The ways they communicated remained a secret, about which white people could only guess.

In the new United States their network linked slaves not just to one another, but to a world where some black people were free and some white people were their allies. Black seafarers arriving from the North at Charleston faced temporary jailing during their ship's stay in the harbor, but they bore free-world news, to share and to spread. A black revolutionary veteran telling his war stories, such as Austin Dabney in Georgia, was bound to recount one version of Americans' struggle for their freedom from Britain if his listeners were white, and another if they were black.

In plantation country, the collective black church became the South's "invisible institution," kept secret from the masters. But it was not cut off from or invisible to the free Black Christian world. Morris Brown, who succeeded Richard Allen as AME bishop in1835, was a Carolinian. Learning what Allen had done in Philadelphia, he established another Free African Society in Charleston, founded Mother Emmanuel AME Church there in 1816, and created a circuit of AME congregations that reached beyond the city's limits. Slave and free, black people mingled in Charleston's public market and in places like it all around the booming cotton South. Whatever they said to one another there cannot be known. But news could be passed on, black sailor to free black Charlestonian, Northern churchman to Southern, free to slave, and deep into plantation country. The church was suppressed in the aftermath of the Denmark Vesey conspiracy of 1822, but the network survived.

Probably most significantly, black Americans South and North, slave and free, knew about Haiti. When the French slave colony exploded early in the

1790s, many refugees, including black people, ended up in the United States, with tales to tell. News continued to arrive: how Haitian leader Toussaint L'Ouverture's black army fought the French to a standstill, how his successors Jean Jacques Desallines and Henri Christophe stepped forward when the French tricked L'Ouverture into captivity, and how both a Republic of Haiti and, for a time, a Kingdom of Haiti emerged from slavery's rubble. For slave-holding Southerners, Haiti's great revolution presented a nightmare of fire, blood, and atrocity, evidence that black people had to be kept down at all costs. Unquestionably, that is what Jefferson had in mind when he wrote during the Missouri crisis that justice was in one scale and self-preservation was in the other.

How slavery ended in Haiti was explosively violent, but the reports that spread in the white world made it seem not just violent but full of atrocities. Horror stories spread widely about what happened, and many people far away from the events believed them. But independent Haiti's many enemies had good reason to exaggerate any tale of horror they heard, and always to believe the worst about it. So fearsome did Southern slave masters find the Haiti story that in deference to them President John Quincy Adams refused to send a delegation to a congress of the new American republics in Panama in 1826, because former Haitian slaves would be there as free men, representing their own free country as an equal, proud member of the world's family of nations.

But black people had good reason to believe otherwise than whites about Haiti, and to see in it not horror but rather inspiration. They knew that in Haiti people much like themselves had overthrown slavery by their own efforts, and those people were building an American nation that was entirely theirs. Until the Civil War, the image of the Haitian Revolution loomed over the entire raging American debate about slavery. For many people who believed the horror stories, Haiti provided reason for holding the lid on American slavery tight. For other people, who also believed them, the explosive end of slavery there offered reason to demolish it in the United States before it could detonate there the same way. But for most black Americans the whole Haitian story offered a beacon telling them that black people had been able to liberate themselves and destroy slavery, by their own efforts.

They learned about Haiti, and a great deal else, because black writers kept them informed. During its two-year run from March 1827 to April 1829 the newspaper *Freedom's Journal* spoke both to the black community and for it. It was the first black-owned and black-produced paper in the United States. Take just a few of its issues. On March 23, 1827, it carried a long account of the life of Captain Paul Cuffee and another about Phillis Wheatley, a report from Jamaica, and reprinted sympathetic articles from the white press. On April 18 it discussed African colonization, commented that freeing slaves by purchasing them amounted to "hiring" the slaveholders to be just, and declared that ending slavery in the United States had to be the business of the whole nation, because the whole nation shared in it. On May 4 it explored the so-called curse of Canaan, dating from the Biblical story of Noah cursing one of his sons, as a supposed justification for slavery. It carried a running series on the life of Haitian hero Toussaint L'Ouverture. There were accounts of people in ancient Egypt and Carthage and contemporary Africa. Readers learned about debates over slavery in the United States Congress and state legislatures, the British Parliament, and public meetings. Nobody possibly could read the paper and think that black people in America were contented or that they were humble, or that they had no history. Nobody could read it and not realize that among them there was strong, insistent determination to bring slavery down, whatever the odds against the effort, and whatever means proved necessary to achieve the goal.[8]

Rebellion offered one possible way. There is no full telling how many plans for rebellion were talked over in the slave quarters during the decades that followed American independence or what the rebels actually discussed. But four great slave uprisings are known. One way or another all four drew on the revolutionary era. Gabriel's Plan in Virginia (1800) sought to complete what the white Virginia revolution had left undone, in the expectation that ordinary white Virginians would join black Virginians and remake the world together. Rebels in Louisiana (1811) intended to do for themselves what the Haitians had achieved. Denmark Vesey's plan in South Carolina (1822) was to escape, not to refuge in a swampland or mountain range but rather to revolutionary Haiti, but the plan emerged from what black people already had made of the possibilities in post-revolutionary America. Nat Turner's rebellion in Southampton County, Virginia, (1831) seemed to end the possibilities that the revolutionary era had opened. All four attempts failed. All were suppressed. Following Nat Turner, there would not be another great slave rising in the United States until the Civil War.

Gabriel formed his plan in 1800, the year of the first tumultuous, fully contested presidential election. He dwelt as Thomas Prosser's slave near Richmond, amid Virginia's growing free black population. Free and slave alike, black Virginians heard the fever-hot rhetoric of Thomas Jefferson's Democratic-Republican politicians, particularly their insistence that they stood for equality and for the rights of common men. Gabriel paid close attention as the Jeffersonians, especially Governor James Monroe, railed against the privileges of merchants and other men of wealth. What he heard was the language of class struggle, not the language of white supremacy. He saw no reason not to think that the politicians' language applied to people like him.

Gabriel's strategy was to take over Richmond with his organization of free and enslaved black men and then to enlist sympathetic white people. He timed the event for a summer Saturday, when such people converging on the town would generate little suspicion. He knew which targets to seize and in what order to do it, including, if Monroe would not live up to his words and cooperate, making the governor a hostage. Taking seriously the Democratic-Republicans' talk about liberty being endangered by merchants' and bankers' supposed greed, he expected that politicians like Monroe and poor white people would realize that their interests and black people's could fuse. The Jeffersonian dream of a small-farmer world would emerge, with slavery gone. Gabriel hoped that he, Gabriel, would join Monroe among the reformed republic's leaders.

As Gabriel's followers moved toward their rendezvous in Richmond, a torrential rainstorm spoiled the plan's execution. Virginia whites of all sorts joined together against the slaves, with Governor Monroe in the lead. One exception may have been a white boatman who helped Gabriel escape down the James River toward Norfolk, only to be betrayed by a fellow black man who hoped that his own freedom would be the reward. Hanging followed upon hanging in the plot's aftermath. But one of the defendants at the brief trials that preceded the hangings put the difference between what Gabriel and his fellows had intended and earlier rebellions perfectly. He had "nothing to offer" in his defense other "than what General Washington would have had to offer, had he been taken by the British and put to trial."[9]

The second great rebellion, in Louisiana in the year 1811, was also the largest. It remains the least-known, because the French planters, American officials, and United States troops who joined forces to put it down made sure that news of it did not spread. It drew on what Haiti's black people made of the larger revolutionary era, rather than directly on the American events with which the era had begun. France had ceded Louisiana to Spain in 1763, as it withdrew from North America. Spain gave it back to France nearly four decades later, as part of French First Consul (later Emperor) Napoleon Bonaparte's plan to reestablish French sugar slavery in the Caribbean, particularly Haiti. Its role in Bonaparte's plan would be to supply foodstuffs to the islands, but southern Louisiana was becoming a sugar region in its own right. Bonaparte sold Louisiana to the United States in 1803 when it became clear that his venture against the Haitians had failed, defeated both by the Haitians' determined bravery and by yellow fever that decimated the French army that Bonaparte had sent to subdue them. In terms of the larger course of American history, buying Louisiana was a brilliant stroke of diplomacy, doubling the size of the republic for a payment of $15,000,000. But the whole process emerged from the problem of slavery during the revolutionary era. For years after the sale, American power in Louisiana remained weak. At the time of the 1811 Louisiana rising, American settlers were just starting to trickle in.

When the United States acquired Louisiana its sugar industry was thriving. North and south of New Orleans, sugar plantations lined the banks of the Mississippi River. Growing, harvesting, and processing Louisiana sugar were just as difficult and just as dangerous for the slaves who did the work as on the Caribbean Islands. Like eighteenth-century French Ste. Domingue and British Jamaica, Louisiana sugar planters wanted all the slaves they possibly could get. When they came under United States dominion in 1803, only five years remained before Congress could constitutionally end the slave trade. So, like South Carolina and Georgia, Louisiana imported Africans. They brought direct memories of their own freedom. Refugees from Haiti came to Louisiana from Haiti as well, with all that they had to tell about what happened there. Its swamplands offered refuge for people who had escaped, much better than any east-coast terrain.

For all these reasons, the arrival of new Africans, knowledge of what had happened in Haiti, and the existence of free Maroon communities that the planters could not destroy, Louisiana's French-speaking planters had reason to fear their slaves. But they were totally unprepared for what erupted on January 8, 1811, as the sugar-processing season ended and the Mardi Gras season arrived. Working together, a combination of trusted slave drivers, Africans who had not forgotten how to lead, escapees hiding in the swamps, and slaves who knew about Haiti had been creating a revolutionary network that stretched across much of the sugar region. They rose almost as one, assembling themselves into an army about five hundred strong, driving the planters out if they did not kill them, and destroying the sugar plantations just as the Haitians had done. But a few of the planters did escape, spreading the alarm, regrouping, and fighting back quickly and ferociously, with the aid of United States troops from the garrison stationed in New Orleans. A fierce pitched battle on January 10 ended the rising, and more than one hundred heads of the defeated black rebels were impaled on high poles along the riverfront for a distance of forty miles, a clear warning to other slaves of the fate that awaited them if they also tried to rise.

Until the rising, Louisiana's French planters had been doubtful about United States rule over them. They thought themselves far more cultured than the rough, crude Americans who were taking over the running of their province. They had resisted the idea of accepting American statehood. But the American officials joined the planters with all the force they could muster to put the rebellion down. Now the planters realized that they needed full membership in the United States for their own safety, and their territory of Louisiana moved swiftly toward statehood, the planters sure that the United States would guarantee their safety. All the planters had to do was ask.

As with New York in 1741, there is some possibility that there was no conspiracy in South Carolina in 1822, only white fears run wild. But the best evidence suggests otherwise. The plan's leader, Denmark Vesey, was West Indies–born, and spent a brief time in pre-revolutionary Ste. Domingue. By the time of the Haitian Revolution, Vesey was in Charleston, where he had gone as a slave in about 1782. A lucky lottery ticket enabled him to purchase his freedom, and he learned the trade of carpentry. Vesey followed the Haiti story more closely and probably with better understanding than most, since he had known the French sugar colony firsthand. Unlike Virginia's Gabriel, Vesey had no reason to expect that he could make common cause with white allies of any sort. No South Carolina white politician ever deployed the political language of human equality that James Monroe and Thomas Jefferson threw about and that made Gabriel believe Monroe and even Jefferson would take his side. Nor did Vesey trust Charleston's free brown people. Most of them, he knew, looked down on black Carolinians just as surely as their counterparts in Ste. Domingue had done. Their Brown Fellowship Society, founded in 1790, denied membership to people who were fully black, such as Vesey.

Vesey's heroes and models were the Haitian leaders Toussaint L'Ouverture and Henri Christophe. But even in South Carolina he benefited from what the American Revolution had made possible. He bought his own freedom with his lottery winnings, which, for a time, the law allowed. He joined a black Presbyterian church. Renting a place that served him as both a shop and a home, he was as secure as any black Carolinian could be against white invasions of his property. Within his four walls, he could talk with others, shape his thoughts, and make plans. He could come and go as he pleased on business. But he was unable to buy out the enslavement of the first of his several wives or the children he had with her. The most basic unit of civil society, a secure family, was denied to him as surely as if he were still enslaved.

Carolina politicians were not Virginia-style Jeffersonian democrats, extolling the virtues of lower-class white people and damning aristocrats and money-changers. But they, too, spoke the language of American republican-ism, and Vesey heard it. But what the Virginians had done to the rebels of 1800 was no secret, and Vesey was a realistic man, not a dreamer. Overturn-ing Carolina slavery directly seemed beyond possibility, so he planned to escape. What looseness there had been was turning solid again. In 1820 the state ended both emancipation of slaves by masters without the legislature's permission, and self-purchase by slaves, such as Vesey himself had done. But Vesey also knew that in the same year, 1820, Haitian president Jean-Pierre Boyer publicly invited black Americans to come south to his island. They would find full freedom there, as citizens of the western hemisphere's revo-lutionary second republic, among heroic black men and women who had destroyed slavery entirely. If Vesey's people could get to the waterfront, they could commandeer ships, which some of them knew how to sail. There was no point at all in heading for the Northern free states. That would only mean being returned. The plan was to reach Haiti.

It did not succeed. One of Vesey's followers talked to a slave who was not in on the secret, and that slave talked to his master. As with Gabriel's plan, it took some time for white Carolina leaders to appreciate the severity of the threat, but, as with the Virginians, summary trials and many hangings fol-lowed. No more than for the Stono rebels in 1739 would there be an escape. What Vesey and his fellows sought was revolutionary, not in the context of South Carolina or even the United States, but of what the American devel-opments had helped to trigger on a world scale. They drew their inspiration both from their pessimistic conclusion that the American Republic could not live up to its own language, and from their historic knowledge that the Republic of Haiti had done what the United States did not seem able to do.

In August 1831 another rebellion exploded, this time in Southampton County, Virginia. Southampton lies in the Virginia Southside, the area between the James River and the North Carolina border. It is just west of the Great Dismal Swamp, where some escaped slaves did find refuge. Almost half of the county's sixteen thousand people in 1830 were slaves. People who knew the rebellion's leader, who went by Nat and was not known, yet, as Nat Turner, described him as highly intelligent. He certainly could read. He studied the Bible carefully, and he breathed the fire of radical black Christi-anity. It seems that he drew most heavily on the Book of Revelations, with its images of a final battle between the forces of good and the forces of evil. Nat believed himself divinely inspired, and his message of divine retribution against the enslavers was inspiring to the people who joined him.

In their two-day insurrection Nat and his followers killed about sixty white people, sparing a few who, they knew, had not dealt in slavery. The local mi-

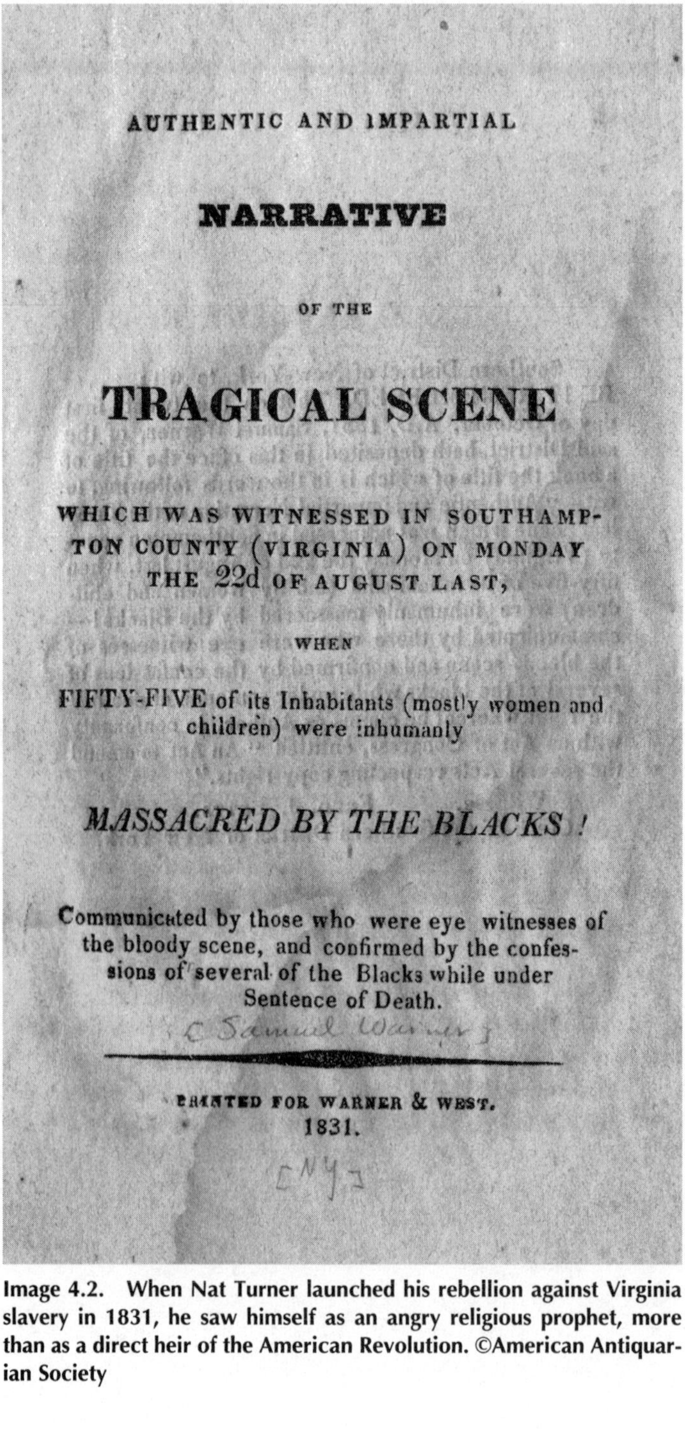

AUTHENTIC AND IMPARTIAL

NARRATIVE

OF THE

TRAGICAL SCENE

WHICH WAS WITNESSED IN SOUTHAMP-
TON COUNTY (VIRGINIA) ON MONDAY
THE 22d OF AUGUST LAST,

WHEN

FIFTY-FIVE of its Inhabitants (mostly women and
children) were inhumanly

MASSACRED BY THE BLACKS !

Communicated by those who were eye witnesses of
the bloody scene, and confirmed by the confessions of several of the Blacks while under
Sentence of Death.

[Samuel Warner]

PRINTED FOR WARNER & WEST.
1831.

[N Y]

Image 4.2.   When Nat Turner launched his rebellion against Virginia slavery in 1831, he saw himself as an angry religious prophet, more than as a direct heir of the American Revolution. ©American Antiquarian Society litia had no trouble putting them down. Forty-five slaves and five free black people went on trial. Thirty were convicted and eighteen of those went to the gallows. The twelve who were spared the noose were sent out of the state. Before they hanged Nat, he got the chance to tell his story to a white man who wrote it down and published it as *The Confessions of Nat Turner*, taking the surname, which Nat never used, of one of the Virginians who had owned him. The rebellion had not spread, but retribution did. Fearful whites killed about two hundred more people across the length and width of the South. Planters warned one another to keep silent. Slaves learned about the rebellion anyway, from overheard accounts, from newspapers if they could read, from their secret ways of sharing news, and from the black Virginians and North Carolinians whom the domestic slave trade brought to their region.

White Southerners drew the appropriate conclusions from the Gabriel and Vesey plots and the Southampton County and Louisiana insurrections. From the year of the Southampton slave rising, 1831, until their own insurrection against the United States in 1861, they kept intense, careful watch over their slaves. They built what they hoped was a wall around their slaves and even around themselves, separating their world of slavery from the free world outside. They developed an elaborate pro-slavery argument, drawing on their reading of both the Bible and American history, and on racist anthropology, sociology, law, and economics.

In 1837 South Carolina's John C. Calhoun declared in the United States Senate that slavery was not an evil at all. It was a "positive good" for everybody involved, including the slaves. When the United States finally broke up, unable to resolve the slavery issue, Confederate Vice-President Alexander Stephens announced that slavery would be the "cornerstone" of the new Southern nation. In his words, the Confederacy rested "upon the great truth that the negro is not equal to the white man; that slavery subordination to the superior race is his natural and normal condition. This, our new government, is the first, in the history of the world, based upon this great physical, philosophical, and moral truth." As the South declared independence, Stephens thought he and his fellows were confirming what the American Revolution had accomplished and solving its mistakes. He even invoked Jefferson as saying that slavery was the "rock upon which the old Union would split."[10] Jefferson might have acknowledged the prophecy, but even as an old man he would not have accepted how Stephens repudiated his own "self-evident" truth of 1776, that all men are created equal.

Like their frightened masters, enslaved black people pondered all that happened in Haiti, and in Richmond, Louisiana, Charleston, and Southampton

County. There was no major rebellion in the South after 1831. But the South's black people were not docile, or accepting. On the South's upper edges, from Delaware to Missouri, resistance could take the form of escape via the Underground Railroad, the informal chain of allies and safe places along which fugitive slaves heading north could journey. The free world was not far away. A person could see it from the Kentucky bank of the Ohio River or the northern Missouri bank of the Mississippi, or at the line where slave Maryland and free Pennsylvania met. Frederick Douglass and Harriet Tubman both got out that way. Some escaped from farther south as well, but they were rare. To find real safety a person had to get to Canada, beyond the reach of the United States Constitution and its protection for the property rights of slave owners rather than the human rights of slaves.

The great black historian John Hope Franklin showed in one of his late-life books that the "Old South" of the 1830s, 1840s, and 1850s still seethed with slave unrest and that most slaves in the Cotton Kingdom resisted where they were. In 1850 the black population of the booming cotton state of Mississippi stood at about three hundred thousand. Only about nine hundred of them were free. Most of those lived in the river port towns, such as Natchez and Vicksburg on the Mississippi and Columbus on the Tombigbee. Outside those places the chances were overwhelming that a Mississippi slave did not meet a free black person directly from one year to the next. Mississippi masters did their very utmost to cut their slaves from any news about the outside world. When Stephen Duncan of Natchez learned in 1831 about Nat Turner's rebellion in faraway Virginia he wrote to a friend that "it behooves to be vigilant, *but silent*."[11]

But despite all the masters' efforts to hold their slaves in a vast, sealed series of slave labor camps, most of them had come to Mississippi from far away. They knew what had happened in Maryland, Virginia, the Carolinas, and Georgia. They heard about Gabriel, Denmark Vesey, and Nat Turner, what those men had dreamed and planned, how their plans had failed, and how the authorities put their rebellions down with blood. They knew that to their north there was freedom and they knew that in Haiti black people had a republic of their own. If they had had a chance to read *Freedom's Journal* or hear somebody talk about it, they had learned about black history. They had heard black ministers preach freedom. They knew that free black communities existed and, even in the South, there were not Maroons hidden in the swamps but open communities with churches, organizations, leaders, and businesses. Moreover, the flow of newcomers to America's slave frontier never let up. Like Africans during the trans-Atlantic slave trade period, these people knew that enslavement did not exist everywhere and that, in some places where it once had existed, it had been destroyed.

We have absolutely no way of knowing what they said to one another. Keeping a written record or telling a white person would have been suicidal. But we can imagine what they thought, based on the anguish of young Frederick Bailey, later known as Frederick Douglass, enslaved in the mid-1830s at Wye Plantation on Maryland's Eastern Shore. Bailey often watched the vessels that plied Chesapeake Bay. Northbound, their prows pointed toward places where slavery did not exist, and, at the bay's northern end, such places were not far away. Southbound, those same prows pointed ever deeper into slavery. Had Bailey been sold south, which came close to happening when one of his escape attempts failed, he might have passed through the notorious slave market in Washington, D.C., in sight of the unfinished United States Capitol, which slaves were constructing. He would have understood the bitter irony in what the Capitol represented. Had that happened, and had he ended up in Alabama, Mississippi, Arkansas, northern Louisiana, or east Texas his only choice would have been to resist where he was, as well as he could. But he would not ever have forgotten that even in the United States there were places where somebody like him was not a slave. He did not go south, of course. In 1838 he successfully made his way north and changed his name to Frederick Douglass.

Between the suppression of Nat Turner's Rebellion of 1831 and the outbreak three decades later of the white South's war to protect slavery by destroying the United States, slaves across the cotton South had good reason for thinking that open revolution made no sense for them. They knew what the whites would do, should they try. Some may have realized that Ste. Domingue had succeeded for reasons that did not hold in the United States. First, it was on an island, separated by mountains from Spanish Santo Domingo. Second, slaves there vastly outnumbered both white and free brown people. Third, most of the slaves were crammed into the lowland sugar-growing regions. Even the coffee plantations on the island's hills were not far away. Fast communication was possible. Fourth, the French Revolution split the French and Franco-American elite. The highest people in the French *Ancien Régime* (old order) lost their will to dominate, in the face of notions about liberty, equality, and fraternity, and confronted by risings in Paris and the French provinces. Ste. Domingue's free brown people demanded the full rights of Frenchmen and Frenchwomen, and sent delegates to state their claims. But like the island's whites, they were slaveholders, and they were blind to the fact that, although they did have grievances, their slaves had far greater grievances of their own.

Some of those conditions had held for a time in the revolutionary and post-revolutionary United States. The American ruling elite did split. Some of its members did lose their faith in their own right to rule, and particularly in their right to hold slaves in absolute dominion. Slavery did crack open, as this book has shown. Slaves escaped by the thousands. Freedom became a possibility. The institution itself began to collapse, starting in Vermont. But by the second quarter of the nineteenth century, the revolutionary time had passed and the system had congealed. Haiti presented a brilliant, inspiring example of black people freeing themselves, but in the United States the road that black Haitians had taken to freedom was closed.

The slavery issue had arisen in revolutionary America. It had spread far beyond the United States. The problem would not go away. But when the Constitution took effect in 1789 and the nation settled down to business, its leaders and most of its white people seemed to want the slavery question to just go away. As one of his last public acts, in 1790, Benjamin Franklin invoked his enormous prestige to support an anti-slavery petition, but it had no effect. The same year, Congress passed an immigration and naturalization bill that granted free access to all comers, if they came from Europe. Nobody from elsewhere would be welcome, and to gain citizenship by naturalization a person had to be white. In 1797 Absalom Jones led a petition campaign to Congress by black Philadelphians on behalf of four North Carolina slaves who had managed to make their way north. James Madison, sitting in the House of Representatives for Virginia, had written privately a decade earlier that where slavery exists the fundamental "republican theory" that what a majority decided was right was simply false. But now, he held, the petitioners had "no claim" on the attention of Congress.[12]

George Washington's decision to free his own slaves in his last will is to his credit. But his will did not take effect until Washington himself was dead. As president while the United States capital was in Philadelphia, he made sure that the slaves who served him rotated back to Mount Vernon every six months. That was so that Pennsylvania's gradual emancipation law, which limited the time that an outside slave could stay within the state, would not take effect applied to them. Eight of the first twelve men who held the presidency also held slaves. John Quincy Adams did not, and he disliked slavery all his life. But as secretary of state, he pressed Britain to return slaves who had joined British troops during the War of 1812, just as Washington had pressed for their return when the British were evacuating in 1783. As president, Adams refused to send delegates to the Panama Conference of 1826 because of the presence of Haitians. Though Britain and the United States abolished the slave trade within a year of each other, in 1807 and 1808 respectively, the United States refused to let its vessels cooperate with the Royal Navy to enforce the law along the African coast. Until the Civil War, many vessels engaged in the illegal African trade flew the Stars and Stripes if a British vessel approached them, secure in the knowledge that the British ship could do nothing to them.

After the Louisiana rising of 1811, the United States troops did not deploy troops to uphold slavery until 1859, when John Brown raided the federal arsenal at Harpers Ferry, Virginia, in the futile hope of seizing arms and launching a rising on the Haitian model. But the prospect always existed. Slaveholders virtually monopolized the presidency. Had any state governor called for federal aid in putting down a slave rising, he would have received it. The ferocity that local authorities used against Gabriel's conspiracy in 1800, the Louisiana rebellion of 1811, the Denmark Vesey plot in 1822, and Nat Turner's rebellion of 1831 in Virginia showed that confronted with even the threat of a slave rising the white South could defend itself with all the violence it could muster. Meanwhile, the North stood by and watched. Slavery in the South would not fall the way that it had fallen in Haiti. It was too strong, even right after independence. Both across the South and in national politics, its strength grew rather than waned. By themselves, black Americans could not bring it down, and allies seemed to be few. North or South, free or still enslaved, black people knew that the overwhelming majority of white Americans either did not want them to be free or did not care. Their enslavers were armed and were ready to use their weapons. Slavery's supporters controlled the institutions of public power and they could deploy the Republic's forces.

What, then, to do? Emigrate, if a person could? For free people it certainly was possible, if they could raise the money to go. Even Richard Allen thought about leaving, first to Africa at the invitation of his friend Paul Cuffee and later to Haiti. But he had come to a different conclusion in 1827: "This land which we have watered with our tears and our blood is now our mother country and we are well satisfied to stay."[13] He had not arrived at that answer easily, and getting to it still left open the question of what to do within the slave-holding American republic. Slavery's world-historic destruction had begun there, but its actual end seemed nowhere in sight.

Notes

1. M. A. Richmond, *Bid the Vassal Soar: Interpretive Essays on the Life and Poetry of Phillis Wheatley (ca. 1753–1784) and George Moses Horton (ca. 1977–1883)* (Washington: Howard University Press, 1974), 54.

2. Kaplan and Kaplan, *Black Presence*, 189.

3. Kaplan and Kaplan, *Black Presence*, 147.

4. *The Poems of Phillis Wheatley*, ed. Julian D. Mason, Jr. (Chapel Hill: University of North Carolina Press, 1989), 53, 50.

5. *The Poems of Phillis Wheatley*, 104.

6. Kaplan and Kaplan, *Black Presence*, 122.

7. Jefferson to John Holmes, April 22, 1820, www.loc.gov/exhibits/jefferson/159 .html, accessed March 11, 2011.

8. The entire press run of *Freedom's Journal* is available online at www.wisconsin history.org/libraryarchives/aanp/freedom/volume1.asp, and www.wisconsinhistory.org/ libraryarchives/aanp/freedom/volume2.asp.

9. Douglas Egerton, *Gabriel's Rebellion: The Virginia Slave Conspiracies of 1800 and 1802* (Chapel Hill: University of North Carolina Press, 1993), 102.

10. Thomas G. West, *Vindicating the Founders: Race, Sex, Class, and Justice in the Origins of America* (Lanham, MD: Rowman & Littlefield, 1997), 34.

11. Winthrop D. Jordan, *Tumult and Silence at Second Creek: An Inquiry into a Civil War Slave Conspiracy* (Baton Rouge: Louisiana State University Press, 1993), 1.

12. Kaplan and Kaplan, *Black Presence*, 272.

13. Richard Allen, *Freedom's Journal*, November 2, 1827, quoted in David Walker, *Appeal to the Coloured Citizens of the World*, ed. Sean Wilentz (New York: Hill & Wang, 1995), 58.

EPILOGUE

~

"You May Rejoice, I Must Mourn"

Slaves, Free Americans, and the Fourth of July

"Now. Americans! I ask you candidly, was your sufferings under Great Britain one hundredth part so cruel and Tyrannical as you have rendered ours under you?"

—David Walker, *Appeal to the Coloured Citizens of the World*, 1829

"This Fourth of July is yours, not mine."

—Frederick Douglass, *What to the Slave is the Fourth of July*,
July 5, 1852

Until the Fifteenth Amendment added the word "male" to the United States Constitution in 1870, the document said nothing at all about who could take part in political society, other than setting age requirements for election to the House of Representatives, the Senate, and the presidency, and requiring that the president be native born. Unlike most of the early state constitutions, it did not have property requirements to vote and hold office. Nor did it mention race or sex. In 1791 the First Amendment specifically forbade taking religion into account as well. Custom and state law, not the Constitution, decreed that to be a full, participating citizen in the young United States a person almost always had to be adult, white, male, and a property owner.

Even at the beginning, there were exceptions. Vermont set no property requirement for voting. In New Jersey free black people and unmarried women who met the property requirement could vote until 1807, when both

113

groups lost that right. During the fifty years that followed independence, state laws setting property requirements fell away and America became democratic, in the sense that virtually any white male could vote and seek office. But restrictions on people who were not white and male grew stronger. Free black people and women lost their right to vote in New Jersey in 1807. In 1821, New York lowered the white requirement for voting to merely paying taxes and one year of residence, but raised it to having property worth $250 and three years of residence for men "of colour."[1] The French observer Alexis de Tocqueville described the new political reality brilliantly in his classic account of *Democracy in America* (2 vol., 1836–1839). He saw there the whole world's future. But like every other outside observer, he also saw American democracy's great flaws. One was what he called the tyranny of the majority. Two others were slavery in the South and the exclusion of free black people everywhere from most of American liberty's blessings. These things were connected. The rise of American democracy, the expansion of Southern slavery, and the less than second-class status of free black people were bound together.

Black people of the young republic did not need the observations of Europeans to understand their situation. Free or enslaved, they knew that they were excluded, surrounded, outnumbered, and, if it came to it, out-gunned. Slaves were stuck wherever and however their masters chose to place them, unless they could escape, one by one. A slave who did escape could be recaptured. The local law of a free state would give no protection. According to the Constitution, a "person held to service or labor in one state, under the Law thereof" was to be "delivered up on Claim of the Party to whom such Service or Labour may be due" and the Constitution was, in its own words, "the supreme law of the land." Freedom was real where state laws mandated it, but the right of masters to recover escaped slaves was national because of the Constitution's fugitive slave clause, and it trumped state law.

Free black people did have the ongoing choice to leave, if they could afford to do it. Massachusetts ship owner and sea captain Paul Cuffee possessed the means to go, and early in the nineteenth century he concluded that there was no point in remaining. He became deeply interested in the British venture to Sierra Leone, and he attracted the serious attention for a time of his friends James Forten and Richard Allen. He hoped that many others would follow. But they did not. Free Haiti offered another possibility. That interested Forten and Allen too, and getting to Haiti was Denmark Vesey's goal in 1822. Some free black people accepted the Haitian government's 1820 invitation to come. But they found that living in a French-speaking officially Catholic country was not easy and most returned to the

United States, despite all the problems that they knew they would face when they got back.

Most free black people, however, did not want to go anywhere, to Africa, to Haiti, or anywhere else outside the United States. In Richard Allen's words, America was now their mother country, however bad a mother it was. They knew where their ancestors had come from, Africa, and they were proud of it. They knew what the black people of Haiti had achieved, and they admired it. But the United States was their home, and the struggle within it was theirs to wage. When Allen and Forten considered the idea of emigration, they found themselves confronting enormous opposition from their own free Philadelphia community. They backed down, and turned their lives, their fortunes, and their talents toward improving the situation where they had been born and raised.

As the Republic reached its first half-century, in 1826, black Americans had to face a new challenge. Some of the country's most prominent white figures began organizing themselves as the American Colonization Society, with the idea of getting free black people to emigrate, at first to Sierra Leone and after 1825 to Liberia. The society offered financial help to anybody who wanted to go. Former president James Madison accepted the society's presidency. The name of Liberia's capital, Monrovia, honors President James Monroe, who leant his prestige to the colonization project, but who as governor of Virginia in 1800 had led the bloody suppression of Gabriel's plan to end slavery there.

Some black Americans did respond. On the surface the new venture looked much like neighboring Sierra Leone, but there were differences between the two. Sierra Leone had emerged from white benevolence, but its British sponsors were veterans of the intense, decades-long struggle in that country to end the African slave trade, which they achieved in 1807. When Britain's slave trade ended, they turned their efforts toward full abolition and they saw Sierra Leone as leading toward ending slavery outright. There were no slaveholders among them. The North American refugees who answered their call were leaving behind the dismal realities of free life in Nova Scotia. The American Colonization Society, however, drew strong slaveholder support. Its call for free black people to leave the United States, and its offer to make departure possible, seemed benevolent, and the society's members probably thought that was so. But, if their plan succeeded, it would mean that what black Americans were creating for themselves would be destroyed. There would be no Richard Allens, no James Fortens, no Denmark Veseys left to struggle against slavery and to offer living examples of freedom. There would be no AME churches, no black-owned businesses, no black organizations or communities where people could meet and make plans. There would be nothing and nobody for enslaved people to see that was different from slavery.

The most notable black man who answered the call was John Brown Russwurm, the first black American college graduate. He edited *Freedom's Journal* during most of its two-year life from 1827 to 1829. The paper vehemently opposed colonization during its too-brief run, and Russwurm's decision to go cost him all the respect he had built up in the free community. He departed anyway, and he went on to a distinguished and successful African life. Liberia, like Sierra Leone and Canada, joined the United States as a direct product of the upheavals and changes of the American Revolution.

But few departed. Most did not go and they did not want to go. The stories of two who stayed, David Walker and Frederick Douglass, show both what black people had to say to a world that did not want to hear and the dilemmas that they faced as they and their people pondered what to do. Each framed his understanding and his vision of black people's future in the United States in terms of what the American Revolution had done and what it had failed to do.

David Walker was born free in Wilmington, North Carolina in 1785. Restless for more than Wilmington could offer, he moved south to Charleston and joined its free black community, which had taken shape during the revolutionary era. There he could find churches (such as Mother Emanuel), organizations (such as Charleston's Free African Society), businesses (like Denmark Vesey's carpentry shop), houses where black people could talk safely, and public places like the market, where free and enslaved Carolinians could mingle and exchange news. In his later writings Walker said very little about what he saw, whom he knew, and what he learned in Charleston's black community during his time there. He knew how dangerous it would be to tell.

Walker left Charleston for the free state of Massachusetts about the time of Denmark Vesey's plan. He settled in Boston. Perhaps he had been involved in the plan himself; he did not say. He took with him the plan's angry spirit and determination to resist; he left behind Vesey's belief that the answer lay in Haiti, other than as an inspiration.

When Walker got to Massachusetts, the whole problem of slavery was entirely behind him, if he wanted it to be. He did not have to fear recapture. He could simply choose to be a free black man in the North. But he did not choose to disappear. He had to support himself, so he opened a used clothes store near the waterfront, where he sold cheap pants, shirts, and jackets, mostly to seafarers, many of them black. He made the most of Boston's libraries and

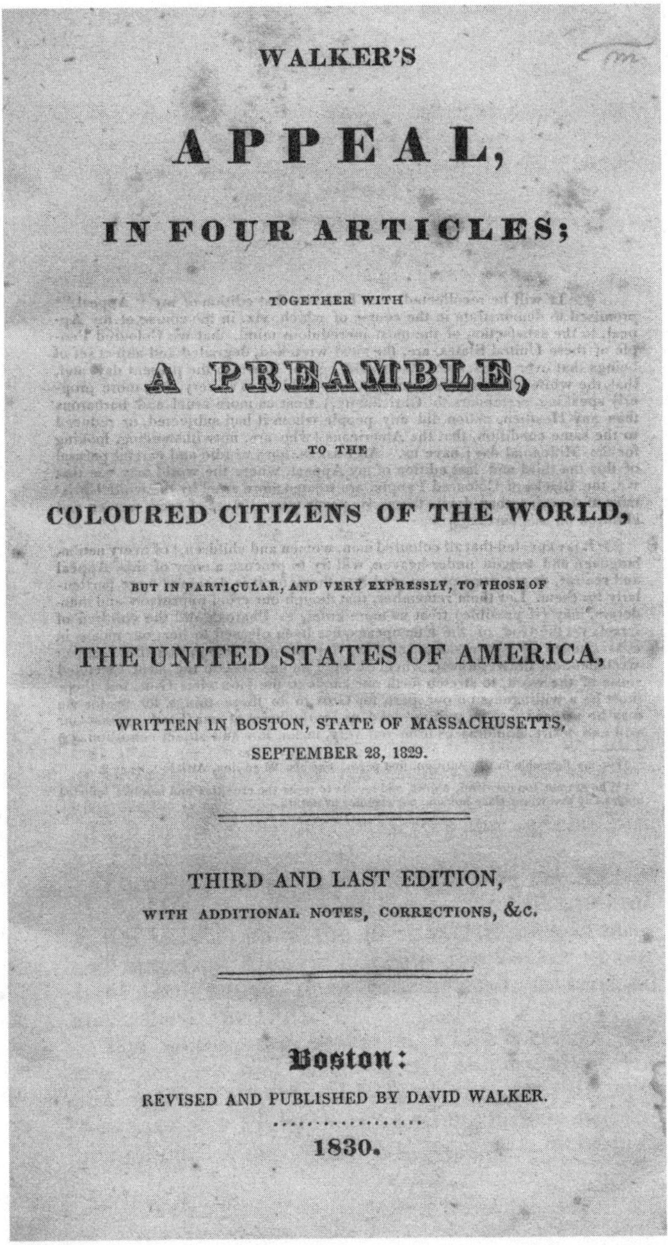

WALKER'S

APPEAL,

IN FOUR ARTICLES;

TOGETHER WITH

A PREAMBLE,

TO THE

COLOURED CITIZENS OF THE WORLD,

BUT IN PARTICULAR, AND VERY EXPRESSLY, TO THOSE OF

THE UNITED STATES OF AMERICA,

WRITTEN IN BOSTON, STATE OF MASSACHUSETTS,
SEPTEMBER 28, 1829.

THIRD AND LAST EDITION,
WITH ADDITIONAL NOTES, CORRECTIONS, &c.

Boston:
REVISED AND PUBLISHED BY DAVID WALKER.
1830.

Image E.1.   Like Nat Turner, Boston writer David Walker invoked the wrath of an angry God against slaveholding America. But he also called on white Americans to live up to the best promises of their revolution. Image courtesy of *Documenting the American South*, the University of North Carolina at Chapel Hill Libraries bookstores, reading widely about the world-wide history of slavery and about black people in the United States. As his knowledge grew, he started speaking out in meetings and writing for *Freedom's Journal*. Some of the essays it carried definitely have his voice. He had something larger in mind, a book to awaken his own people, express their rage, and set the world alight.

In 1829 Walker published his great, impassioned, ferociously angry *Appeal to the Coloured Citizens of the World*. He addressed it to black people like himself, "the coloured citizens of the world, but in particular, and very expressly . . . those of the United States of America." His great goal was to rouse them for a task of historic proportions, "to prove to the Americans and the World that we are MEN and not *brutes*" and to bring "*entire emancipation . . . all over the world*." They needed to be shocked, for "We . . . are the *most wretched, degraded* and *abject* set of beings that *ever lived* since the world began." White people had inflicted slavery upon them, but black Americans had allowed it to endure. White people were very unlikely to end what they had begun. It was up to black people, not anybody else, to change their situation: "men of colour . . . for you particularly is my APPEAL designed. . . . *Go to work and enlighten your brethren*." Walker had grasped the deepest lesson that the American Revolution could teach, which is that people who suffer have the right and the duty to end their own suffering and must do so if they can. He understood that doing it would require great courage and greater determination.[2]

But repeatedly in the book he turned to white America, to condemn its faults without excuse or exception. Walker knew he would have white readers. He knew that he was risking his life with what he had to say, and he did not care: "if you wish . . . to murder me, know ye, that I . . . count my life not dear." He urged "you of the United States" to change your ways, "if you will hear."[3] One way he sought to reach them was by praising the British. What could July 4th, the Declaration of Independence, the Constitution, and the pretensions of Americans' "*Republican land of liberty*" hold for his own people? Britons, he thought, were "the best friends the coloured people have upon earth." Almost certainly Walker's wide reading had taught him about the British record during the revolutionary era, from Somerset's case to the great exodus of 1783. He knew that British people who had campaigned against the slave trade had gone on to push for ending slavery altogether, wherever the Union Jack flew. By 1829 they were close to that goal, while white America seemed only to look away.

Walker had read very widely in black and slave history, from the ancient world to "Hayti, the glory of the blacks and terror of tyrants." He had learned how Fray Bartholomé de las Casas, the Spanish campaigner against enslaving

Native Americans, had assured early Spanish colonists that Africans were readily available for enslavement. Always, he wrote, "the whites have . . . been an unjust, jealous, avaricious, and blood-thirsty set of beings." But the "white Christians of America . . . treat us more cruel and barbarous than any heathen nation did any people."

Walker had studied Thomas Jefferson, particularly his *Notes on the State of Virginia*. "The very learned and penetrating" Jefferson had taught him about slavery in ancient Rome. He recognized that the Virginian was "one of as great characters as ever lived among the whites." He quoted Jefferson's fine language about human equality. But to Walker, Jefferson had "injured us more [and] been as great a barrier to our emancipation as any thing that has ever been advanced against us," with what he said about black people in *Notes on Virginia*. He took particular aim at what Jefferson had said about artistic talent, and how Jefferson had contrasted ancient Roman slave artists with black Americans, including his dismissal of Phillis Wheatley and Benjamin Banneker. Walker understood Jefferson's tactic, perhaps better than did Jefferson himself. Natural difference, which amounted for Jefferson to natural inferiority, would outweigh Jefferson's own self-evident truth of human equality. Perhaps Walker recognized that Jefferson was torturing his own mind, but that was beside the point. Jefferson was dead, and resolving the matter was up to black people, for "unless we try to refute Mr. Jefferson's arguments respecting us, we will only establish them."

But Walker despised the idea of emigration. He gave his greatest praise not to the black heroes of the revolution in Haiti but rather to Richard Allen, who had been showing Americans ever since the Revolution what black people could do for themselves. He quoted what Allen had written in 1827 in *Freedom's Journal: "This land which we have watered with our tears and our blood is now our mother country and we are well satisfied to stay."* Almost prefiguring Martin Luther King, he wrote "what a happy country this will be, if the whites will listen." Almost despite himself, however, Walker honored the Revolution. Emulating the Constitution's structure, he divided his book into a preamble and four articles. At the very end, he quoted extensively from the best language of the Declaration of Independence and called on white Americans to live up to it, if they could. But Walker knew that well-meaning white people could not and would not solve the problem, and he knew as well that in his time very few white Americans were willing to listen.[4]

Walker's book went through three editions in just one year. Free black people in the North devoured it. Seafarers smuggled copies into Southern ports, sewn into the cheap clothing that they bought at Walker's shop.

The mayor of Savannah read the book and wrote in outrage to his Boston counterpart, asking that he silence Walker. The Bostonian had read it too. He replied that he did not like what Walker had written, but that he had no legal authority to silence him. The white reformer William Lloyd Garrison read Walker, reacted at first against Walker's seeming call for violence, and then began to make his historic turn from supporting colonization to denouncing it, and to heeding Walker's cry that "America is as much our country as it is yours."[5]

Walker certainly had more to say, and he might have found a political home in the Abolitionist movement that he helped inspire Garrison to launch. But he was found dead in 1830, only a year after the book came out. Perhaps somebody murdered him; people certainly suspected that was the case. There is no good evidence either way. Certainly there were Southerners who wanted him dead, and equally certainly there were Northerners who would not have stopped an assassin bent on killing him. But for all the scorn and anger that he poured out, Walker was telling the American Republic to live up to what it had said about itself at its birth, or it would fail. He knew that the United States was where the struggle had to be waged.

Twenty-three years later, on July 5, 1852, Frederick Douglass asked the Ladies Anti-Slavery Society of Rochester, New York, to ponder the same question. "What," he asked, "to the Slave is the Fourth of July?"[6] Walker had been relatively obscure when he published his book, but in 1852 Douglass was the most famous black man in the world, known on both sides of the Atlantic. Thanks to advances in print technology, images of his face circulated widely. Nobody who did not know Walker personally would have recognized him on the street, but Douglass was a head-turning celebrity, the first in black history.

He had escaped slavery in Maryland, worked for Garrison's American Anti-Slavery Society, moved from Boston to Rochester, and founded his own newspaper, *The North Star*. He opposed Garrison's belief that slavery's opponents had to stay out of politics, because, Garrison thought, the entire political system was corrupted by slavery. He also opposed his fellow black leader Henry Highland Garnet, debating him in 1849 about taking up arms. Garnet wanted a solution on the model of Haiti; Douglass thought that trying to do it would be suicide and achieve nothing. Douglass supported the women's rights movement that was emerging out of anti-slavery and he took part in the Women's Rights Convention of 1848. He chose the date for his 1852 speech, July 5 rather than July 4, deliberately. The national holiday and the revolution that it honored were well worth celebrating. But they did not belong to him.

Like David Walker, Frederick Douglass understood that black people had to free themselves, and in 1852 freedom looked far away. But like Phillis Wheatley and Benjamin Banneker, he also understood that controlled, directed anger can be just as effective as rage let free. He was a master orator by 1852, one of the very best in a nation that valued the skills of public speaking. He opened his great July 5th address with a tribute to America's white revolutionaries. George Washington, Thomas Jefferson, and their generation had been great men, and they had accomplished great things. Then as he turned his attention from the great story of how white Americans had won their freedom to the problem of enduring black slavery, Douglass conjured up a powerful image, the heavy iron ringbolt that holds the rigging of a sailing vessel to the hull. Rochester faces Lake Ontario, where powerful storms often blow. Douglass's listeners knew what could happen when a storm's winds pushed a vessel's masts, its rigging, and the ringbolt that held the whole vessel together to their limits. Should the ringbolt snap, the vessel and all aboard it were doomed.

The ringbolt was the principles announced in the Declaration of Independence. The storm was the great struggle over slavery. "Stand by [those] principles," Douglass proclaimed, meaning equality and the unalienable human rights to life, liberty, and the pursuit of happiness. "Be true to them," he urged his listeners, "on all occasions, in all places, against all foes, and at whatever cost." The signers of 1776 had been brave, great men. They had understood that "justice, liberty and humanity" rather than slavery and oppression were ultimate values. He put almost no limits on his praise for the Republic's founders. "You may well cherish" their memory, he told his listeners. But their work remained unfinished. "You may rejoice" at this national celebration, but "I must mourn" because "the character and the conduct of this nation never looked blacker to me than on this 4th of July."

Then Douglass took his audience on a tour of slavery, as he had known it. Beyond the national celebrations he heard "the mournful cry of millions." Prefiguring Walt Whitman's first great poem, "Song of Myself" (1855), Douglass recited a litany of all that black men and women were doing in his America. There was absolutely nothing that white Americans were doing that black Americans were not doing as well. But, just as Walker had written, black people were called upon to prove what white people could take for granted, "that we are men!" Douglass went on to describe the horrors of the internal slave trade, which to him was a terrible reality. He had seen the slave markets of Baltimore and the advertisements of traveling slave traders, headed "CASH FOR NEGROES." He had heard the nighttime "dead, heavy footsteps . . . of the chained gangs that passed our door." He had watched slave ships set sail with their human cargoes. Still worse, the Fugitive Slave Law of 1850 had "obliterated" the Mason-Dixon line that separated the slave states from the free. Slavery had become "an institution of the whole United States." What the revolutionary generation had achieved was well on its way to being undone.

Hope did remain, in the form of the American Revolution's final great document, the United States Constitution. Despite its three-fifths clause, fugitive slave clause, and allowance of the African slave trade for two long decades after it took effect, the Constitution was a "GLORIOUS LIBERTY DOCUMENT." For Douglass, nothing in it actually supported slavery, and its "principles and purposes" were "entirely hostile to the existence of slavery." There was hope as well from "the obvious tendencies" of the age, not just in Douglass's America but in the world that the American Revolution had inaugurated. Africa itself, he said at the very end, "must rise and put on her yet unwoven garment." Like Walker, he was addressing the United States. But again like Walker he was reaching beyond his own country to "the Coloured citizens of the world."

The first American Revolution, for independence, republicanism, and national existence, did not end slavery. In all probability, it could not have done so. As the Revolution's events, struggles, conflicts, hopes, fears, triumphs and failures receded into the past and into patriotic, flag-waving, heroic history books, as the people who had made the real difficult, transforming, liberating Revolution died off, and as slavery thrived across the Cotton Kingdom, the United States sank into what seemed to be a new normality in which slavery thrived rather than withered. For decade after decade between George Washington's accession to the presidency in 1789 and Abraham Lincoln's in 1861, most of its citizens and almost all of its politicians agreed that the slavery issue was not to be raised, and did all they could to keep it down.

But the issue had emerged, thanks in good part to what black people of the revolutionary era made of their chances during that time. Once raised, the issue had spread from revolutionary America around a revolutionary Atlantic world. Once it had come forth, it could not be fully repressed, thanks first of all to the black people of the young American republic who would not allow that to happen. They had white allies, of course, but they, more than any others, kept the American Revolution's full promise alive. Douglass, willingly, and Walker, almost despite himself, were sons of an American Revolution that both of them knew had been left incomplete. Neither man is imaginable without what the Revolution had achieved, however incomplete it was.

The American Revolution broke the colonial period's hemisphere-wide assumptions that slavery was just part of life and that any black person probably was a slave. Out of it there emerged the first places in the western hemisphere where every single person, black and white alike, was presumed to be free, not enslaved. There emerged a network of free black communities and organizations where people organized their own civil society, communicated with one another, defended themselves against the hostility of the society that surrounded them, and embarked on the huge project of bringing slavery down.

But the Revolution fostered slavery too. Out of it there also emerged a slave economy more powerful than any that the world had seen, strong enough to dominate the American Republic for decades, to strike for its own independence in order to protect slavery, and to wage an enormous, bloody struggle before it finally failed. There emerged an intense, determined racism, supported, seemingly, by science, religion, law, and history. All across the country, the combination of the actual power of Southern slavery and of racism's new justification for denying that black people really could be equal served to nullify the American Revolution's best promises. In the South, John C. Calhoun could announce in 1837 that slavery was positively good. In the North, the vast majority of white people came to not care about the slavery issue at all. But South and North alike, they found that the problem would not disappear, primarily because the black people all around them would not let it disappear.

One of the revolutionary principles of 1776, that an aggrieved people may overturn an oppressive government, underpinned the white South's abortive attempt for separate, slave-holding nationhood between 1861 and 1865. The secessionists regarded themselves as an aggrieved people, and they made that plain. Preserving slavery and the way of life it made possible for them was more important than preserving the United States.

But the secessionists made it even more plain that they were seeking nationhood in outright denial of the other great principles of 1776, which are that all men are created equal and that life, liberty, and the pursuit of happiness are human rights. They were denying that black Americans could be members of the People of the United States, and that they, as much as anybody else, deserved what the Constitution called the "blessings of liberty." Everybody knew as the United States broke up that slavery was the underlying issue. White Southerners said so openly. Black people both North and South knew it too. Abraham Lincoln admitted it in his greatest speech, as he accepted the presidency for the second time in 1865. Ending slavery's long reincarnation as Jim Crow required yet another intense struggle, in the form of the twentieth-century movement for Civil Rights. That struggle likewise exacted a huge cost.

The shadow of American slavery is not fully gone yet. But from the time of Phillis Wheatley and Elizabeth Freeman through that of Civil Rights activists Rosa Parks and Fannie Lou Hamer to that of former Secretary of State Condoleezza Rice and first lady Michelle Obama, from the era that spanned Benjamin Banneker, Richard Allen, James Forten, David Walker, and Frederick Douglass to the epoch of first black Supreme Court Justice Thurgood Marshall, Malcolm X, Martin Luther King, former Secretary of State Colin Powell, and President Barack Obama, black Americans have called and called again upon the United States to live up to the high, still-unfinished task that it set for itself when it first began to assume its separate and equal station among the powers of the earth. The black Americans who began to force slavery open during the founding era, and the black Americans ever since then who have struggled, protested, and fought whenever the country has backslid, deserve as much honor as anybody in the pages of American history. None have earned such honor against greater odds.

Notes

1. New York State Constitution of 1821, Article II, Section 1.

2. David Walker, *Appeal to the Coloured Citizens of the World, but in particular, and very expressly, to those of the United States of America*, ed. Sean Wilentz (New York: Hill & Wang, 1995), iii, 30, 28, 29, xxvi.

3. Walker, *Appeal*, 72, 69–70.

4. Walker, *Appeal*, 21, 35-36, 40–41, 26–28, 41, 57, 70.

5. Walker, *Appeal*, 70.

6. All remaining quotations from Frederick Douglass, "What to the Slave is the Fourth of July" (July 5, 1852), *The Frederick Douglass Papers*, ed. John W. Blassingame, series 1, vol. 2 (New Haven: Yale University Press, 1982), 359–88.

~

Documents

The Beginnings of American Slave Law

The two excerpts that follow illustrate the differences between the law of slavery in the New World, as imported by Spanish colonizers and as created by British colonists. The Spanish document lists the many separate headings of medieval Spanish slave law in Las Siete Partidas, codified by King Alfonso el Sabio ("the Wise"). The actual text covers many pages. Even the headings indicate the complexity of Spanish law, the existence of rights and privileges for slaves, and many paths to freedom that a slave might follow. The Virginia Code of 1703, by contrast, was made in Virginia, to serve masters' purposes. Note that, although Spanish law made "injury to slave" a ground for ending enslavement, Virginia law protected masters who injured their slaves against all criminal charges.

The Headings of Medieval Spanish Slave Law

Partida 4:

Title XXI: Slavery

Law I: Nature and Sources

Law II: When One Parent is Free

Law III: Sons of Priests are Slaves of the Church

Law IV: Christians Become Slaves by Aiding the Enemy

Law V: Slave's Duty to Protect Master

Law VI: Master's Authority Over Slave

Law VII: Master's Right to Slave's *Peculium*

Law VIII: Christians Cannot Be Slaves of Non-Christians

Title XXII: Freedom
Law I: Nature and Source
Law II: Enfranchisement When Slave Has Two Masters
Law III: Emancipation for Good Conduct
Law IV: Emancipation by Injury to Slave
Law V: Emancipation by Marriage
Law VI: Emancipation by Receiving Holy Orders
Law VII: Emancipation by Prescription
Law VIII: Emancipated Slave's Duties
Law IX: Re-Enslavement After Emancipation
Law X: Master's Right in Emancipated Slave's Property
Source: *Las Siete Partidas, Volume 4*
Family, Commerce, and the Sea: The Worlds of Women and Merchants (Partidas
IV and V), Translated by Samuel Parsons Scott. Edited by Robert I. Burns,
S.J, xlix.

Virginia Law of Slavery, 1705

An act concerning Servants and Slaves . . .
IV. And also be it enacted, by the authority aforesaid, and it is hereby enacted,
That all servants imported and brought into this country, by sea or land, who
were not christians in their native country, (except Turks and Moors in amity
with her majesty, and others that can make due proof of their being free in
England, or any other christian country, before they were shipped, in order to
transportation hither) shall be accounted and be slaves, and as such be here
bought and sold notwithstanding a conversion to christianity afterwards. . . .
XI. And for a further christian care and usage of all christian servants, Be it also
enacted, by the authority aforesaid, and it is hereby enacted, That no negros,
mulattos, or Indians, although christians, or Jews, Moors, Mahometans, or
other infidels, shall, at any time, purchase any christian servant, nor any other,
except of their own complexion, or such as are declared slaves by this act: And
if any negro, mulatto, or Indian, Jew, Moor, Mahometan, or other infidel, or
such as are declared slaves by this act, shall, notwithstanding, purchase any
christian white servant, the said servant shall, ipso facto, become free and
acquit from any service then due, and shall be so held, deemed, and taken:
And if any person, having such christian servant, shall intermarry with any
such negro, mulatto, or Indian, Jew, Moor, Mahometan, or other infidel, every
christian white servant of every such person so intermarrying, shall, ipso facto,
become free and acquit from any service then due to such master or mistress so
intermarrying, as aforesaid. . . .
XXIII. And for encouragement of all persons to take up runaways, Be it enacted, by the authority aforesaid, and it is hereby enacted, That for the taking

up of every servant, or slave, if ten miles, or above, from the house or quarter where such servant, or slave was kept, there shall be allowed by the public, as a reward to the taker-up, two hundred pounds of tobacco; and if above five miles, and under ten, one hundred pounds of tobacco: Which said several rewards of two hundred, and one hundred pounds of tobacco, shall also be paid in the county where such taker-up shall reside, and shall be again levied by the public upon the master or owner of such runaway, for re-imbursement of the same to the public. And for the greater certainty in paying the said rewards and re-imbursement of the public, every justice of the peace before whom such runaway shall be brought, upon the taking up, shall mention the proper-name and sur-name of the taker-up, and the county of his or her residence, together with the time and place of taking up the said runaway; and shall also mention the name of the said runaway, and the proper-name and sur-name of the master or owner of such runaway, and the county of his or her residence, together with the distance of miles, in the said justice's judgment, from the place of taking up the said runaway, to the house or quarter where such runaway was kept. . . .

XXVI. Provided always, and be it further enacted, That when any servant or slave, in his or her running away, shall have crossed the great bay of Chesapeak, and shall be brought before a justice of the peace, the said justice shall, instead of committing such runaway to the constable, commit him or her to the sheriff, who is hereby required to receive every such runaway, according to such warrant, and to cause him, her, or them, to be transported again across the bay, and delivered to a constable there; and shall have, for all his trouble and charge herein, for every such servant or slave, five hundred pounds of tobacco, paid by the public; which shall be re-imbursed again by the master or owner of such runaway, as aforesaid, in manner aforesaid. . . .

XXXII. And also be it enacted, by the authority aforesaid, and it is hereby enacted, That no master, mistress, or overseer of a family, shall knowingly permit any slave, not belonging to him or her, to be and remain upon his or her plantation, above four hours at any one time, without the leave of such slave's master, mistress, or overseer, on penalty of one hundred and fifty pounds of tobacco to the informer; cognizable by a justice of the peace of the county wherein such offence shall be committed. . . .

XXXIV. And if any slave resist his master, or owner, or other person, by his or her order, correcting such slave, and shall happen to be killed in such correction, it shall not be accounted felony; but the master, owner, and every such other person so giving correction, shall be free and acquit of all punishment and accusation for the same, as if such accident had never happened: And also, if any negro, mulatto, or Indian, bond or free, shall at any time, lift his or her hand, in opposition against any christian, not being negro, mulatto, or Indian, he or she so offending, shall, for every such offence, proved by the oath of the party, receive on his or her bare back, thirty lashes, well laid on;

cognizable by a justice of the peace for that county wherein such offence shall be committed. . . .

XXXVI. And also it is hereby enacted and declared, That baptism of slaves doth not exempt them from bondage; and that all children shall be bond or free, according to the condition of their mothers, and the particular directions of this act.

Source: www.law.du.edu/russell/lh/alh/docs/virginiaslaverystatutes.html, accessed May 5, 2011.

From the Trial Records of the New York City Slave Conspiracy, 1741

White servant Mary Burton worked in John Hughson's New York tavern where a plot was supposedly hatched among slaves and poor white New Yorkers to burn the city. The testimony that she provided was recorded in the volume published by Justice Daniel Horsmanden, who presided over the trials that condemned both black slaves and supposed white accomplices to death for their parts in the plot. She was instrumental in bringing about several of the death sentences. After her testimony several of the accused slaves were brought before the court. In contrast to Burton's testimony, the record contains only what was said to them and provides no information as to what they had to say on behalf of themselves.

Supreme Court
  Wednesday, April 22 [1741]
  Deposition, No. 1—Mary Burton [a servant], being sworn, deposeth,
  1. "That Prince [Mr. Auboyneau's slave] and Caesar [Mr. Varack's slave] brought the things which they had robbed . . . to her master, John Hughson's house . . . about two or three o'clock on a Sunday morning [March 1, 1740]."
  2. "That Caesar, Prince and Mr. Philipse's Negro man (Cuffee) used to meet frequently at her master's house, and that she had heard them (the Negroes) talk frequently of burning the fort; and that they would go down to the Fly [the city's east end] and burn the whole town; and that her master and mistress said, they would aid and assist them as much as they could."
  3. "That in their common conversation they used to say, that when all this was done, Caesar should be governor, and Hughson, her master, should be king."
  4. "That Cuffee used to say, that a great many people had too much, and others too little; that his old master had a great deal of money, but that, in a short time, he should have less, and that he (Cuffee) should have more. . . ."
  7. "That she had known at times, seven or eight guns in her master's house, and some swords, and that she had seen twenty or thirty Negroes at one time in her master's house. . . ."

This evidence of a conspiracy, not only to burn the city, but also destroy and murder the people, was most astonishing to the grand jury, and that any white people should become so abandoned as to confederate with slaves in such an execrable and detestable purpose, could not but be very amazing to every one that heard it. . . .

[A Justice administers the sentence to Quack and Cuffee]

You both now stand convicted of one of the most horrid and detestable pieces of villainy, that ever satan instilled into the heart of human creatures to put in practice; ye, and the rest of your colour, though you are called slaves in this country; yet are you all far from the condition of other slaves in other countries; nay, your lot is superior to that of thousands of white people. You are furnished with all the necessaries of life, meat, drink, and clothing, without care, in a much better manner than you could provide for yourselves, were you at liberty; as the miserable condition of many free people here of your complexion might abundantly convince you. What then could prompt you to undertake so vile, so wicked, so monstrous, so execrable and hellish a scheme, as to murder and destroy your own masters and benefactors? nay, to destroy root and branch, all the white people of this place, and to lay the whole town in ashes.

I know not which is more astonishing, the extreme folly, or wickedness, of so base and shocking a conspiracy. . . . What could it be expected to end in, in the account of any rational and considerate person among you, but your own destruction?

Source: www.digitalhistory.uh.edu/documents/documents_p2.cfm?doc=231, accessed May 5, 2011.

Samuel Sewall, *The Selling of Joseph*

Samuel Sewall may have written The Selling of Joseph *to atone for his role as a judge on the court that had condemned the accused Salem witches during that village's witchcraft scare of 1691–1692. The pamphlet is one of the earliest English-language attacks on human slavery and set the tone for future Christian anti-slavery writing.*

The Selling of JOSEPH
A Memorial.
And seeing GOD hath said, *He that Stealeth a Man and Selleth him, or if he be found in his hand, he shall surely be put to Death.* Exod. 12.16. This Law being of Everlasting Equity, wherein Man Stealing is ranked amongst the most atrocious of Capital Crimes: What louder Cry can there be made of the Celebrated Warning,

And all thing considered, it would conduce more to the Welfare of the Province, to have White Servants for a Term of Years, than to have Slaves for Life. Few can endure to hear of a Negro's being made free; and indeed they can seldom use their freedom well; yet their continual aspiring after their forbidden Liberty, renders them Unwilling Servants. And there is such a disparity in their Conditions, Color & Hair, that they can never embody with us, and grow up into orderly Families, to the Peopling of the Land: but still remain in our Body Politick as a kind of extra-vasat Blood. As many Negro men as there are among us, so many empty places there are in our Train Bands, and the places taken up of Men that might make Husbands for our Daughters. And the Sons and Daughters of *New England* would become more like *Jacob*, and *Rachel*, if this Slavery were thrust quite out of doors. Moreover it is too well known what Temptations Masters are under, to connive at the Fornification of their Slaves; lest they should be obliged to find them Wives, or pay their Fines. It seems to be practically pleaded that they might be Lawless; 'tis thought much of, that the Law should have Satisfaction for their Thefts, and other Immoralities; by which means, *Holiness to the Lord*, is more rarely engraven upon this sort of Servitude. It is likewise most lamentable to think, how in taking Negros out of *Africa*, and Selling of them here, That which GOD ha's joyned together men do boldly rend asunder; Men from their Country, Husbands from their Wives, Parents from their Children. How horrible is the Uncleanness, Mortality, if not Murder, that the Ships are guilty of that bring great Crouds of these miserable Men, and Women. Methinks, when we are bemoaning the barbarous Usage of our Friends and Kinsfolk in *Africa*: it might not be unseasonable to enquire whether we are not culpable in forcing the *Africans* to become Slaves amongst our selves. And it may be a question whether all the Benefit received by *Negro* Slaves, will balance the Accompt of Cash laid out upon them; and for the Redemption of our own enslaved Friends out of *Africa*. Besides all the Persons and Estates that have perished there.

Obj. 1. *These Blackamores are of the Posterity of* Cham, *and therefore are under the Curse of Slavery.* Gen. 9.25, 26, 27.

Answ. Of all Offices, one would not begg this; *viz.* Uncall'd for, to be an Executioner of the Vindictive Wrath of God; the extent and duration of which is to us uncertain. If this ever was a Commission; How do we know but that it is long since out of date? Many have found it to their Cost, that a Prophetical Denunciation of Judgment against a Person or People, would not warrant them to inflict that evil. If it would, *Hazael* might justify himself in all he did against his Master, and the *Israelites*, from 2 *Kings* 8. 10, 12.

But it is possible that by cursory reading, this Text may have been mistaken. For *Canaan* is the Person Cursed three times over, without the mentioning of *Cham*. Good Expositors suppose the Curse entailed on him, and that this Prophesie was accomplished in the Extirpation of the *Canaanites*, and in the

Servitude of the *Gibeonites, Vide Pareum*. Whereas the Blackmores are not descended of *Canaan*, but of *Cush*. Psal. 68. 31. *Princes shall come out of Egypt* [Mizraim] *Ethopia* [Cush] *shall soon stretch out her hands unto God*. Under which Names, all *Africa* may be comprehended; and the Promised Conversion ought to be prayed for. *Jer.* 13, 23. *Can the Ethiopian change his skin?* This shews that Black Men are the Posterity of *Cush:* Who time out of mind have been distinguished by their Colour.

Obj. 2. *The* Nigers *are brought out of a Pagan Country, into places where the Gospel is Preached.*

Answ. Evil must not be done, that good may come of it. The extraordinary and comprehensive Benefit accruing to the Church of God, and to *Joseph* personally, did not rectify his brethrens Sale of him.

Obj. 3. *The* Africans *have Wars with one another: our Ships bring lawful Captives taken in those Wars.*

Answ. For ought is known, their Wars are much such as were between *Jacob's* Sons and their Brother *Joseph*. If they be between Town and Town; Provincial, or National: Every War is upon one side Unjust. An Unlawful War can't make lawful Captives. And by Receiving, we are in danger to promote, and partake in their Barbarous Cruelties. I am sure, if some Gentlemen should go down to the *Brewsters* to take the Air, and Fish: And a stronger party from *Hull* should Surprise them, and Sell them for Slaves to a Ship outward bound: they would think themselves unjustly dealt with; both by Sellers and Buyers. And yet 'tis to be feared, we have no other kind of Title to our *Nigers. Therefore all things whatsoever ye would that men should do to you, do ye even so to them: for this is the Law and the Prophets.* Matt. 7. 12.

Obj. 4. Abraham *had servants bought with his Money, and born in his House.*

Answ. Until the Circumstances of *Abraham's* purchase be recorded, no Argument can be drawn from it. In the mean time, Charity obliges us to conclude, that He knew it was lawful and good.

It is Observable that the *Israelites* were strictly forbidden the buying, or selling one another for Slaves. *Levit.* 25. 39, 46. *Jer.* 34. 8–22. And GOD gaged His Blessing in lieu of any loss they might conceipt they suffered thereby. *Deut.* 15. 18. And since the partition Wall is broken down, inordinate Self love should likewise be demolished. GOD expects that Christians should be of a more Ingenuous and benign frame of spirit. Christians should carry it to all the World, as the *Israelites* were to carry it one towards another. And for men obstinately to persist in holding their Neighbours and Brethren under the Rigor of perpetual Bondage, seems to be no proper way of gaining Assurance that God ha's given them Spiritual Freedom. Our Blessed Saviour ha's altered the Measures of the Ancient Love-Song, and set it to a most Excellent New Tune, which all ought to be ambitious of Learning. *Matt.* 5. 43, 44. *John* 13. 34. These *Ethiopians*, as black as they are; seeing they are the Sons and Daughters of the

First *Adam*, the Brethren and Sister of the Last ADAM, and the Offspring of GOD; They ought to be treated with a Respect agreeable.

BOSTON of the Massachusetts;

Source: Printed by *Bartholomew Green*, and *John Allen*, June, 24th. 1700.

Lord Mansfield's Opinion in *Somerset* [or Sommersett, Somersett] *v. Steuart* [or Stewart], 1772

Although anti-slavery opinion was building in Britain as well as in America during the years immediately prior to American Independence, the decision in the Somerset case was the first public position on the matter by a high British official. Note Lord Mansfield's clear indications that he is troubled by having to rule in favor of James Somerset rather than in favor of his alleged master Charles Steuart (or Stewart). Note also how Mansfield follows the logic of the law, and how he limits his opinion to Somerset's own case, with no explicit expansion of the matter to a general anti-slavery enactment. Compare Mansfield's language here with Thomas Jefferson's language on slavery in the Declaration of Independence *(1776) (discussed in chapter 2) and with Massachusetts Chief Justice William Cushing's language in the* Quok Walker *case (1783, below).*

Lord *Mansfield.*—On the part of Sommerset, the case which we gave notice should be decided this day, the Court now proceeds to give its opinion.

I shall recite the return to the writ of Habeas Corpus, as the ground of determination; omitting only words of form.

The captain of the ship on board of which the negro was taken, makes his return to the writ in terms signifying that there have been, and still are, slaves to a great number in Africa, and that the trade in them is authorized by the laws and opinions of Virginia and Jamaica; that they are goods and chattels; and, as such, saleable and sold.

That James Sommerset, is a negro of Africa, and long before the return of the king's writ was brought to be sold, and was sold to Charles Stewart, Esq. then in Jamaica, and has not been manumitted since; that Mr. Stewart, having occasion to transact business, came over hither, with an intention to return; and brought Sommerset, to attend and abide with him, and to carry him back as soon as the business should be transacted.

That such intention has been, and still continues; and that the negro did remain till the time of his departure, in the service of his master Mr. Stewart, and quitted it without his consent; and thereupon, before the return of the king's writ, the said Charles Stewart did commit the slave on board the "Ann and Mary," to save custody, to be kept till he should set sail, and then to be taken with him to Jamaica, and there sold as a slave.

And this is the cause why he, captain Knowles, who was then and now is commander of the slave vessel, then and now lying in the river of [19] Thames, did the said negro, committed to his custody, detain; and on which he now surrenders him to the order of the Court.

We pay all due attention to the opinion of sir Philip Yorke, and lord chancellor Talbot whereby they pledged themselves to the British planters, for all the legal consequences of slaves coming over to this kingdom or being baptized, recognized by lord Hardwicke, sitting as chancellor on the 19th of October 1749, that trover would lie: that a notion had prevailed, if a negro came over, or became a Christian, he was emancipated, but no ground in law; that he and Lord Talbot, when Attorney and Solicitor-General, were of opinion, that no such claim for freedom was valid; that though the Statute of Tenures had abolished "*villeins regardant to a manor*," yet he did not conceive but that a man might still become a "*villein in gross*," by confessing himself such in open Court.

We are so well agreed, that we think there is no occasion of having it argued (as I intimated an intention at first,) before all the judges, as is usual, for obvious reasons, on a return to a Habeas Corpus. The only question before us is, whether the cause on the return is sufficient. If it is, the negro must be remanded [to the master]; if it is not, he must be discharged [freed].

Accordingly, the return states, that the slave departed [fled] and refused to serve; whereupon he was kept [detained without due process], to be sold abroad.

So high an act of dominion must be recognized by the law of the country where it is used. The power of a master over his slave has been exceedingly different, in different countries.

The state of slavery is of such a nature, that it is incapable of being introduced on any reasons, moral or political, but only by positive [written] law, which preserves its force long after the reasons, occasion, and time itself from whence it was created, is erased from memory. It is so odious, that nothing can be suffered to support it, but positive law.

Whatever inconveniences, therefore, may follow from the decision, I cannot say this case is allowed or approved by the law of England; and therefore the black must be discharged.

Source: 20 Howell's State Trials 1, 79–82.

The Emergence of Black Protest

It is extremely difficult to listen in on the thoughts and voices of enslaved black people during the colonial period. But the independence crisis brought the chance to speak and to write about their case. The petition of Peter Bestes, Sambo Freeman, Felix Holbrook, and Chester Joie in 1773 offers a prime example. They offered their petition prior to the final crisis, which began with the destruction of East India Company tea by Bostonians at the end of 1773. It was not yet clear that Britain and the colonies would separate, but Bestes, Freeman, Holbrook, and Joie were paying close attention. Note their use of the white revolutionaries' own language, their assertion of their right to reparations for what they had endured, their understanding of the differences between their enslavement and enslavement under Spanish law, and their desire to return to Africa. This petition is just one example of how black people began to speak out on their own behalf as relations worsened between Britain and white colonists.

Sir, The efforts made by the legislative of this province in their last sessions to free themselves from slavery, gave us, who are in that deplorable state, a high degree of satisfaction. We expect great things from men who have made such a noble stand against the designs of their *fellow-men* to enslave them. . . .

We do not pretend to dictate to you Sir, or to the honorable Assembly, of which you are a member: We acknowledge our obligations to you for what you have already done, but as the people of this province seem to be actuated by the principles of equity and justice, we cannot but expect your house will again take our deplorable case into serious consideration, and give us that ample relief which, as men, we have a natural right to.

But since the wise and righteous governor of the universe, has permitted our fellow men to make us slaves, we bow in submission to him, and determine to behave in such a manner, as that we may have reason to expect the divine approbation of, and assistance in, our peaceable and lawful attempts to gain our freedom.

We are willing to submit to such regulations and laws, as may be made relative to us, until we leave the province, which we determine to do as soon as we can from our joynt labours procare money to transport ourselves to some part of the coast of *Africa*, where we propose a settlement. We are very desirous that you should have instructions relative to us, from your town, therefore we pray you to communicate this letter to them, and ask this favor for us.

In behalf of our fellow slaves in this province,
And by order of their Committee,

PETER BESTES,
SAMBO FREEMAN,
FELIX HOLBROOK,
CHESTER JOIE.

For the REPRESENTATIVE of the town of Thompson
April 20, 1773.

Source: Boston, no printer, 1773.

The Continental Association, 1774

Late in the summer of 1774 the First Continental Congress gathered in Philadelphia to work out a common American position in response to Britain's punishment of Boston for destroying East India Company tea in December, 1773. The result was the Continental Association, a voluntary agreement to end all commerce with Britain until the punishments were rescinded. One of its provisions was an absolute end to the slave trade. The ban marked the high point of white Americans acting as a whole against slavery until the Thirteenth Amendment to the Constitution in 1865. Note how the Congress linked stopping the slave trade directly to the American cause by making it the second item on the Association.

We, his majesty's most loyal subjects, the delegates of the several colonies of New-Hampshire, Massachusetts-Bay, Rhode-Island, Connecticut, New-York, New-Jersey, Pennsylvania, the three lower counties of Newcastle, Kent and Sussex on Delaware, Maryland, Virginia, North-Carolina, and South-Carolina, deputed to represent them in a continental Congress, held in the city of Philadelphia, on the 5th day of September, 1774, avowing our allegiance to his majesty, our affection and regard for our fellow-subjects in Great-Britain and elsewhere, affected with the deepest anxiety, and most alarming apprehensions, at those grievances and distresses, with which his Majesty's American subjects are oppressed; and having taken under our most serious deliberation, the state of the whole continent, find, that the present unhappy situation of our affairs is occasioned by a ruinous system of colony administration, adopted by the British ministry about the year 1763, evidently calculated for enslaving these colonies, and, with them, the British Empire. In prosecution of which system, various acts of parliament have been passed, for raising a revenue in America, for depriving the American subjects, in many instances, of the constitutional trial by jury, exposing their lives to danger, by directing a new and illegal trial beyond the seas, for crimes alleged to have been committed in America: And in prosecution of the same system, several late, cruel, and oppressive acts have been passed, respecting the town of Boston and the Massachusetts-Bay, and also an act for extending the province of Quebec, so as to border on the western frontiers of these colonies, establishing an arbitrary government therein, and discouraging the settlement of British subjects in that wide extended country; thus, by the influence of civil principles and ancient prejudices, to dispose the inhabitants to act with hostility against the free Protestant colonies, whenever a wicked ministry shall chuse so to direct them. To obtain redress of these grievances, which threaten destruction to the lives, liberty, and property of his majesty's subjects, in North-America, we are of opinion, that a non-importation, non-consumption, and non-exportation agreement, faithfully adhered to, will prove the most speedy, effectual, and peaceable measure: And, therefore, we do, for ourselves, and the inhabitants of the several colonies, whom we represent, firmly agree and associate, under the sacred ties of virtue, honour and love of our country, as follows:

1. That from and after the first day of December next, we will not import, into British America, from Great-Britain or Ireland, any goods, wares, or merchandise whatsoever, or from any other place, any such goods, wares, or merchandise, as shall have been exported from Great-Britain or Ireland; nor will we, after that day, import any East-India tea from any part of the world; nor any molasses, syrups, paneles, coffee, or pimento, from the British planta-tions or from Dominica; nor wines from Madeira, or the Western Islands; nor foreign indigo.

2. We will neither import nor purchase, any slave imported after the first day of December next; after which time, we will wholly discontinue the slave trade, and will neither be concerned in it ourselves, nor will we hire our vessels, nor sell our commodities or manufactures to those who are concerned in it.

Source: Journals of the Continental Congress, October 20, 1774.

Lord Dunmore's Proclamation and the Patriot Response, November, 1774

When war broke out in Massachusetts in April, 1775, word spread very fast. In Williamsburg, Virginia, slaves approached the province's royal governor John Mur-ray, Earl of Dunmore, in the spring of 1775, offering their aid. Dunmore sent them away. He finally responded to their offer in November, 1774. Note that Dunmore was not offering a general emancipation, just freedom for slaves and servants of rebels who were willing to fight on the king's side. Nonetheless, together with Lord Mansfield, he seemed to be aligning the royal side with the interests of slaves. The response of the Virginia leaders showed their fright at his action, and their unwilling-ness to link the slavery issue to their own protests.

By His Excellency the Right Honourable John, Earl of Dunmore, His Maj-esty's Lieutenant and Governor of the Colony and Dominion of Virginia, A PROCLAMATION

As I have ever entertained Hopes, that an Accommodation might have taken Place between GREAT-BRITAIN and this Colony, without being

compelled by my Duty to this most disagreeable but now absolutely necessary Step, rendered so by a Body of armed Men unlawfully assembled, firing
on His MAJESTY'S Tenders, and the formation of an Army, and that Army
now on their March to attack his MAJESTY'S Troops and destroy the well
disposed subjects of the Colony. To defeat such treasonable Purposes, and
that all such Traitors, and their Abettors, may be brought to Justice, and that
the Peace, and good Order of this Colony may be again restored, which the
ordinary Course of the Civil Law is unable to effect; I have thought fit to issue
this my Proclamation, hereby declaring, that until the aforesaid good Purpose
can be obtained, I do in Virtue of the Power and Authority to ME given, by
His MAJESTY, determine to execute Martial Law, and cause the same to be
executed throughout this Colony: and to end that the Peace and good Order
may the sooner be restored, I do require every Person capable of bearing Arms,
to resort to His MAJESTY'S STANDARD, or be looked upon as Traitors
to His MAJESTY'S Crown and Government, and thereby become liable to
the Penalty the Law inflicts upon such Offenses; such as forfeiture of Life,
confiscation of Lands, &. &. And I do hereby further declare all indented
Servants, Negroes, or others, (appertaining to Rebels,) free that are able and
willing to bear Arms, they joining His MAJESTY'S Troops as soon as may be,
foe the more speedily reducing this Colony to a proper Sense of their Duty,
to His MAJESTY'S Crown and Dignity. I do further order, and require, all
His MAJESTY'S Liege Subjects, to retain their Quitrents, or any other Taxes
due or that may become due, in their own Custody, till such a Time as Peace
may be again restored to this at present most unhappy Country, or demanded
of them for their former salutary Purposes, by Officers properly authorized to
receive the same.

GIVEN under my Hand on board the Ship WILLIAM by Norfolk, the 7th Day
of November in the SIXTEENTH Year of His MAJESTY'S Reign.
DUNMORE
(GOD save the KING.)

Source: By His Excellency the Right Honourable John Earl of Dunmore, His
Majesty's lieutenant and governour-general of the colony and dominion of
Virginia, and vice admiral of the same: a proclamation (Norfolk, Va.: John
H. Holt, 1775).

A Patriot Response

The second class of people, for whose sake a few remarks upon this proclamation seem necessary, is the *Negroes*. They have been flattered with their
freedom, if they be able to bear arms, and will spedily join Lord *Dunmore's*
troops. To none then is freedom promised but to such as are able to do Lord

Dunmore service: The aged, the infirm, the women and children, are still to remain the property of their masters, masters who will be provoked to severity, should part of their slaves desert them. Lord *Dunmore's* declaration, therefore, is a cruel declaration to the Negroes. He does not even pretend to make it out of any tenderness to them, but solely on his own account; and should it meet with success, it leaves by far the greater number at the mercy of an enraged and injured people. But should there be any amongst the Negroes weak enough to believe that *Dunmore* intends to do them a kindness, and wicked enough to provoke the fury of the Americans against their defenceless fathers and mothers, their wives, their women and children, let them only consider the difficulty of effecting their escape, and what they must expect to suffer if they fall into the hands of the Americans. Let them farther consider what must be their fate, should the English prove conquerors in this dispute. If we can judge of the future from the past, it will not be much mended. Long have the Americans, moved by compassion, and actuated by sound policy, endeavoured to stop the progress of slavery. Our Assemblies have repeatedly passed acts laying heavy duties upon imported Negroes, by which they meant altogether to prevent the horrid traffick; but their humane intentions have been as often frustrated by the cruelty and covetousness of a set of English merchants, who prevailed upon the King to repeal our kind and merciful acts, little indeed to the credit of his humanity. Can it then be supposed that the Negroes will be better used by the English, who have always encouraged and upheld this slavery, than by their present masters, who pity their condition, who wish, in general, to make is as easy and comfortable as possible, and who would willingly, were it in their power, or were they permitted, not only prevent any more Negroes from losing their freedom, but restore it to such as have already unhappily lost it. No, the ends of Lord *Dunmore* and his party being answered, they will either give up the offending Negroes to the rigour of the laws they have broken, or sell them in the West Indies, where every year they sell many thousands of their miserable brethren, to perish either by the inclemency of the weather, or the cruelty of barbarous masters. Be not then, ye Negroes, tempted by this proclamation to ruin yourselves. I have given you a faithful view of what you are to expect; and I declare, before GOD, in doing it, I have considered your welfare, as well as that of the country. Whether you will profit by my advice I cannot tell; but this I know, that whether we suffer or not, if you desert us, you most certainly will.

Source: *Virginia Gazette*, November 5, 1775.

Phillis Wheatley's Emerging Language of Liberty

Phillis Wheatley's poetry and letters reveal her growing sense of the wrongfulness of slavery. Compare her poem "On Being Brought from Africa to America," in which she accepts her captivity, her poetic address to Lord Dartmouth, colonial secretary in London, in which she links her own situation to the colonial outcry, and her letter to Mohegan Indian minister Reverend Samson Occum, in which she makes common cause with Native Americans. The two poems appeared in the volume of her poetry published in London in 1773. They are undated, but apparently are arranged in the order in which she wrote them.

On Being Brought from Africa to America

'Twas <u>mercy</u> brought me from my Pagan land,
Taught my <u>benighted</u> soul to understand
That there's a God, that there's a <u>Saviour too</u>:
<u>Once</u> I redemption neither sought nor knew.
Some view our <u>sable</u> race with scornful eye,
"Their colour is a <u>diabolic die</u>."
<u>Remember, Christians</u>, Negros, black as <u>Cain</u>,
May be <u>refin'd</u> and join th'angelic train.

To the Right Honorable William, Earl of Dartmouth

Hail, happy day, when, smiling like the morn,
Fair Freedom rose New-England to adorn:
The northern clime beneath her genial ray,
Dartmouth, congratulates thy blissful sway:
Elate with hope her race no longer mourns,
Each soul expands, each grateful bosom burns,
While in thine hand with pleasure we behold
The silken reins, and Freedom's charms unfold.
Long lost to realms beneath the northern skies

She shines supreme, while hated faction dies:
Soon as appear'd the Goddess long desir'd,
Sick at the view, she languish'd and expir'd;
Thus from the splendors of the morning light
The owl in sadness seeks the caves of night.
No more, America, in mournful strain
Of wrongs, and grievance unredress'd complain,
No longer shalt thou dread the iron chain,
Which wanton Tyranny with lawless hand
Had made, and with it meant t' enslave the land.

Should you, my lord, while you peruse my song,
Wonder from whence my love of Freedom sprung,

Whence flow these wishes for the common good,
By feeling hearts alone best understood,
I, young in life, by seeming cruel fate
Was snatch'd from Afric's fancy'd happy seat:
What pangs excruciating must molest,
What sorrows labour in my parent's breast?
Steel'd was that soul and by no misery mov'd
That from a father seiz'd his babe belov'd:
Such, such my case. And can I then but pray
Others may never feel tyrannic sway?

For favours past, great Sir, our thanks are due,
And thee we ask thy favours to renew,
Since in thy pow'r, as in thy will before,
To sooth the griefs, which thou did'st once deplore.
May heav'nly grace the sacred sanction give
To all thy works, and thou for ever live
Not only on the wings of fleeting Fame,
Though praise immortal crowns the patriot's name,
But to conduct to heav'ns refulgent fane,
May fiery coursers sweep th' ethereal plain,
And bear thee upwards to that blest abode,
Where, like the prophet, thou shalt find thy God.

Source: Phillis Wheatley, *Poems on Various Subjects, Religious and Moral* (London: A. Bell, 1773).

Wheatley Shares her Mind with Reverend Samson Occum

Rev'd and honor'd Sir,

I have this Day received your obliging kind Epistle, and am greatly satisfied with your Reasons respecting the Negroes, and think highly reasonable what you offer in Vindication of their natural Rights: Those that invade them cannot be insensible that the divine Light is chasing away the thick Darkness which broods over the Land of Africa; and the Chaos which has reign'd so long, is converting into beautiful Order, and [r]eveals more and more clearly, the glorious Dispensation of civil and religious Liberty, which are so inseparably Limited, that there is little or no Enjoyment of one Without the other: Otherwise, perhaps, the Israelites had been less solicitous for their Freedom from Egyptian slavery; I do not say they would have been contented without it, by no means, for in every human Breast, God has implanted a Principle, which we call Love of Freedom; it is impatient of Oppression, and pants for

Deliverance; and by the Leave of our modern Egyptians I will assert, that the same Principle lives in us. God grant Deliverance in his own Way and Time, and get him honour upon all those whose Avarice impels them to countenance and help forward tile Calamities of their fellow Creatures. This I desire not for their Hurt, but to convince them of the strange Absurdity of their Conduct whose Words and Actions are so diametrically, opposite. How well the Cry for Liberty, and the reverse Disposition for the exercise of oppressive Power over others agree. . . .

Source: *Massachusetts Gazette*, 24 March 1774.

Vermont, Pennsylvania, and Massachusetts Abolish Slavery

The destruction of slavery in the Northern states was a state-by-state process. Vermont ended it in one stroke, by the first clause in the bill of rights that the state adopted in 1777, when it declared its independence from New York. Pennsylvania began to end it by the gradual manumission law that it adopted in 1780, but the act took effect very slowly and it had not completely finished its work by the time of the Civil War. Slavery died in Massachusetts by decision of the chief justice of the commonwealth in 1783, on the basis of the Massachusetts Bill of Rights adopted in 1780. Note the contrast between the terse, tight language of the Vermont Bill of Rights and the Massachusetts decision and the wordiness of Pennsylvania's law. Note also the self-congratulation of Pennsylvania's lawmakers, as if the gradual abolition law finished what, in fact, it had barely begun.

Vermont: A Declaration of the Rights of the Inhabitants of the State of Vermont

I. That all men are born equally free and independent, and have certain natural, inherent, and unalienable rights, amongst which are the enjoying and defending life and liberty; acquiring, possessing, and protecting property, and pursuing and obtaining happiness and safety. Therefore, no male person, born in this country, or brought from over sea, ought to be holden by law, to serve any person, as a servant, slave, or apprentice, after he arrives to the age of twenty-one years; nor female, in like manner, after she arrives to the age of eighteen years, unless they are bound by their own consent, after they arrive to such age, or bound by law for the payment of debts, damages, fines, costs, or the like.

Source: vermont-archives.org/govhistory/constitut/con77.htm, accessed May 11, 2011.

Pennsylvania: An ACT for the GRADUAL ABOLITION of SLAVERY

When we contemplate our Abhorence of that Condition to which the Arms and Tyranny of Great Britain were exerted to reduce us, when we look back on the Variety of Dangers to which we have been exposed, and how miraculously our Wants in many Instances have been supplied and our Deliverances wrought, when even Hope and human fortitude have become unequal to the Conflict; we are unavoidably led to a serious and grateful Sense of the manifold Blessings which we have undeservedly received from the hand of that Being from whom every good and perfect Gift cometh. Impressed with these Ideas we conceive that it is our duty, and we rejoice that it is in our Power, to extend a Portion of that freedom to others, which hath been extended to us; and a Release from that State of Thraldom, to which we ourselves were tyrannically doomed, and from which we have now every Prospect of being delivered. It is not for us to enquire, why, in the Creation of Mankind, the Inhabitants of the several parts of the Earth, were distinguished by a difference in Feature or Complexion. It is sufficient to know that all are the Work of an Almighty Hand, We find in the distribution of the human Species, that the most fertile, as well as the most barren parts of the Earth are inhabited by Men of Complexions different from ours and from each other, from whence we may reasonably as well as religiously infer, that he, who placed them in their various Situations, hath extended equally his Care and Protection to all, and that it becometh not us to counteract his Mercies.

We esteem a peculiar Blessing granted to us, that we are enabled this Day to add one more Step to universal Civilization by removing as much as possible the Sorrows of those, who have lived in undeserved Bondage, and from which by the assumed Authority of the Kings of Britain, no effectual legal Relief could be obtained. Weaned by a long Course of Experience from those narrow Prejudices and Partialities we had imbibed, we find our Hearts enlarged with Kindness and Benevolence towards Men of all Conditions and Nations; and we conceive ourselves at this particular Period extraordinarily called upon by the Blessings which we have received, to manifest the Sincerity of our Profession and to give a substantial Proof of our Gratitude.

And whereas, the Condition of those Persons who have heretofore been denominated Negroe and Mulatto Slaves, has been attended with Circumstances which not only deprived them of the common Blessings that they were by Nature entitled to, but has cast them into the deepest Afflictions by an unnatural Separation and Sale of Husband and Wife from each other, and from their Children; an Injury the greatness of which can only be conceived, by supposing that we were in the same unhappy Case. In Justice therefore to Persons so unhappily circumstanced and who, having no Prospect before them whereon they may rest their Sorrows and their hopes have no reasonable Inducement to render that Service to Society, which they otherwise might; and also ingrateful Commemoration of our own happy Deliverance, from that State of unconditional Submission, to which we were doomed by the Tyranny of Britain.

Be it enacted and it is hereby enacted by the Representatives of the Freemen of the Commonwealth of Pennsylvania in General Assembly met and by the Authority of the same, That all Persons, as well Negroes, and Mulattos, as others, who shall be born within this State, from and after the Passing of this Act, shall not be deemed and considered as Servants for Life or Slaves; and that all Servitude for Life or Slavery of Children in Consequence of the Slavery of their Mothers, in the Case of all Children born within this State from and after the passing of this Act as aforesaid, shall be, an hereby is, utterly taken away, extinguished and for ever abolished.

Provided always and be it further enacted by the Authority aforesaid, That every Negroe and Mulatto Child born within this State after the passing of this Act as aforesaid, who would in Case this Act had not been made, have been born a Servant for Years or life or a Slave, shall be deemed to be and shall be, by Virtue of this Act the Servant of such person or his or her Assigns, who would in such Case have been entitled to the Service of such Child until such Child shall attain unto the Age of twenty eight Years, in the manner and on the Conditions whereon Servants bound by Indenture for four Years are or may be retained and holden; and shall be liable to like Correction and punishment, and intitled to like Relief in case he or she be evilly treated by his or her master or Mistress; and to like Freedom dues and other Privileges as Servants bound by Indenture for Four Years are or may be intitled unless the Person to whom the Service of any such Child Shall belong, shall abandon his or her Claim to the same, in which Case the Overseers of the Poor of the City Township or District, respectively where such Child shall be so abandoned, shall by Indenture bind out every Child so abandoned as an Apprentice for a Time not exceeding the Age herein before limited for the Service of such Children.

And be it further enacted by the Authority aforesaid, That every Person who is or shall be the Owner of any Negroe or Mulatto Slave or Servant for life or till the Age of thirty one Years, now within this State, or his lawful Attorney shall on or before the said first day of November next, deliver or cause to be delivered in Writing to the Clerk of the Peace of the County or to the Clerk of the Court of Record of the City of Philadelphia, in which he or she shall respectively inhabit, the Name and Sirname and Occupation or Profession of such Owner, and the Name of the County and Township District or Ward where he or she resideth, and also the Name and Names of any such Slave and Slaves and Servant and Servants for Life or till the Age of thirty one Years together with their Ages and Sexes severally and respectively set forth and annexed, by such Person owned or statedly employed, and then being within this State in order to ascertain and distinguish the Slaves and Servants for Life and Years till the Age of thirty one Years within this State who shall be such on the said first day of November next, from all other persons, which particulars shall by said Clerk of the Sessions and Clerk of said City Court be entered in Books to be provided for that Purpose by the said Clerks; and that no Negroe or Mulatto now within this State shall from and after the said first day of November by deemed a slave or Servant for life or till the Age of thirty one Years unless his or her name shall be entered as aforesaid on such Record except such Negroe and Mulatto Slaves and Servants as are hereinafter excepted; the said Clerk to be entitled to a fee of Two Dollars for each Slave or Servant so entered as aforesaid, from the Treasurer of the County to be allowed to him in his Accounts.

Provided always, That any Person in whom the Ownership or Right to the Service of any Negro or Mulatto shall be vested at the passing of this Act, other than such as are herein before excepted, his or her Heirs, Executors, Administrators and Assigns, and all and every of them severally Shall be liable to the Overseers of the Poor of the City, Township or District to which any such Negroe or Mulatto shall become chargeable, for such necessary Expence, with Costs of Suit thereon, as such Overseers may be put to through the Neglect of the Owner, Master or Mistress of such Negroe or Mulatto, notwithstanding the Name and other descriptions of such Negroe or Mulatto shall not be entered and recorded as aforesaid; unless his or her Master or Owner shall before such Slave or Servant attain his or her twenty eighth Year execute and record in the proper County, a deed or Instrument securing to such Slave or Servant his or her Freedom.

And be it further enacted by the Authority aforesaid, That the Offences and Crimes of Negroes and Mulattos as well as Slaves and Servants and Freemen, shall be enquired of, adjudged, corrected and punished in like manner as the Offences and Crimes of the other Inhabitants of this State are and shall be enquired of adjudged, corrected and punished, and not otherwise except that a Slave shall not be admitted to bear Witness agaist [sic] a Freeman.

And be it further enacted by the Authority aforesaid, That no Man or Woman of any Nation or Colour, except the Negroes or Mulattoes who shall be registered as aforesaid shall at any time hereafter be deemed, adjudged or holden, within the Territories of this Commonwealth, as Slaves or Servants for Life, but as freemen and Freewomen; and except the domestic Slaves attending upon Delegates in Congress from the other American States, foreign Ministers and Consuls, and persons passing through or sojourning in this State, and not becoming resident therein; and Seamen employed in Ships, not belonging to any Inhabitant of this State nor employed in any Ship owned by any such Inhabitant, Provided such domestic Slaves be not aliened or sold to any Inhabitant, nor (except in the Case of Members of Congress, foreign Ministers and Consuls) retained in this State longer than six Months.

Provided always and be it further enacted by the Authority aforesaid, That this Act nor any thing in it contained shall not give any Relief or Shelter to any absconding or Runaway Negroe or Mulatto Slave or Servant, who has absented himself or shall absent himself from his or her Owner, Master or Mistress, residing in any other State or Country, but such Owner, Master or Mistress, shall have like Right and Aid to demand, claim and take away his Slave or Servant, as he might have had in Case this Act had not been made.

Be it therefore enacted by the Authority aforesaid, That no Covenant of personal Servitude or Apprenticeship whatsoever shall be valid or binding on a Negroe or Mulatto for a longer Time than Seven Years; unless such Servant or Apprentice were at the Commencement of such Servitude or Apprenticeship under the Age of Twenty one Years; in which Case such Negroe or Mulatto may be holden as a Servant or Apprentice respectively, according to the Covenant, as the Case shall be, until he or she shall attain the Age of twenty eight Years but no longer.

John Bayard, Speaker

Enacted into a Law at Philadelphia on Wednesday the first day of March, Anno Domini One thousand seven hundred Eighty Thomas Paine, Clerk of the General Assembly

Source: State of Pennsylvania, An Act for the Gradual Abolition of Slavery (Philadelphia, no printer, 1781).

Massachusetts: Chief Justice William Cushing's Charge to the Jury in *Quok Walker v. Jennison*, 1783

The people of this commonwealth have solemnly bound themselves to each other - to declare - that all men are born free and equal; and that every subject is entitled to liberty, and to have it guarded by the laws as well as his life and property. In short, without resorting to implication in constructing the constitution, slavery is in my judgment as effectively abolished as it can be by the granting of rights and privileges wholly incompatible and repugnant to its existence. The court are therefore fully of the opinion that perpetual servitude can no longer be tolerated in our government, and that liberty can only be forfeited by some criminal conduct or relinquished by personal consent or contract. And it is therefore unnecessary to consider whether the promises of freedom to Quaco, on the part of his master and mistress, amounted to a manumission or not.

Source: www.mass.gov/courts/sjc/constitution_and_slavery.html#e, accessed May 11, 2011.

Thomas Jefferson on Slavery and on Black People

Thomas Jefferson wrote two different passages on the problem of slavery in his Notes on the State of Virginia. In one of those passages, on the manners and customs of Virginians, he presented a sharp, insightful discussion of the damage that slavery does to masters and slaves alike. As the master of hundreds of slaves, he had reason to know. In the other, he offered his reasons why black people would have to leave America if slavery did end. John Adams regarded the passage on manners as "worth diamonds." The second passage brought forth every racist belief of Jefferson's era. Jefferson had written the book for a French friend. Initially, he resisted publication because he feared what his neighbors would make of his description of slavery's effects. The second passage, from the query on "laws," begins with his proposals for amendments to existing Virginia law, including a law to begin the abolition of slavery. His discussion of black people in terms of supposedly inferior nature and his "suspicion only" of separate creation is painful to read, and not just for somebody with a modern sensibility, as David Walker shows below.

Jefferson on the Effects of Slavery

Manners

It is difficult to determine on the standard by which the manners of a nation may be tried, whether *catholic*, or *particular*. It is more difficult for a native to bring to that standard the manners of his own nation, familiarized to him by habit. There must doubtless be an unhappy influence on the manners of our people produced by the existence of slavery among us. The whole commerce between master and slave is a perpetual exercise of the most boisterous passions, the most unremitting despotism on the one part, and degrading submissions on the other. Our children see this, and learn to imitate it; for man is an imitative animal. This quality is the germ of all education in him. From his cradle to his grave he is learning to do what he sees others do. If a parent could find no motive either in his philanthropy or his self-love, for restraining the intemperance of passion towards his slave, it should always be a sufficient one that his child is present. But generally it is not sufficient. The parent storms, the child looks on, catches the lineaments of wrath, puts on the same airs in the circle of smaller slaves, gives a loose to his worst of passions, and thus nursed, educated, and daily exercised in tyranny, cannot but be stamped by it with odious peculiarities. The man must be a prodigy who can retain his manners and morals undepraved by such circumstances. And with what execration should the statesman be loaded, who permitting one half the citizens thus to trample on the rights of the other, transforms those into despots, and these into enemies, destroys the morals of the one part, and the amor patriae of the other. For if a slave can have a country in this world, it must be any other in preference to that in which he is born to live and labour for another: in which he must lock up the faculties of his nature, contribute as far as depends on his individual endeavours to the evanishment of the human race, or entail his own miserable condition on the endless generations proceeding from him. With the morals of the people, their industry also is destroyed. For in a warm climate, no man will labour for himself who can make another labour for him. This is so true, that of the proprietors of slaves a very small proportion indeed are ever seen to labour. And can the liberties of a nation be thought secure when we have removed their only firm basis, a conviction in the minds of the people that these liberties are of the gift of God? That they are not to be violated but with his wrath? Indeed I tremble for my country when I reflect that God is just: that his justice cannot sleep for ever: that considering numbers, nature and natural means only, a revolution of the wheel of fortune, an exchange of situation, is among possible events: that it may become probable by supernatural interference! The Almighty has no attribute which can take side with us in such a contest. -- But it is impossible to be temperate and to pursue this subject through the various considerations of policy, of morals, of history natural and civil. We must be contented to hope they will force their way into every one's mind. I think a change already perceptible, since the origin of the present revolution. The spirit of the master is abating, that of the slave rising from the dust, his condition mollifying, the way I hope preparing, under the auspices of heaven, for a total emancipation, and that this is disposed, in the order of events, to be with the consent of the masters, rather than by their extirpation.

Jefferson on Ending Slavery

The following are the most remarkable alterations proposed:
To emancipate all slaves born after passing the act. The bill reported by the revisors does not itself contain this proposition; but an amendment containing it was prepared, to be offered to the legislature whenever the bill should be taken up, and further directing, that they should continue with their parents to a certain age, then be brought up, at the public expence, to tillage, arts or sciences, according to their geniusses, till the females should be eighteen, and the males twenty-one years of age, when they should be colonized to such place as the circumstances of the time should render most proper, sending them out with arms, implements of houshold and of the handicraft arts, feeds, pairs of the useful domestic animals, &c. to declare them a free and independant people, and extend to them our alliance and protection, till they shall have acquired strength; and to send vessels at the same time to other parts of the world for an equal number of white inhabitants; to induce whom to migrate hither, proper encouragements were to be proposed. It will probably be asked, Why not retain and incorporate the blacks into the state, and thus save the expence of supplying, by importation of white settlers, the vacancies they will

leave? Deep rooted prejudices entertained by the whites; ten thousand recollections, by the blacks, of the injuries they have sustained; new provocations; the real distinctions which nature has made; and many other circumstances, will divide us into parties, and produce convulsions which will probably never end but in the extermination of the one or the other race. -- To these objections, which are political, may be added others, which are physical and moral. The first difference which strikes us is that of colour. Whether the black of the negro resides in the reticular membrane between the skin and scarf-skin, or in the scarf-skin itself; whether it proceeds from the colour of the blood, the colour of the bile, or from that of some other secretion, the difference is fixed in nature, and is as real as if its seat and cause were better known to us. And is this difference of no importance? Is it not the foundation of a greater or less share of beauty in the two races? Are not the fine mixtures of red and white, the expressions of every passion by greater or less suffusions of colour in the one, preferable to that eternal monotony, which reigns in the countenances, that immoveable veil of black which covers all the emotions of the other race? Add to these, flowing hair, a more elegant symmetry of form, their own judgment in favour of the whites, declared by their preference of them, as uniformly as is the preference of the Oranootan for the black women over those of his own species. The circumstance of superior beauty, is thought worthy attention in the propagation of our horses, dogs, and other domestic animals; why not in that of man? Besides those of colour, figure, and hair, there are other physical distinctions proving a difference of race. They have less hair on the face and body. They secrete less by the kidnies, and more by the glands of the skin, which gives them a very strong and disagreeable odour. This greater degree of transpiration renders them more tolerant of heat, and less so of cold, than the whites. Perhaps too a difference of structure in the pulmonary apparatus, which a late ingenious experimentalist has discovered to be the principal regulator of animal heat, may have disabled them from extricating, in the act of inspiration, so much of that fluid from the outer air, or obliged them in expiration, to part with more of it. They seem to require less sleep. A black, after hard labour through the day, will be induced by the slightest amusements to sit up till midnight, or later, though knowing he must be out with the first dawn of the morning. They are at least as brave, and more adventuresome. But this may perhaps proceed from a want of forethought, which prevents their seeing a danger till it be present. When present, they do not go through it with more coolness or steadiness than the whites. They are more ardent after their female: but love seems with them to be more an eager desire, than a tender delicate mixture of sentiment and sensation. Their griefs are transient. Those numberless afflictions, which render it doubtful whether heaven has given life to us in mercy or in wrath, are less felt, and sooner forgotten with them. In general, their existence appears to participate more of sensation than reflection. To this must be ascribed their disposition to sleep when abstracted from their diversions, and unemployed in labour. An animal whose body is at rest, and who does not reflect, must be disposed to sleep of course. Comparing them by their faculties of memory, reason, and imagination, it appears to me, that in memory they are equal to the whites; in reason much inferior, as I think one could scarcely be found capable of tracing and comprehending the investigations of Euclid; and that in imagination they are dull, tasteless, and anomalous. It would be unfair to follow them to Africa for this investigation. We will consider them here, on the same stage with the whites, and where the facts are not apocryphal on which a judgment is to be formed. It will be right to make great allowances for the difference of condition, of education, of conversation, of the sphere in which they move. Many millions of them have been brought to, and born in America. Most of them indeed have been confined to tillage, to their own homes, and their own society: yet many have been so situated, that they might have availed themselves of the conversation of their masters; many have been brought up to the handicraft arts, and from that circumstance have always been associated with the whites. Some have been liberally educated, and all have lived in countries where the arts and sciences are cultivated to a considerable degree, and have had before their eyes samples of the best works from abroad. The Indians, with no advantages of this kind, will often carve figures on their pipes not destitute of design and merit. They will crayon out an animal, a plant, or a country, so as to prove the existence of a germ in their minds which only wants cultivation. They astonish you with strokes of the most sublime oratory; such as prove their reason and sentiment strong, their imagination glowing and elevated. But never yet could I find that a black had uttered a thought above the level of plain narration; never see even an elementary trait of painting or sculpture. In music they are more generally gifted than the whites with accurate ears for tune and time, and they have been found capable of imagining a small catch. Whether they will be equal to the composition of a more extensive run of melody, or of complicated harmony, is yet to be proved. Misery is often the parent of the most affecting touches in poetry. -- Among the blacks is misery enough, God knows, but no poetry. Love is the peculiar oestrum of the poet. Their love is ardent, but it kindles the senses only, not the imagination. Religion indeed has produced a Phyllis Whately; but it could not produce a poet. The compositions published under her name are below the dignity of criticism. The heroes of the Dunciad are to her, as Hercules to the author of that poem. Ignatius Sancho has approached nearer to merit in composition; yet his letters do more honour to the heart than the head. They breathe the purest effusions of friendship and general philanthropy, and shew how great a degree of the latter may be compounded with strong religious zeal. He is often happy in the turn of his compliments, and his stile is easy and familiar, except when he affects a Shandean fabrication of words. But his imagination is wild and extravagant, escapes incessantly from every restraint of reason and taste, and, in the course of its vagaries, leaves a tract of thought as incoherent and eccentric, as is the course of a meteor through the sky. His subjects should often have led him to a process of sober reasoning: yet we find him always substituting sentiment for demonstration. Upon the whole, though we admit him to the first place among those of his own colour who have presented themselves to the public judgment, yet when we compare him with the writers of the race among whom he lived, and particularly with the epistolary class, in which he has taken his own stand, we are compelled to enroll him at the bottom of the column. This criticism supposes the letters published under his name to be genuine, and to have received amendment from no other hand; points which would not be of easy investigation. The improvement of the blacks in body and mind, in the first instance of their mixture with the whites, has been observed by every one, and proves that their inferiority is not the effect merely of their condition of life. We know that among the Romans, about the Augustan age especially, the condition of their slaves was much more deplorable than that of the blacks on the continent of America. The two sexes were confined in separate apartments, because to raise a child cost the master more than to buy one. Cato, for a very restricted indulgence to his slaves in this particular, took from them a certain price. But in this country the slaves multiply as fast as the free inhabitants. Their situation and manners place the commerce between the two sexes almost without restraint. -- The same Cato, on a principle of oeconomy, always sold his sick and superannuated slaves. He gives it as a standing precept to a master visiting his farm, to sell his old oxen, old waggons, old tools, old and diseased servants, and every thing else become useless. 'Vendat boves vetulos, plaustrum vetus, ferramenta vetera, servum senem, servum morbosum, & si quid aliud supersit vendat.' Cato de re rusticâ. c. 2. The American slaves cannot enumerate this among the injuries and insults they receive. It was the common practice to expose in the island of Aesculapius, in the Tyber, diseased slaves, whose cure was like to become tedious. The Emperor Claudius, by an edict, gave freedom to such of them as should recover, and first declared, that if any person chose to kill rather than to expose them, it should be deemed homicide. The exposing them is a crime of which no instance has existed with us; and were it to be followed by death, it would be punished capitally. We are told of a certain Vedius Pollio, who, in the presence of Augustus, would have given a slave as food to his fish, for having broken a glass. With the Romans, the regular method of taking the evidence of their slaves was under torture. Here it has been thought better never to resort to their evidence. When a master was murdered, all his slaves, in the same house, or within hearing, were condemned to death. Here punishment falls on the guilty only, and as precise proof is required against him as against a freeman. Yet notwithstanding these and other discouraging circumstances among the Romans, their slaves were often their rarest artists. They excelled too in science, insomuch as to be usually employed as tutors to their master's children. Epictetus, Terence, and Phaedrus, were slaves. But they were of the race of whites. It is not their condition then, but nature, which has produced the distinction. -- Whether further observation will or will not verify the conjecture, that nature has been less bountiful to them in the endowments of the head, I believe that in those of the heart she will be found to have done them justice. That disposition to theft with which they have been branded, must be ascribed to their situation, and not to any depravity of the moral sense. The man, in whose favour no laws of property exist, probably feels himself less bound to respect those made in favour of others. When arguing for ourselves, we lay it down as a fundamental, that laws, to be just, must give a reciprocation of right: that, without this, they are mere arbitrary rules of conduct, founded in force, and not in conscience: and it is a problem which give to the master to solve, whether the religious precepts against the violation of property were not framed for him as well as his slave? And whether the slave may not as justifiably take a little from one, who has taken all from him, as he may slay one who would slay him? That a change in the relations in which a man is placed should change his ideas of moral right and wrong, is neither new, nor peculiar to the colour of the blacks. Homer tells us it was so 2600 years ago.

Jove fix'd it certain, that whatever day
Makes man a slave, takes half his worth away.

But the slaves of which Homer speaks were whites. Notwithstanding these considerations which must weaken their respect for the laws of property, we find among them numerous instances of the most rigid integrity, and as many as among their better instructed masters, of benevolence, gratitude, and unshaken fidelity. -- The opinion, that they are inferior in the faculties of reason and imagination, must be hazarded with great diffidence. To justify a general conclusion, requires many observations, even where the subject may be submitted to the Anatomical knife, to Optical glasses, to analysis by fire, or by solvents. How much more then where it is a faculty, not a substance, we are examining; where it eludes the research of all the senses; where the conditions of its existence are various and variously combined; where the effects of those which are present or absent bid defiance to calculation; let me add too, as a circumstance of great tenderness, where our conclusion would degrade a whole race of men from the rank in the scale of beings which their Creator may perhaps have given them. To our reproach it must be said, that though for a century and a half we have had under our eyes the races of black and of red men, they have never yet been viewed by us as subjects of natural history. I advance it therefore as a suspicion only, that the blacks, whether originally a distinct race, or made distinct by time and circumstances, are inferior to the whites in the endowments both of body and mind. It is not against experience to suppose, that different species of the same genus, or varieties of the same species, may possess different qualifications. Will not a lover of natural history then, one who views the gradations in all the races of animals with the eye of philosophy, excuse an effort to keep those in the department of man as distinct as nature has formed them? This unfortunate difference of colour, and perhaps of faculty, is a powerful obstacle to the emancipation of these people. Many of their advocates, while they wish to vindicate the liberty of human nature, are anxious also to preserve its dignity and beauty. Some of these, embarrassed by the question 'What further is to be done with them?' join themselves in opposition with those who are actuated by sordid avarice only. Among the Romans emancipation required but one effort. The slave, when made free, might mix with, without staining the blood of his master. But with us a second is necessary, unknown to history. When freed, he is to be removed beyond the reach of mixture.

Source: Thomas Jefferson, *Notes on the State of Virginia* (Philadelphia: Pritchard and Hall, 1788), Query XVIII and Query XIV.

Benjamin Banneker Responds to Jefferson, 1791

Phillis Wheatley was dead by the time that Jefferson wrote his dismissal of her work. She knew about racism and about being dismissed as a writer because she was black, and had she lived to read his words she might have been able to shrug them off. Benjamin Banneker did read what Jefferson wrote, and he responded. His tone is deferential and polite; he was writing, after all, to a world famous man who at the time was secretary of state of the United States. But his resolute opposition to what Jefferson had to say about black people, including him, runs through the letter.

Maryland, Baltimore County, Near Ellicott's Lower Mills
August 19th 1791.

Thomas Jefferson Secretary of State.

Sir, I am fully sensible of the greatness of that freedom which I take with you on the present occasion; a liberty which Seemed to me Scarcely allowable, when I reflected on that distinguished, and dignifiyed station in which you Stand; and the almost general prejudice and prepossession which is so previlent in the world against those of my complexion.

I suppose it is a truth too well attested to you, to need a proof here, that we are a race of Beings who have long laboured under the abuse and censure of the world, that we have long been looked upon with an eye of contempt, and that we have long been considered rather as brutish than human, and Scarcely capable of mental endowments.

Sir, I hope I may Safely admit, in consequence of that report which hath reached me, that you are a man far less inflexible in Sentiments of this nature, than many others; that you are measurably friendly and well disposed towards us, and that you are willing and ready to Lend your aid and assistance to our relief from those many distresses and numerous calamities to which we are reduced.

Now, Sir, if this is founded in truth, I apprehend you will readily embrace every opportunity to eradicate that train of absurd and false ideas and opinions which so generally prevail with respect to us, and that your Sentiments are concurrent with mine, which are that one universal Father hath given being to us all, and that he hath not only made us all of one flesh, but that he hath also without partiality afforded us all the same Sensations, and endued us all with the same faculties, and that however variable we may be in Society or religion, however diversified in Situation or colour, we are all of the Same Family, and Stand in the Same relation to him.

Sir, if these are Sentiments of which you are fully persuaded, I hope you cannot but acknowledge, that it is the indispensible duty of those who maintain for themselves the rights of human nature, and who profess the obligations of Christianity, to extend their power and influence to the relief of every part of the human race, from whatever burthen or oppression they may unjustly labour under; and this I apprehend a full conviction of the truth and obligation of these principles should lead all to.

Sir, I have long been convinced, that if your love for your Selves and for those inesteemable laws which preserve to you the rights of human nature, was founded on Sincerity, you could not but be Solicitous, that every Individual of whatsoever rank or distinction, might with you equally enjoy the blessings thereof, neither could you rest Satisfyed, short of the most active diffusion of your exertions, in order to their promotion from any State of degradation, to which the unjustifyable cruelty and barbarism of men may have reduced them.

Sir, I freely and Chearfully acknowledge, that I am of the African race, and, in that colour which is natural to them of the deepest dye*; and it is under a Sense of the most profound gratitude to the Supreme Ruler of the universe, that I now confess to you, that I am not under that State of tyranical thraldom, and inhuman captivity, to which too many of my brethren are doomed; but that I have abundantly tasted of the fruition of those blessings which proceed from that free and unequalled liberty with which you are favoured and which I hope you will willingly allow you have received from the immediate Hand of that Being from whom proceedeth every good and perfect gift.

Sir, Suffer me to recall to your mind that time in which the Arms and tyranny of the British Crown were exerted with every powerful effort, in order to reduce you to a State of Servitude; look back I intreat you on the variety of dangers to which you were exposed, reflect on that time in which every human aid appeared unavailable, and in which even hope and fortitude wore the aspect of inability to the Conflict, and you cannot but be led to a

Serious and grateful Sense of your miraculous and providential preservation; You cannot but acknowledge, that the present freedom and tranquility which you enjoy you have mercifully received, and that it is the peculiar blessing of Heaven.

This, Sir, was a time in which you clearly saw into the injustice of a State of Slavery, and in which you had Just apprehensions of the horrors of its condition, it was now Sir, that your abhorrence thereof was so excited, that you publickly held forth this true and invaluable doctrine, which is worthy to be recorded and remembered in all

Succeeding ages. "We hold these truths to be Self evident, that all men are created equal, and that they are endowed by their creator with certain inalienable rights, that amongst these are life, liberty, and the persuit of happiness."

Here, Sir, was a time in which your tender feelings for your selves engaged you thus to declare, you were then impressed with proper ideas of the great valuation of liberty, and the free possession of those blessings to which you were entitled by nature; but Sir how pitiable is it to reflect, that altho you were so fully convinced of the benevolence of the Father of mankind, and of his equal and impartial distribution of those rights and privileges which he had conferred upon them, that you should at the Same time counteract his mercies, in detaining by fraud and violence so numerous a part of my brethren under groaning captivity and cruel oppression, that you should at the Same time be found guilty of that most criminal act, which you professedly detested in others, with respect to yourselves.

Sir, I suppose that your knowledge of the situation of my brethren is too extensive to need a recital here; neither shall I presume to prescribe methods by which they may be relieved, otherwise than by recommending to you, and all others, to wean yourselves from those narrow prejudices which you have imbibed with respect to them, and as Job proposed to his friends "Put your Souls in their Souls' stead," thus shall your hearts be enlarged with kindness and benevolence towards them, and thus shall you need neither the direction of myself or others in what manner to proceed herein.

And now, Sir, altho my Sympathy and affection for my brethren hath caused my enlargement thus far, I ardently hope that your candour and generosity will plead with you in my behalf, when I make known to you, that it was not originally my design; but that having taken up my pen in order to direct to you as a present, a copy of an Almanack which I have calculated for the Succeeding year, I was unexpectedly and unavoidably led thereto.

This calculation, Sir, is the production of my arduous study, in this my advanced Stage of life; for having long had unbounded desires to become Acquainted with the Secrets of nature, I have had to gratify my curiosity herein thro my own assiduous application to Astronomical Study, in which I need not to recount to you the many difficulties and disadvantages which I have had to encounter.

And altho I had almost declined to make my calculation for the ensuing year, in consequence of that time which I had allotted therefor being taking up at the Federal Territory by the request of Mr. Andrew Ellicott, yet finding myself under Several engagements to printers of this state to whom I had communicated my design, on my return to my place of residence, I industriously apply'd myself thereto, which I hope I have accomplished with correctness and accuracy, a copy of which I have taken the liberty to direct to you, and which I humbly request you will favourably receive, and altho you may have the opportunity of perusing it after its publication, I chose to send it to you in manuscript previous thereto, that thereby you might not only have an earlier inspection but that you might also view it in my own hand writing.

And now Sir, I Shall conclude and Subscribe my Self with the most profound respect,

> Your most Obedient humble Servant
> Benjamin Banneker.

Source: *Copy of a Letter from Benjamin Banneker to the Secretary of State* (Philadelphia: Daniel Lawrence, 1792).

Reverend Richard Allen and Reverend Absalom Jones Defend Philadelphia's Black Community against Charges of Profiteering from its Service during the Yellow Fever Epidemic of 1793

The yellow fever epidemic that swept through Philadelphia in 1793 devastated the entire city. Nobody understood the sources of the contagion, and a mistaken belief prevailed that black people were immune. Perhaps in response to that belief, the black community took on much of the task of tending the sick and disposing of the bodies of the dead, only to be accused by printer Matthew Carey of asking for exorbitant fees. Richard Allen and Absalom Jones, who had organized the effort, responded at length. As with Phillis Wheatley's emerging language of liberty and as with Benjamin Banneker's response to Thomas Jefferson, their outrage at the accusations is tightly controlled, but unmistakable. They also linked their defense of the black community to a stinging indictment of slavery.

IN consequence of a partial representation of the conduct of the people who were employed to nurse the sick, in the late calamitose state of the city of Philadelphia, we are solicited, by a number of those who feel themselves injured thereby, and by the advice of several respectable citizens, to step forward and declare facts as they really were; seeing that from our situation, on account of the charge we took upon us, we had it more fully and generally in our power, to know and observe the conduct and behavior of those that were also employed. Early in September, a solicitation appeared in the Public papers, to the people of colour to come forward and assist the distressed, perishing, and neglected sick; with a kind of assurance, that people of our colour were not liable to take the infection. Upon which we and a few others met and consulted how to act on so truly alarming and melancholy an occasion. After some conversations, we found a freedom to go forth, confining in him who can preserve in the midst of a burning fiery furnace, sensible that it was our duty to do all the good we could to our suffering fellow mortals. We set out to see where we could be useful. The first we visited was a man in Emsley's alley, who was dying, and his wife lay dead at the time in the house, there were none to assist but two poor helpless children. We administered what relief we could, and applied to the overseers of the poor to have the woman buried. We visited upwards of twenty families that day- they were scenes of woe indeed! The Lord was pleased to strengthen, and remove all fear from us, and disposed our hearts to be as useful as possible.

In order the better to regulate our conduct, we called on the mayor next day, to consult with him how to proceed, so as to be most useful. The first object he recommended, was a strict attention to the sick, and the procuring of nurses. This was attended to by Absalom Jones and William Gray; and, in order that the distressed might know where to apply, the mayor advertised the public that upon application to them they would be supplied. Soon after, the mortality increasing, the difficulty of getting a corpse taken away, was such, that few were willing to do it, when offered great rewards. The black people were looked to. We then offered our services in the public papers, by advertising that we would remove the dead and procure nurses. Our services were the production of real sensibility;—we sought not fee nor reward, until the increase of the disorder rendered our labour so arduous that we were not adequate to the service we had assumed. The mortality increasing rapidly, obliged us to call in the assistance of five hired men, in the awful discharge of interring the dead. They, with great reluctance, were prevailed upon to join us. It was very uncommon, at this time, to find any one that would go near, much more, handle, a sick or dead person. When the sickness became general, and several of the physicians died, and most of the survivors were exhausted by sickness or fatigue; that good man, Doctor Rush, called us more immediately to attend upon the Sick, knowing we could both bleed; he told us we could increase our utility, by attending to his instructions, and accordingly directed us where to procure medicine duly prepared with proper directions how to administer them, and at what stages of the disorder to bleed; and when we found ourselves incapable of judging what was proper to be done, to apply to him, and he would, if able, attend them himself, or send Edward Fisher, his pupil, which he often did; and Mr. Fisher manifested his humanity, by an affectionate attention for their relief.-This has been no small satisfaction to us; for, we think, that when a physician was not attainable, we have been the instruments, in the hand of God, for saving the lives of some hundreds of our suffering fellow mortals.

We feel ourselves sensibly aggrieved by the censorious epithets of many, who did not render the least assistance in the time of necessity, yet are liberal of their censure of us, for the prices paid for our services, when no one knew how to make a proposal to any one they wanted to assist them. At first we made no charge, but let it to those we served in removing their dead, to give what they thought fit-we set no price, until the reward was fixed by those we had served. After paying the people we had to assist us, our compensation is much less than many will believe.

We do assure the public, that *all* the money we have received, for burying, and for coffins which we ourselves purchased and procured, has not defrayed the expense of wages which we had to pay to those whom we employed to assist us. The following statement is accurately made:

CASH RECEIVED.

The whole amount of cash we received for burying the dead, and for burying beds, is, - - - - £233 10 4

CASH PAID.

For coffins, for which we have received nothing - £33 0 0

For the hire of five men, 3 of them 70 days each, and the other two, 63 days each, at 22/6 per day, - - - 378 0 0

411 0 0

Debts due us, for which we expect but little, - £110 0 0

From the statement, for the truth of which we solemnly vouch, it is evident, and we sensibly feel the operation of the fact, that we are out of pocket, - - - - - £177 9 8

Besides the cost of hearses, maintenance of our families for 70 days, (being the period of our labours) and the support of the five hired men, during the respective times of their being employed; which expences, together with sundry gifts we occasionally made to poor families, might reasonably and properly be introduced, to shew our actual situation with regard to profit-but it is enough to exhibit to the public, from the above specified items, *of cash paid and cash received*, without taking into view the other expences, that, by the employment we were engaged in, we have lost £177 9 8. But, if the other expences, which we have actually paid, are added to that sum, how much then may we not say we have suffered! We leave the public to Judge.

It may possibly appear strange to some who know how constantly we were employed, that we should have received no more cash than £233 10 4. But repeat our assurance, that this is the fact, and we add another, which will serve the better to explain it: We have buried *several hundreds* of poor persons and strangers, for which service we have never received, nor never asked any compensation.

That there were some few black people guilty of plundering the distressed, we acknowledge; but in that they only are pointed out, and made mention of, we esteem partial and injurious; we know as many whites who were guilty of it; but this is looked over, while the blacks are held up to censure.- Is it a greater crime for a black to pilfer, than for a white to privateer?

We wish not to offend, but when an unprovoked attempt is made, to make us blacker than we are, it becomes less necessary to be over cautious on that account; therefore we shall take the liberty to tell of the conduct of some of the whites.

We know, six pounds was demanded by, and paid, to a white woman, for putting a corpse into a coffin; and forty dollars was demanded, and paid, to four white men, for bringing it down the stairs.

Mr. and Mrs. Taylor both died in one night; a white woman had the care of them; after they were dead she called on Jacob Servoss, esq. for her pay, demanding six pounds for laying them out; upon seeing a bundle with her, he suspected she had pilfered; on searching her, Mr. Taylor's buckles were found in her pocket, with other things.

An elderly lady, Mrs. Malony, was given into the care of a white woman, she died, we were called to remove the corpse, when we came the women was laying so drunk that she did not know what we were doing, but we know she had one of Mrs. Malony's rings on her finger, and another in her pocket.

It is unpleasant to point out the bad and unfeeling conduct of any colour, yet the defence we have undertaken obliges us to remark that although "hardly any of good character at that time could be procured" yet only two black women were, at this time in the hospital, and they were retained and the others discharged when it was reduced to order and good government.

Absalom Jones.

Richard Allen.

January 7th 1794

****

Having, during the prevalence of the late malignant disorder, had almost daily opportunities of seeing the conduct of Absalom Jones and Richard Allen, and the people employed by them, to bury the dead—I with cheerfulness give this testimony of my approbation of their proceedings, as far as the same came under my notice. Their diligence, attention and decency of deportment, afforded me, at the time, much satisfaction.

MATTHEW CLARKSON, Mayor.

Philadelphia, January 23, 1794

Source: *A narrative of the proceedings of the black people, during the late awful calamity in Philadelphia, in the year 1793: and a refutation of some censures, thrown upon them in some late publications* (Philadelphia: William H. Woodward, 1794).

Slavery and Public Policy in the Young Republic

In 1787 the federal convention drafted and proposed the United States Constitution, which does not use the word "slavery" but which provided explicit protection for its power in national politics and the privilege of slaveholders to recover slaves who had escaped into free states. As the convention was working in Philadelphia, the Confederation Congress, meeting in New York, passed an act for organizing the "Northwest Territory" (now Ohio, Indiana, Illinois, Michigan, and Wisconsin), forbidding slavery in the region. In 1790 the new United States Congress passed the first immigration and naturalization act, opening American immigration freely to Europeans, but closing them to all others. In 1797, at the urging of James Madison, the House of Representatives flatly rejected a petition from the free black Philadelphia community on behalf of slaves who had escaped from North Carolina. Taken together, these official documents show the ambiguity of the young republic toward slavery, opening a problem in American legal, social, political, economic, and cultural life that would not be resolved until the end of the Civil War, and whose shadow still remains.

The United States Constitution and the Slavery Problem, 1787

Article 1, Section 9: The migration or importation of such persons as any of the states now existing shall think proper to admit, shall not be prohibited by the Congress prior to the year 1808, but a tax or duty may be imposed on such importations, not exceeding 10 dollars for each person.

Article 4, Section 2: No person held to service or labour in one state, under the laws thereof, escaping into another, shall, in consequence of any law or regulation therein, be discharged from such service or labour, but shall be delivered up on claim of the party to whom such service or labour may be due.

Source: avalon.law.yale.edu/18th_century/usconst.asp, accessed May 30, 2011.

Slavery in the Northwest Ordinance, 1787

Art. 6. There shall be neither slavery nor involuntary servitude in the said territory, otherwise than in the punishment of crimes whereof the party shall have been duly convicted: *Provided, always,* That any person escaping into the same, from whom labor or service is lawfully claimed in any one of the original States, such fugitive may be lawfully reclaimed and conveyed to the person claiming his or her labor or service as aforesaid.

Source: avalon.law.yale.edu/18th_century/nworder.asp, accessed May 30, 2011.

United States Congress, "An act to establish an uniform Rule of Naturalization" (March 26, 1790)

Be it enacted by the Senate and House of Representatives of the United States of America, in Congress assembled, That any Alien being a free white person, who shall have resided within the limits and under the jurisdiction of the United States for the term of two years, may be admitted to become a citizen thereof on application to any common law Court of record in any one of the States wherein he shall have resided for the term of one year at least, and making proof to the satisfaction of such Court that he is a person of good character, and taking the oath or affirmation prescribed by law to support the Constitution of the United States, which Oath or Affirmation such Court shall administer, and the Clerk of such Court shall record such Application, and the proceedings thereon; and thereupon such person shall be considered as a Citizen of the United States. And the children of such person so natural-ized, dwelling within the United States, being under the age of twenty one years at the time of such naturalization, shall also be considered as citizens of the United States. And the children of citizens of the United States that may be born beyond Sea, or out of the limits of the United States, shall be considered as natural born Citizens: Provided, that the right of citizenship shall not descend to persons whose fathers have never been resident in the United States: Provided also, that no person heretofore proscribed by any States, shall be admitted a citizen as aforesaid, except by an Act of the Leg-islature of the State in which such person was proscribed.

Source: Linda Grant De Pauw, et al., eds. *Documentary History of the First Federal Congress of the United States of America, March 4, 1789–March 3, 1791.* Baltimore: Johns Hopkins University Press, 1972–1995. 6: 1516–522.

Four Black North Carolinians Petition Congress, 1797

Unlike most states, North Carolina made achieving freedom more difficult rather than easier during the revolutionary period. In 1775 the colonial legislature forbade masters to free their slaves without special permission. That ban survived the in-dependence struggle and the new state government continued it. North Carolina had a significant population of white Protestants who had come to oppose slavery, including Moravians and Quakers. Many of these tried to free their slaves, in defiance of the ban. The freed slaves, however, were subject to recapture. In 1797 four of them brought petitions for help to Congress, with the assistance of Absalom Jones. The resulting debate pitted Northern against Southern members and laid bare the question of whether black people in America enjoyed the rights guaranteed by the first ten amendments, known as the Bill of Rights. Congressman James Madison of Virginia, who had been the author of those amendments, as well as the main author of the Constitution, opposed the petitioners.

Annals of Congress, 1797

Mr. SWANWICK presented the following petition: To the President, Senate, and House of Representatives. The Petition and Representation of the undernamed Freemen, respectfully showeth: —

THAT, being of African descent, late inhabitants and natives of North Carolina, to you only, under God, can we apply with any hope of effect, for redress of our grievances, having been compelled to leave the State wherein we had a right of residence, as freemen liberated under the hand and seal of humane and conscientious masters, the validity of which act of justice, in restoring us to our native right of freedom, was confirmed by judgment of the Superior Court of North Carolina, wherein it was brought to trial; yet, not long after this decision, a law of that State was enacted, under which men of cruel disposition, and void of just principle, received countenance and authority in violently seizing, imprisoning, and selling into slavery, such as had been so emancipated; whereby we were reduced to the necessity of separating from some of our nearest and most tender connexions, and of seeking refuge in such parts of the Union where more regard is paid to the public declaration in favor of liberty and the common right of man, several hundreds, under our circumstances, having in consequence of the said law, been hunted day and night, like beasts of the forest, by armed men with dogs, and made a prey of as free and lawful plunder.

Among others thus exposed, I, JUPITER NICHOLSON, of Perquimans county, N.C., after being set free by my master, Thomas Nicholson, and having been about two years employed as a seaman in the service of Zachary Nickson, on coming on shore, was pursued by men with dogs and arms; but was favored to escape by night to Virginia, with my wife, who was manumitted by Gabriel Cosand, where I resided about four years in the town of Portsmouth, chiefly employed in sawing boards and scantling; from thence I removed with my wife to Philadelphia, where I have been employed, at times, by water, working alongshore, or sawing wood. I left behind me a father and mother, who were manumitted by Thomas Nicholson and Zachary Dickson; they have since been taken up, with a beloved brother, and sold into cruel bondage.

I, JACOB NICHOLSON, also of North Carolina, being set free by my master, Joseph Nicholson, but continuing to live with him till, being pursued at night and day, I was obliged to leave my abode, sleep in the woods, and stacks in the fields, &c, to escape the hands of violent men who, induced by the profit afforded them by law, followed this course as a business; at length, by night, I made my escape, leaving a mother, one child, and two brothers, to see whom I dare not return.

I, JOE ALBERT, manumitted by Benjamin Albertson, who was my careful guardian to protect me from being afterwards taken and sold, providing me with a house to accommodate me and my wife, who was liberated by William Robertson; but we were night and day hunted by men with guns, swords, and pistols, accompanied with mastiff dogs; from whose violence, being one night, apprehensive of immediate danger, I left my dwelling, locked and barred, and fastened with a chain, being at some distance from it, while my wife was by my kind master locked up under his roof. I heard them break into my house where, not finding their prey, they got but a small booty, a handkerchief of about a dollar value, and some provisions; but, not long after, I was discovered and seized by Alexander Stafford, William Stafford, and Thomas Creesy, who were armed with guns and clubs. After binding me with my hands behind me, and a rope round my arms and body, they took me about four miles to Hartford prison, where I lay four weeks, suffering much from want of provision; from thence, with the assistance of a fellow-prisoner, (a white man,) I made my escape, and for three dollars was conveyed, with my wife, by a humane person, in a covered wagon by night, to Virginia, where, in the neighborhood of Portsmouth, I continued unmolested about four years, being chiefly engaged in sawing boards and plank. On being advised to move Northward, I came with my wife to Philadelphia, where I have labored for a livelihood upwards of two years, in Summer mostly, along shore in vessels and stores, and sawing wood in the Winter. My mother was set free by Phineas Nickson, my sister by John Trueblood, and both taken up and sold into slavery, myself deprived of the consolation of seeing them, without being exposed to the like grievous oppression.

I, THOMAS PRITCHET, was set free by my master Thomas Pritchet, who furnished me with land to raise provisions for my use, where I built myself a house, cleared a sufficient spot of woodland to produce ten bushels of corn; the second year about fifteen; and the third, had as much planted as I suppose would have produced thirty bushels; this I was obliged to leave about one month before it was fit for gathering, being threatened by Holland Lockwood, who married my said master's widow, that if I would not come and serve him, he would apprehend me, and send me to the West Indies; Enoch Ralph also threatening to send me to jail, and sell me for the good of the country; being thus in jeopardy, I left my little farm, with my small stock and utensils, and my corn standing, and escaped by night into Virginia, where shipping myself for Boston, I was, through stress of weather landed in New York, where I served as a waiter for seventeen months; but my mind being distressed on account of the situation of my wife and children, I returned to Norfolk in Virginia, with a hope of at least seeing them, if I could not obtain their freedom; but finding I was advertised in the newspaper, twenty dollars the reward for apprehending me, my dangerous situation obliged me to leave Virginia, disappointed of seeing my wife and children, coming to Philadelphia, where I resided in the employment of a waiter upward of two years.

The petitioners summarize the similar situation of an unnamed African American who escaped from North Carolina to Philadelphia, where he lived and worked for eleven years before being recaptured and imprisoned. WE BE-SEECH YOUR IMPARTIAL ATTENTION to our hard condition, not only with respect to our personal sufferings, as freemen, but as a class of that people who, distinguished by color, are therefore with a degrading partiality, considered by many, even of those in eminent stations, as unentitled to that public justice and protection which is the great object of Government. We indulge not a hope, or presume to ask for the interposition of your honorable body, beyond the extent of your constitutional power or influence, yet are willing to believe your serious, disinterested, and candid consideration of the premises, under the benign impressions of equity and mercy, producing upright exertion of what is in your power, may not be without some salutary effect, both for our relief as a people, and toward the removal of obstructions to public order and well-being.

IF, NOTWITHSTANDING all that has been publicly avowed as essential principles respecting the extent of human right to freedom; notwithstanding we have had that right restored to us, so far as was in the power of those by whom we were held as slaves, we cannot claim the privilege of representation in your councils, yet we trust we may address you as fellow-men, who, under God, the sovereign Ruler of the Universe, are intrusted with the distribution of justice, for the terror of evil-doers, the encouragement and protection of the innocent, not doubting that you are men of liberal minds, susceptible of benevolent feelings and clear conception of rectitude to a catholic extent, who can admit that black people (servile as their condition generally is throughout this Continent) have natural affections, social and domestic attachments and sensibilities; and that, therefore, we may hope for a share in your sympathetic attention while we represent that the unconstitutional bondage in which multitudes of our fellows in complexion are held, is to us a subject sorrowfully affecting; for we cannot conceive this condition (more especially those who have been emancipated and tasted the sweets of liberty, and again reduced to slavery by kidnappers and man-stealers) to be less afflicting or deplorable than the situation of citizens of the United States, captured and enslaved through the unrighteous policy prevalent in Algiers. We are far from considering all those who retain slaves as wilful oppressors, being well assured that numbers in the State from whence we are exiles, hold their slaves in bondage, not of choice, but possessing them by inheritance, feel their minds burdened under the slavish restraint of legal impediments to doing justice which they are convinced is due to fellow-rationals. May we not be allowed to consider this stretch of power, morally and politically, a Governmental defect, if not a direct violation of the declared fundamental principles of the Constitution; and finally, is not some remedy for an evil of such magnitude highly worthy of the deep inquiry and unfeigned zeal of the supreme Legislative body of a free and enlightened people?

SUBMITTING OUR CAUSE TO GOD, and humbly craving your best aid and influence, as you may be favored and directed by that wisdom which is from above, wherewith that you may be eminently dignified and rendered conspicuously, in the view of nations, a blessing to the people you represent, is the sincere prayer of your petitioners.

JACOB NICHOLSON,

JUPITER NICHOLSON, his mark,

JOB ALBERT, his mark,

THOMAS PRITCHET, his mark.

PHILADELPHIA, January 23, 1797.

Slaves, Free Americans, and the Fourth of July

These final documents address the problem of what the American Revolution has meant to African-Americans historically. David Walker and Frederick Douglass looked back on it from their nineteenth-century vantage points, during the great campaign against slavery that preceded the Civil War. Though their strategies of persuasion were different, both of these spokesmen for free and enslaved black Americans found the Revolution incomplete. Both of them set out to shock their readers and (for Douglass) their listeners into realizing that that the Revolution's

business remained unfinished as long as slavery persisted. Despite Walker's fero-
ciously angry language and outright scorn for white Americans, he did call on them
to live up to what the revolutionary era had promised. Despite Douglass's professed
admiration for the revolutionaries and what they had achieved, his anger at the
situation in 1852, when he gave the speech, is clear. So is his sense that, unless
the slavery problem was resolved, the United States would fail. The last documents
are brief excerpts from Dr. Martin Luther King, Jr.'s great speech at the civil rights
march on Washington in August, 1963, and from Senator Barack Obama's speech
on race during the presidential campaign of 2008. They, too, found the Revolu-
tion's promise incomplete. They too have called on the United States to live up,
finally, to what it had begun at the time of its founding.

David Walker on the Meaning of the American Revolution, 1829

In conclusion, I ask the candid and unprejudiced of the whole world, to
search the pages of historians diligently, and see if the Antideluvians—the
Sodomites—the Egyptians—the Babylonians—the Ninevites—the Carthage-
nians—the Persians—the Macedonians—the Greeks—the Romans—the
Mahometans—the Jews—or devils, ever treated a set of human beings, as
the white Christians of America do us, the blacks, or Africans. I also ask the
attention of the world of mankind to the declaration of these very American
people, of the United States.

A declaration made July 4, 1776.

It says

"When in the course of human events, it becomes necessary for one people to
dissolve the political bands which have connected them with another, and to
assume among the Powers of the earth, the separate and equal station to which
the laws of nature and of nature's God entitle them. A decent respect for the
opinions of mankind requires, that they should declare the causes which impel
them to the separation. —We hold these truths to be self evident—that all
men are created equal, that they are endowed by their Creator with certain
unalienable rights: that among these, are life, liberty, and the pursuit of happiness that, to secure these rights, governments are instituted among men,
deriving their just powers from the consent of the governed; that when ever
any form of government becomes destructive of these ends, it is the right of
the people to alter or to abolish it, and to institute a new government laying
its foundation on such principles, and organizing its powers in such form, as
to them shall seem most likely to effect their safety and happiness. Prudence,
indeed, will dictate, that governments long established should not be changed
for light and transient causes; and accordingly all experience hath shewn, that
mankind are more disposed to suffer, while evils are sufferable, than to right
themselves by abolishing the forms to which they are accustomed. But when

a long train of abuses and usurpations, pursuing invariably the same object, evinces a design to reduce them under absolute despotism, it is their right it is their duty to throw off such government, and to provide new guards for their future security." See your Declaration Americans!!! Do you understand your own language? Hear your language, proclaimed to the world, July 4th, 1776— "We hold these truths to be self evident—that ALL MEN ARE CREATED EQUAL!! that they *are endowed by their Creator with certain unalienable rights;* that among these are life, *liberty,* and the pursuit of happiness!!" Compare your own language above, extracted from your Declaration of Independence, with your cruelties and murders inflicted by your cruel and unmerciful fathers and yourselves on our fathers and on us—men who have never given your fathers or you the least provocation!!!!!!

Hear your language further! "But when a long train of abuses and usurpation, pursuing invariably the same object, evinces a design to reduce them under absolute despotism, it is their *right,* it is their *duty,* to throw off such government, and to provide new guards for their future security."

Now, Americans! I ask you candidly, was your sufferings under Great Britain, one hundredth part as cruel and tyranical as you have rendered ours under you? Some of you, no doubt, believe that we will never throw off your murderous government and "provide new guards for our future security." If Satan has made you believe it, will he not deceive you?

Do the whites say, I being a black man, ought to be humble, which I readily admit? I ask them, ought they not to be as humble as I? or do they think that they can measure arms with Jehovah? Will not the Lord yet humble them? or will not these very coloured people whom they now treat worse than brutes, yet under God, humble them low down enough? Some of the whites are ignorant enough to tell us, that we ought to be submissive to them, that they may keep their feet on our throats. And if we do not submit to be beaten to death by them, we are bad creatures and of course must be damned, &c. If any man wishes to hear this doctrine openly preached to us by the American preachers, let him go into the Southern and Western sections of this country—I do not speak from hear say—what I have written, is what I have seen and heard myself. No man may think that my book is made up of conjecture—I have travelled and observed nearly the whole of those things myself, and what little I did not get by my own observation, I received from those among the whites and blacks, in whom the greatest confidence may be placed.

The Americans may be as vigilant as they please, but they cannot be vigilant enough for the Lord, neither can they hide themselves, where he will not find and bring them out.

Source: David Walker, *Walker's Appeal, With a Brief Sketch of his Life by Henry Highland Garnet and also Garnet's Address to the Slaves of the United States of America* (New York: J. Tobitt, 1848), 84–87.

Frederick Douglass on the Meaning of the
American Revolution, 1852

Fellow Citizens, I am not wanting in respect for the fathers of this republic. The signers of the Declaration of Independence were brave men. They were great men, too—great enough to give frame to a great age. It does not often happen to a nation to raise, at one time, such a number of truly great men. The point from which I am compelled to view them is not, certainly, the most favorable; and yet I cannot contemplate their great deeds with less than admiration. They were statesmen, patriots and heroes, and for the good they did, and the principles they contended for, I will unite with you to honor their memory. . . .

Fellow-citizens! I will not enlarge further on your national inconsistencies. The existence of Slavery in this country brands your republicanism as a sham, your humanity as a base pretence, and your Christianity as a lie. It destroys your moral power abroad; it corrupts your politicians at home. It saps the foundation of religion; it makes your name a hissing, and a by-word to the mocking earth. It is the antagonistic force in your government, the only thing that seriously disturbs and endangers your *Union*. It fetters your progress; it is the enemy of improvement, the deadly foe of education; it fosters pride; it breeds insolence; it promotes vice; it shelters crime; it is a curse to the earth that supports it; and yet, you cling to it, as if it were the sheet anchor of all your hopes. . . .

Fellow-citizens! There is no matter in respect to which, the people of the North have allowed themselves to be so ruinously imposed upon, as that of the pro-slavery character of the Constitution. In *that* instrument I hold there is neither warrant, license, nor sanction of the hateful thing; but, interpreted as it *ought* to be interpreted, the Constitution is a GLORIOUS LIBERTY DOCU-MENT. Read its preamble, consider its purposes. Is slavery among them? Is it at the gateway? Or is it in the temple? It is neither.

Source: Frederick Douglass, "The Celebration at Corinthian Hall," *Frederick Douglass's Paper*, July 9, 1852.

Martin Luther King, Jr., on the Meaning of the
American Revolution, 1963

In a sense we have come to our nation's capital to cash a check. When the architects of our republic wrote the magnificent words of the Constitution and the Declaration of Independence, they were signing a promissory note to which every American was to fall heir. This note was a promise that all men, yes, black men as well as white men, would be guaranteed the unalienable rights of life, liberty, and the pursuit of happiness.

It is obvious today that America has defaulted on this promissory note insofar as her citizens of color are concerned. Instead of honoring this sacred obligation, America has given the Negro people a bad check, a check which has come back marked "insufficient funds." But we refuse to believe that the bank of justice is bankrupt. We refuse to believe that there are insufficient funds in the great vaults of opportunity of this nation. So we have come to cash this check—a check that will give us upon demand the riches of freedom and the security of justice. We have also come to this hallowed spot to remind America of the fierce urgency of now. This is no time to engage in the luxury of cooling off or to take the tranquilizing drug of gradualism. Now is the time to make real the promises of democracy. Now is the time to rise from the dark and desolate valley of segregation to the sunlit path of racial justice. Now is the time to lift our nation from the quick sands of racial injustice to the solid rock of brotherhood. Now is the time to make justice a reality for all of God's children.

Source: mlk-kpp01.stanford.edu/kingweb/publications/speeches/address_at_march_on_washington.pdf, accessed May 6, 2011.

Senator Barack Obama on the Meaning of the American Revolution, 2008

"We the people, in order to form a more perfect union . . ."—221 years ago, in a hall that still stands across the street, a group of men gathered and, with these simple words, launched America's improbable experiment in democracy. Farmers and scholars, statesmen and patriots who had traveled across an ocean to escape tyranny and persecution finally made real their declaration of independence at a Philadelphia convention that lasted through the spring of 1787.

The document they produced was eventually signed but ultimately unfinished. It was stained by this nation's original sin of slavery, a question that divided the colonies and brought the convention to a stalemate until the founders chose to allow the slave trade to continue for at least 20 more years, and to leave any final resolution to future generations.

Of course, the answer to the slavery question was already embedded within our Constitution—a Constitution that had at its very core the ideal of equal citizenship under the law; a Constitution that promised its people liberty and justice and a union that could be and should be perfected over time.

And yet words on a parchment would not be enough to deliver slaves from bondage, or provide men and women of every color and creed their full rights and obligations as citizens of the United States. What would be needed were Americans in successive generations who were willing to do their part—

through protests and struggles, on the streets and in the courts, through a civil war and civil disobedience, and always at great risk—to narrow that gap between the promise of our ideals and the reality of their time.

Source: www.npr.org/templates/story/story.php?storyId=88478467, accessed May 6, 2011.

~

Bibliographical Essay

Library shelves are laden with studies of the American Revolution, and this is not the place to list them all. I used about two hundred separate books to write this account of just one subject, Black Americans and the revolutionary era, and this is not the place to list all of them either, let alone the many articles that have appeared in academic journals. Instead, I will try to suggest the most important, at least in my experience. The literature in scholarly journals and anthologies is just as large, but I will not attempt to cover it. A seriously interested reader or student can find the essays and articles by following footnotes or doing online searches of such journals as *The American Historical Review*, *The Journal of American History*, *The Journal of African-American History*, *Slavery and Abolition*, *The William and Mary Quarterly*, and *Early American Studies*, as well as many others.

Classics and Overviews

Nineteenth-century African-American writers understood the importance of black people to American history long before "mainstream" (white) scholars began to turn to the subject. In 1855 William Cooper Nell published *Colored Patriots of the American Revolution, With Sketches of Several Distinguished Colored Persons* (Boston: R. F. Wallcut). George Washington Williams told a larger story in his two-volume *History of the Negro Race in America, 1619–1880* (1883, reprinted New York: Arno Press, 1968). W. E. B. Du Bois launched his remarkable seven-decade career of writing and political action when he published *The Suppression of the African Slave-Trade to the United States of America, 1638–1870* (New York: Longmans, Green, 1896).

Modern book-length scholarship on black people in the revolutionary era begins with Herbert Aptheker, *American Negro Slave Revolts* (New York: Columbia University Press, 1943) and Benjamin Quarles, *The Negro in the American Revolution* (Chapel Hill: University of North Carolina Press, 1961). Eugene D. Genovese placed the revolutionary events in black North American history in a larger perspective in *From Rebellion to Revolution: Afro-American Slave Revolts in the Making of the New World* (Baton Rouge: Louisiana State University Press, 1979), as has done David Brion Davis in *Revolutions: Reflections on American Equality and Foreign Liberations* (Cambridge, MA: Harvard University Press, 1990) and *Challenging the Boundaries of Slavery* (Cambridge, MA: Harvard University Press, 2003). Drawing on a lifetime of study of the American Revolution "from below," Gary B. Nash has published two overview accounts, *Race and Revolution* (Madison, WI: Madison House, 1990) and *The Forgotten Fifth: African Americans in the Age of Revolution* (Cambridge, MA: Harvard University Press, 2006). Douglas R. Egerton, *Death or Liberty: African-Americans and Revolutionary America* (New York: Oxford University Press, 2009) draws on his deep research on Southern rebellions in the Revolution's aftermath. Ira Berlin and Ronald Hoffman, eds., *Slavery and Freedom in the Age of the American Revolution* (Charlottesville: University Press of Virginia, 1983) assembles essays by the best scholars working on the subject during the era of the revolutionary bicentennial. Sidney Kaplan and Emma Nogrady Kaplan assembled a collage of primary sources and interpretive essays in *The Black Presence in the Era of the American Revolution* (revised ed., Amherst: University of Massachusetts Press, 1989). Woody Holton, *Black Americans in the Revolutionary Era: A Brief History with Documents* (Boston: Bedford St. Martins, 2009) also assembles primary sources.

Understanding the Revolution

Short overview accounts of the American Revolution include Edward Countryman, *The American Revolution* (revised ed., New York: Hill & Wang, 2003); Edmund S. Morgan, *The Birth of the Republic* (Chicago: University of Chicago Press, 1956); and Gordon S. Wood, *The American Revolution: A History* (New York: Modern Library, 2002). They differ markedly in their handling of the problem of slavery during the era. Longer accounts, again with very different perspectives, include John E. Ferling, *A Leap in the Dark: The Struggle to Create the American Republic* (New York: Oxford University Press,

2003); Robert M. Middlekauff, *The Glorious Cause: The American Revolution, 1763–1789* (New York: Oxford University Press, 2005); and Gary B. Nash, *The Unknown American Revolution: The Unruly Birth of Democracy and the Struggle to Create America* (New York: Viking, 2005). On the general issue of whether the American Revolution was a transforming social experience, rather than simply a struggle for national liberation, are Ronald Hoffman and Peter J. Albert, eds., *The Transforming Hand of Revolution; Reconsidering the American Revolution as a Social Movement* (Charlottesville: University Press of Virginia, 1995) and Alfred F. Young, *Liberty Tree: Ordinary People and the American Revolution* (New York: New York University Press, 2006). Young and Gregory H. Nobles, *Whose American Revolution Was It? Historians Interpret the Founding* (New York: New York University Press, 2011) bring understanding of the Revolution's social dimensions up to the present, at the time of this writing.

Origins of American Slavery

I owe the globe-spanning approach to how American slavery began that I have followed to several monumental studies. They include three books by David Brion Davis, *The Problem of Slavery in Western Culture* (Ithaca, NY: Cornell University Press, 1967), *The Problem of Slavery in the Age of Revolution, 1770–1823* (New York: Oxford University Press, 1976), and *Inhuman Bondage: The Rise and Fall of Slavery in the New World* (New York: Oxford University Press, 2006). They also include Winthrop D. Jordan, *White Over Black: American Attitudes Toward the Negro, 1550–1812* (Chapel Hill: University of North Carolina Press, 1968); two books by Robin Blackburn, *The Overthrow of Colonial Slavery, 1776–1848* (London: Verso, 1988) and *The Making of New World Slavery: From the Baroque to the Modern, 1492–1800* (London: Verso, 1997); two by Michael A. Gomez, *Reversing Sail: A History of the African Diaspora* (Cambridge, England: Cambridge University Press, 2005) and *Black Crescent: The Experience and Legacy of African Muslims in the Americas* (Cambridge, England: Cambridge University Press, 2005); and, most recently, Seymour Drescher, *Abolition: A History of Slavery and Antislavery* (Cambridge, England: Cambridge University Press, 2009). Betty Wood has a trenchant, short account of *The Origins of American Slavery: Freedom and Bondage in the English Colonies* (New York: Hill & Wang, 1997), which segues into her *Slavery in Colonial America, 1619–1776* (Lanham, MD: Rowman & Littlefield, 2005). Edward Countryman, ed., *How Did American Slavery Begin?* (Boston: Bedford St. Martins, 1999) shows how historians have approached the problem that its title poses.

We must begin a list of more specific studies not in America, but rather in Africa. Sterling Stuckey, *Slave Culture: Nationalist Theory and the Foundations of Black America* (New York: Oxford University Press, 1987) looms over most other scholarship. Philip D. Curtin, *The Atlantic Slave Trade, A Census* (Madison: University of Wisconsin Press, 1969) long stood as the major quantitative study. David Eltis, *The Trans-Atlantic Slave Trade: A Database on CD-ROM* (Cambridge, England: Cambridge University Press, 1999) makes the raw data readily available and updates Curtin's numbers. Linda M. Heywood and John K. Thornton, *Central Africans, Atlantic Creoles, and the Foundation of the Americas, 1585–1660* (Cambridge, England: Cambridge University Press, 2007) shows Africans as participants in the early modern Atlantic world, including enslavement, rather than simply as victims of it. The best account of how the slave trade reached deep into Africa is Joseph C. Miller, *Way of Death: Merchant Capitalism and the Angolan Slave Trade, 1730–1830* (Madison: University of Wisconsin Press, 1988). Stephanie Smallwood, *Saltwater Slavery: A Middle Passage from Africa to American Diaspora* (Cambridge, MA: Harvard University Press, 2007) and Marcus Rediker, *The Slave Ship: A Human History* (New York: Viking, 2007) take the reader into the experience of enslavement as the people involved lived it. James A. McMillin, *The Final Victims: Foreign Slave Trade to North America, 1783–1810* (Columbia: University of South Carolina Press, 2004) significantly increases knowledge of the Africans brought to the United States after the Revolutionary War. Both Margaret Washington Creel, *A Peculiar People: Slave Religion and Community Culture Among the Gullahs* (New York: New York University Press, 1988) and James Sidbury, *Becoming African in America: Race and Nation in the Early Black Atlantic* (New York: New York University Press, 2007) explore the continuation and transformation of African ways in the colonial era. So does Michael A. Gomez, *Exchanging Our Country Marks: The Transformation of African Identities in the Colonial and Ante-Bellum South* (Chicago: University of Chicago Press, 1998). I cannot leave this topic without praising the children's account *Amos Fortune, Free Man* (New York: E. P. Dutton, 1950) by Elizabeth Yates, which takes its subject from Africa to New Hampshire. This book introduced me to African-American history more than half a century ago and it deservedly remains in print

Three path-breaking books from the mid-1970s launched modern study of slavery in early North America: Richard S. Dunn, *Sugar and Slaves: The Rise of the Planter Class in the English West Indies, 1624–1713* (Chapel Hill: University of North Carolina Press, 1972); Peter H. Wood, *Black Majority: Negroes in Colonial South Carolina From 1670 Through the Stono Rebellion* (New York: Knopf, 1975); and Edmund S. Morgan, *American Slavery, American*

Freedom: The Ordeal of Colonial Virginia (New York: Norton, 1975). Many excellent studies have built upon them. Among the most important on the Southern colonies are: Alan Kulikoff, *Tobacco and Slaves: The Development of Southern Cultures in the Chesapeake, 1680–1800* (Chapel Hill: University of North Carolina Press, 1986); Ira Berlin, *Many Thousands Gone: The First Two Centuries of Slavery in North America* (Cambridge, MA: Harvard University Press, 1998); and Philip D. Morgan, *Slave Counterpoint: Black Culture in the Eighteenth-Century Chesapeake & Lowcountry* (Chapel Hill: University of North Carolina Press, 1998). Outside the plantation zone the major studies include: Gary B. Nash, *Forging Freedom: The Formation of Philadelphia's Black Community, 1720–1840* (Cambridge, MA: Harvard University Press, 1988); Thelma Wills Foote, *Black and White Manhattan: The History of Racial Formation in Colonial New York City* (New York: Oxford University Press, 2004); Jill Lepore, *New York Burning: Liberty, Slavery, and Conspiracy in Eighteenth-Century Manhattan* (New York: Knopf, 2005); Graham Russell Hodges, *Root and Branch: African-Americans in New York and East Jersey, 1613–1863* (Chapel Hill: University of North Carolina Press, 1999); and William D. Pierson, *Black Yankees: The Development of an Afro-American Sub-Culture in Eighteenth-Century New England* (Amherst: University of Massachusetts Press, 1988).

This book is about African and African-American people. But colonial-era slavery reached Native Americans as well, transforming their world as fully as it transformed Africa and mingling the two peoples' histories. Jack D. Forbes, *Black Africans and Native Americans: Color, Race, and Caste in the Evolution of Red-Black Peoples* (Oxford: Basil Blackwell, 1988) opened the subject for modern study. Allan Gallay, *The Indian Slave Trade: The Rise of the English Empire in the American South, 1760–1717* (New Haven: Yale University Press, 2002) is fundamental for understanding the subject, as is James R. Brooks, *Captives and Cousins: Slavery, Kinship, and Community in the Southwest Borderlands* (Chapel Hill: University of North Carolina Press, 2002).

Slavery in the Revolutionary Era

Many of the studies listed under the categories above also address the problem of slavery during the American Revolutionary era and need not be listed again. One perennial problem, especially in popular consciousness, is the relationship between slavery and the great figures who usually dominate study of the Revolution as a whole. Some of the best studies of that topic are: Annette Gordon-Reed, *Thomas Jefferson and Sally Hemings: An*

American Controversy (Charlottesville: University of Virginia Press, 1997) and *The Hemingses of Monticello: An American Family* (New York: Norton, 2008); Henry Wiencek, *An Imperfect God: George Washington, His Slaves, and the Creation of America* (New York: Farrar, Straus and Giroux, 2003); David Waldstreicher, *Runaway America: Benjamin Franklin, Slavery, and the American Revolution* (New York: Hill & Wang, 2004); and, in more general terms, Paul Finkelman, *Slavery and the Founders: Race and Liberty in the Age of Jefferson* (Armonk, NY: Sharpe, 1996).

The subject of the relationship between such figures and slavery probably will remain compelling for as long as the United States endures. So will the problem of slavery's relationship to their greatest creative achievement, the United States Constitution. Among many studies of that issue, David Waldstreicher, *Slavery's Constitution: From Revolution to Ratification* (New York: Hill & Wang, 2009) and George William Van Cleve, *A Slaveholder's Union: Slavery, Politics, and the Constitution in the Early American Republic* (Chicago: University of Chicago Press, 2010) stand out. Arthur Zilversmit, *The First Emancipation: The Abolition of Slavery in the North* (Chicago: University of Chicago Press, 1967) provides an overview. Shane White, *Somewhat More Independent: The End of Slavery in New York City, 1770–1810* (Athens: University of Georgia Press, 1991) and David N. Gellman, *Emancipating New York: The Politics of Slavery and Freedom, 1777–1827* (Baton Rouge: Louisiana State University Press, 2006) explore the death of slavery in the Northern state where it had been strongest during the colonial era. Sylvia R. Frey, *Water From the Rock: Black Resistance in a Revolutionary Age* (Princeton, NJ: Princeton University Press, 1991) remains the best account of slavery in the revolutionary-era South.

The real historical advances have lain in exploring what black people did for themselves during the Revolution. One has been the way that many black people found their freedom on the British side. Simon Schama, *Rough Crossings: Britain, The Slaves and the American Revolution* (New York: Penguin, 2005) and Cassandra Pybus, *Epic Journeys of Freedom: Runaway Slaves of the American Revolution and their Global Quest for Liberty* (Boston: Beacon, 2006) complement each other well. Lawrence Hill, *The Book of Negroes* (New York: HarperCollins, 2007) is fiction, but is the product of serious historical research and is a superb read. The title of Stephen M. Wise, *Though the Heavens May Fall: The Landmark Trial That Led to the End of Human Slavery* (Cambridge, MA: Da Capo, 2005) overstates the importance of Somerset's case in the context of the whole era but provides a readable account of what white British anti-slavery activists achieved. Peter Linebaugh and Marcus Rediker, *The Many-Headed Hydra: Sailors, Slaves, Commoners, and the Hidden*

History of the Revolutionary Atlantic (Boston: Beacon, 2000) reverses that perspective, taking the struggles of "ordinary" people as its subject and linking such people into a continuous web of resistance.

From the point of view of enslaved people, the most revolutionary events of the era came in Haiti. Readers of *Freedom's Journal* had the chance to read histories of the Haitian Revolution during the newspaper's two-year print run from 1827 to 1829. Modern study of the Haitian Revolution begins with C. L. R. James, *The Black Jacobins: Toussaint L'Ouverture and the San Domingo Rebellion* (New York: Vintage, 1963 [orig. pub. 1938]). The scholarship on the subject since James published his book is enormous; one recent account is Laurent Dubois, *Avengers of the New World: The Story of the Haitian Revolution* (Cambridge: Harvard University Press, 2004). Any reader wanting to take the subject further can start with David Geggus and Norman Fiering, eds., *The World of the Haitian Revolution* (Bloomington: Indiana University Press, 2009). Both Geggus's earlier collection *The Impact of the Haitian Revolution in the Atlantic World* (Columbia: University of South Carolina Press, 2001) and Matthew J. Clavin, *Toussaint L'Ouverture and the American Civil War* (Philadelphia: University of Pennsylvania Press, 2010) address the importance of the Haitian events for Americans, black and white alike.

After Independence

The four direct rebellions, or attempts at rebellion, in the post-revolutionary United States did not begin to approach the scale of the Haitian events, for reasons discussed in this book. Nonetheless, they were important both as examples (heroic, foolhardy, or both) to black Americans and as warnings to white ones. The best studies of the Gabriel conspiracy in Virginia in 1800 are James Sidbury, *Ploughshares into Swords: Race, Rebellion and Identity in Gabriel's Virginia, 1730–1810* (Cambridge, England: Cambridge University Press, 1997) and Douglas R. Egerton, *Gabriel's Rebellion: The Virginia Slave Conspiracies of 1800 and 1802* (Chapel Hill: University of North Carolina Press, 1993). Daniel Rasmussen has reconstructed the little-known revolt of 1811 in Louisiana in *American Uprising: The Untold Story of America's Largest Slave Revolt* (New York: Harper, 2011). Douglas Egerton also has written *He Shall Go Free: The Lives of Denmark Vesey* (Madison, WI: Madison House, 1999). In October, 2001, and January, 2002, the *William and Mary Quarterly* carried an extended scholarly debate on the nature and extent of the events that centered on Vesey and on one scholar's proposition that the conspiracy to rebel was a figment of white Carolinian imaginations.

Studies of the Southampton County (Nat Turner) Rebellion in Virginia of 1831 start with Herbert Aptheker, *Nat Turner's Slave Rebellion* (New York: Humanities, 1966) and Stephen B. Oates, *The Fires of Jubilee: Nat Turner's Fierce Rebellion* (New York: Harper & Row, 1975). Novelist William Styron's fictional *The Confessions of Nat Turner* (New York: Random House, 1967) led quickly to John Henrik Clarke, ed., *William Styron's Nat Turner: Ten Black Writers Respond* (Boston: Beacon, 1968). Without question Turner's rebellion is the most famous in North American history. The question of how its history and its imagery intersect is the subject of *Nat Turner: A Slave Rebellion in History and Memory* (New York: Oxford University Press, 2003) and of Scot French, *The Rebellious Slave: Nat Turner in American Memory* (Boston: Houghton Mifflin, 2004).

Biographies

Many of the major black figures of the revolutionary era left behind enough material for full biographies. Here are some, in alphabetical order by subject: *Richard Allen:* Richard S. Newman, *Freedom's Prophet: Bishop Richard Allen, The AME Church, and the Black Founding Fathers* (New York: New York University Press, 1998); *Benjamin Banneker:* Silvio A. Benedini, *The Life of Benjamin Banneker: The First African-American Man of Science* (Baltimore: Maryland Historical Society, 1999); *Paul Cuffe:* Rosalind Cobb Wiggins, *Captain Paul Cuffe's Logs and Letters, 1808–1817* (Washington: Howard University Press, 1996); *James Forten:* Julie Winch, *A Gentleman of Color: The Life of James Forten* (New York: Oxford University Press, 2002); *Ibrahima Ibn Sori:* Terry Alford, *Prince Among Slaves* (New York: Oxford University Press, 2007); *Olaudah Equiano:* Vincent Caretta, *Equiano the African: Biography of a Self-Made Man* (Athens: University of Georgia Press, 2005); *Sally Hemings and Her Family:* Gordon-Reed, *The Hemingses of Monticello*, cited above; *David Walker:* Peter P. Hinks, *To Awaken My Afflicted Brethren: David Walker and the Problem of Antebellum Slave Resistance* (University Park, PA: Pennsylvania State University Press, 1997); *Phillis Wheatley:* Henry Louis Gates, Jr., *The Trials of Phillis Wheatley: America's First Black Poet and her Encounters with the Founding Fathers* (New York: Basic Civitas Books, 2003) and John C. Shields, *Phillis Wheatley's Poetics of Liberation: Backgrounds and Context* (Knoxville: University of Tennessee Press, 2008).

Wheatley's complete poetry and her other writings are available in Julian D. Mason, Jr., ed., *The Poems of Phillis Wheatley* (rev. ed., Chapel Hill: University of North Carolina Press, 1989). Margaret Washington's long study of *Sojourner Truth's America* (Urbana and Chicago: University of Illinois Press,

2009) reached me at the very final stage of preparing this book. Its subject's major career came in the mid-nineteenth century, but her enslavement in post-independence New York tells a great deal about slavery's declining years in the North.

Each of these lives takes us deeply into the experience of slavery's partial breakup in the Northern states and the Atlantic world, and of its continuation as the South's increasingly "peculiar" but also increasingly powerful institution.

One major argument in the main text is that the great task of free black Americans was to form their own "civil" society, given their more or less complete exclusion from "political" society's world of elections, office-holding, and making of public policy. For that exclusion, see Don E. Fehrenbacher, *The Slaveholding Republic: An Account of the United State's Government's Relations to Slavery* (New York: Oxford University Press, 2001), although Matthew Mason, *Slavery and Politics in the Early American Republic* (Chapel Hill: University of North Carolina Press, 2006) demonstrates that, despite politicians' best efforts, the issue of slavery could not be fully repressed and that it ignited sectional passions each time it came to the surface, even prior to the Missouri Compromise of 1820.

The theme of how black people dealt with their political exclusion (as opposed to how white people enforced or debated it) is covered in Ira Berlin's classic study, *Slaves Without Masters: The Free Negro in the Antebellum South* (New York: Random House, 1974) and in his more recent *Generations of Captivity: A History of African-American Slaves* (Cambridge, MA: Harvard University Press, 2003). The same theme runs through such accounts as Barbara Jeanne Fields, *Slavery and Freedom on the Middle Ground: Maryland During the Nineteenth Century* (New Haven, CT: Yale University Press, 1985); Suzanne Lebsock, *The Free Women of Petersburg: Status and Culture in a Southern Town, 1784–1860* (New York: Norton, 1984); Graham Russell Hodges, *Slavery and Freedom in the Rural North: African-Americans in Monmouth County, New Jersey, 1665–1865* (Madison, WI: Madison House, 1997); Nash, *Forging Freedom*, cited above; Christopher Phillips, *Freedom's Port: The African American Community of Baltimore, 1790–1860* (Urbana and Chicago: University of Illinois Press,1997); and Shane White, *Stories of Freedom in Black New York* (Cambridge, MA: Harvard University Press, 2002). So do the contrasting accounts of black efforts in James Oliver Horton and Lois E. Horton, *In Hope of Liberty: Culture, Community and Protest Among Northern Free Blacks, 1700–1860* (New York: Oxford University Press, 1997) and John Hope Franklin and Loren Schweninger, *Runaway Slaves: Rebels on the Plantation* (New York: Oxford University Press, 1999).

For a very long time historians of post-revolutionary white society simply ignored the presence, actions, and importance of black people in the same times and places. Thankfully, that is changing, as David Waldstreicher, *In the Midst of Perpetual Fetes: The Making of American Nationalism, 1776–1820* (Chapel Hill: University of North Carolina Press, 1997) and John Brooke, *Columbia Rising: Civil Life on the Upper Hudson from the Revolution to the Age of Jackson* (Chapel Hill: University of North Carolina Press, 2010) both demonstrate. But as the essays collected by James Oliver Horton and Lois E. Horton in *Slavery and Public History* (Chapel Hill: University of North Carolina Press, 2006) demonstrate, slavery remains the tough stuff of American memory. Barack Obama noted in his speech on race in the 2008 presidential campaign that "The past isn't dead and buried. . . . It isn't even past." The author of the phrase was the great novelist William Faulkner, a white Mississippian who wrote profoundly about slavery, freedom, race, and class in his home place. The place of race and of slavery's memory in the United States will remain unquiet until Americans fully realize that both the history of black people in America, including American history's great events, and the history of white people in America remain incomplete until we fully grasp how each is wrapped around the other, and how ultimately the two merge into the most profound, tragic, and inspiring of American stories.

Index

~

About the Author

Edward Countryman is the University Distinguished Professor of American History at Southern Methodist University. He has written numerous books on the social and political consequences of cultural clashes in early America, including *A People in Revolution*, which won the Bancroft Prize in 1981. He is also the author of *The American Revolution*, which is assigned in college courses across the country.